The Life of Alcibiades

THE LIFE OF ALCIBIADES
The Idol of Athens

E. F. Benson

Edited and Introduced by
Dr. Craig Paterson

VP

Los Angeles, California
2010

Published by Viewforth Press, Los Angeles, California, 2010.
1st Viewforth Classics edition. Introduction, notes, index, cover, and layout © 2010 by Viewforth Press. All rights reserved. Printed and distributed by createspace.com.

LCCN: 2010939675

ISBN: 1456303333
EAN-13: 9781456303334

CONTENTS

EDITOR'S INTRODUCTION		IX
PREFACE		XIII
BIBLIOGRAPHY		XVII
I.	HISTORICAL INTRODUCTION	1
II.	THE BOYHOOD OF ALCIBIADES	21
III.	ALCIBIADES'S FIRST MILITARY SERVICE	53
IV.	HISTORICAL INTERLUDE	67
V.	ALCIBIADES'S ENTRY INTO POLITICAL LIFE	79
VI.	THE SICILIAN EXPEDITION	111
VII.	ALCIBIADES AT SPARTA	141
VIII.	AT THE COURT OF TISSAPHERNES	163
IX.	THE SAMIAN COMMAND	195
X.	THE CAMPAIGN IN THE HELLESPONT	213
XI.	THE RETURN TO ATHENS	235
XII.	THE FINAL DISASTER	247
XIII.	"MAGNUS CIVIS OBIT"	265
INDEX		279

EDITOR'S INTRODUCTION

EDWARD Frederic Benson was born at Wellington College, Crowthorne, Berkshire on the 24th of July 1867. He died on the 29th of February 1940 aged 72 from throat cancer at University College Hospital, London. He never married.

Benson was the fourth of six children (third son) of Edward White Benson (1829-1896) and his wife Mary Sidwick (1841-1918), sister of the famous utilitarian philosopher Henry Sidgwick (1838-1900). His elder siblings were Martin Benson (1860-1878), Arthur Christopher Benson (1862-1925), Mary Eleanor Benson 1863-1890), and Margaret Benson (1865–1916). He had a younger brother called Robert Hugh Benson (1871-1914).

Benson's father was a clergyman destined to rise in ecclesiastical office first to the Chancellorship of Lincoln Cathedral in 1872, thence to become the first Bishop of Truro in 1877, later becoming the Lord Archbishop of Canterbury in 1882.

Throughout his education at *Temple Grove*, his private, *Marlborough*, his public, and at *King's College, Cambridge*, Benson was steeped in a classical tradition of education. He certainly must have had aptitude for it, for he graduated from Cambridge with a double first in classics and archaeology. After graduating from Cambridge, Benson worked from 1892 to 1895 in Athens for the *British School of Archaeology* and later he worked in Egypt for the *Society for the Promotion of Hellenic Studies*.

In the years to come Benson would enjoy a considerable reputation as a writer of fiction. From 1893 until his death in 1940, he published at least one, if not two books each year. Amongst his literary output are some works of autobiography and biography. Of his biographical writings—*Sir Francis Drake*, *Queen Victoria*, *Daughters of Queen Victoria*, *King Edward VII*, *Charlotte Brontë*—*The Life of Alcibiades: The Idol of Athens* stands out as his best biographical work. It was a work that he was very well qualified to write, combining as it did his skills and interests in classics, archaeology and writing to considerable effect. While his other biographies are well researched and excellently written, often witty and insightful, they did not quite capture the depth of Benson's imagination as the subject matter of Alcibiades undoubtedly did.

Alcibiades (ca. 450 BC-ca. 404 BC), was the charismatic and controversial bisexual Athenian general and politician who promoted the Peloponnesian war against rival Sparta, who subsequently inspired Athens's failed Sicilian Expedition, and who later allied himself with two of Athens's biggest enemies: Sparta and Persia. His actions gravely affected the future of Athens and his motives and reasons for acting as he did are indeed the stuff of fascinating biography.

Alcibiades's extraordinary beauty, great wealth, ostentatious vanity, male and female amours, debaucheries, and impious revels earned him notoriety not only in Athens but throughout the Hellenic world. In subsequent ages his name was used as a near by-word for all kinds of excess. But, as Benson argues, reappraising Alcibiades's reputation, great as were his vices, his virtues were even greater ...

Although *The Life of Alcibiades* was originally published in 1928, and there have been other newer detailed works published on Alcibiades since then—notably, Steven Forde's *The Ambition to Rule: Alcibiades and the Politics of Imperialism in Thucydides*, 1989, and Walter Ellis's *Alcibiades*, 1989—neither work captures the passion and the excitement of the brilliant but erratic career of Alcibiades as Benson's biography does. As the reader will discover, Benson evidently has much sympathy for his subject and this brings the entire biography very much to life. He combines detailed research, especially his use of primary materials from Thucydides and Plutarch, with writing flare, not an easy accomplishment. In short, Benson's biography of Alcibiades remains unsurpassed in terms of psychological insight and writing style.

Long out of print, *The Life of Alcibiades* richly deserves to be read by new generations of readers in a modern revised edition. The aim of this Viewforth Press edition is to make the text available again to the public in just such a new corrected edition. Typographical errors have been addressed and a new print layout chosen. An editorial decision was also made to leave out of the revised edition Benson's short appendix on Mussolini who had risen to prominence in Italy at the time of writing. It was a brash and ill considered attempt to compare the personalities of Alcibiades and Mussolini. Should any person wish to consult it, he or she will have to get hold of a prior edition of the text. The soul of E. F. Benson, I hope, will not condemn me for the omission.

All those who are interested in the life of Alcibiades, Athenian society and culture, Greek city states, the lives of the ancients in general, or who are interested in brilliant military careers laced with political intrigue, will find this an excellent biography to pick up and read.

Dr. Craig Paterson,
Los Angeles, California, 2010.

PREFACE

THE sources of our information about Alcibiades, such as Thucydides, a contemporary historian, Plato, a contemporary philosopher, or subsequent biographers like Plutarch or gossips like Athenæus, are all accessible to everybody, and the ensuing pages do not pretend to contain facts with which students of his life are not already familiar. But facts, however familiar, can possibly be grouped in new combinations and looked at in new lights, and the study of these has led me to think (and here to set forth) that in certain respects subsequent historians have rendered scant justice to the amazing ability of Alcibiades, his almost magical insight and the breadth of view his statesmanship showed, in their condemnation of his character.

Let us concede then at once that he had the morals of a Satyr, the vanity of a peacock, and that for several years he devoted the energies of the most brilliant brains in Greece to raining calamities on the city of his birth. But having admitted that, it is but just to look into the morals of the day as well as into his, to consider whether a boy so industriously spoiled by his adoring Athens could have avoided being eaten up with vanity, and to examine impartially whether he had not suffered a monstrous injustice at her hands. To ascribe to him any nobility of character would be preposterous, but it would be equally preposterous in a biographer to shut his eyes to his genius and refuse him the due which is proverbially accorded to devils.

Alcibiades has fared hardly with historians: Thucydides alone does not weight the scale against him, but remarks that his public career as a statesman and a General has nothing to do with the scandals of his private life. That is not, it is true, our modern way; a politician's career nowadays can be completely ruined by his private irregularities; but we must not judge Alcibiades by our present standards, but by those prevailing at Athens in his day.

Others, like Mr. Grote, have been so stupefied by his sad pranks and practices that they even deny his ability, and prejudge him as wholly worthless without hearing his defence, much like a certain notable English Judge of darker days, who, at the conclusion of the case for the Crown, said to the prisoner, "I can see that you are a most abandoned wretch," and sentenced him to the maximum penalty. That was a parody of justice, and it is no less a parody of justice that has been served up to this highly sinister but consummately able man by those who, because he was undoubtedly wicked, condemn him as worthless, and rule out such evidence as Thucydides gives with one of his rare flashes of enthusiasm. "He appears," he says, "to have done as eminent a service to the State as any man ever did." To those who are acquainted with the bleak impartiality of the prince of historians, such unusual fervour will carry weight.

If we want to regard him justly now, we must study how he struck his contemporaries. In boyhood and youth he was the idol of the public for his beauty and the charm which even those who disapproved of him most could not resist: while not yet thirty he was of Cabinet rank, and at thirty-five was chosen as one of the three Generals to conduct the Sicilian campaign. In his absence, Athens condemned him to death for blasphemy without a trial, and for three years, in revenge, he directed the course of the Peloponnesian war against her. And yet his countrymen recalled him, welcoming him home with honours meet for a demi-god, knowing that he was the one man who could restore Athens from the ruin of calamity he had rained on her, and their confidence was justified, for he won back her Empire. Once more, in a fit of childish petulance, they deposed him from the dictatorship of the State, and still once more, banished and disgraced, his advice would have saved her from final defeat. Though he was now an exile in Persia, victorious Sparta felt no security while he lived, for once already he had pulled Athens out of the abyss, and she procured his assassination.

Here then are the bare bones of the career which we must clothe with the energy, the charm and the devilishness of him. There is little edification to be gleaned from his story, but a man who was so tinglingly alive, whose brain lost Athens her Empire and won it back for her, was surely something more than a contemptible and swaggering fop. If we employ only our moral sense on his ways and works, no doubt we shall be right in beggaring the dictionary of opprobrious epithets, but there is much to be said for letting the good that men do live after them, and interring the evil with their bones. King David was guilty of offences which would ruin a modern statesman, and yet we are quite right to use his psalms: besides, it somehow seems rather gratuitous to be shocked at what happened so many centuries ago. ... And Alcibiades had charm, colossal charm, and he was witty, and his mouth was full of laughter. It is in the hopes of realizing for modern readers some semblance of his charm, no less than of attempting to do justice to one of the most gifted and unprincipled men who ever lived, that I have written this book.

E. F. Benson.

BIBLIOGRAPHY

Ancient
Homer: "Iliad."
Hesiod: "Works and Days."
Pindar.
Herodotus.
Thucydides.
Plato:
    "Symposium."
    "Protagoras."
    "Euthydemus."
    "Alcibiades I."
    "Republic."
    "Laws."
    -"Phaedrus."
    "Menexenus."
    "Lysis."
    "Hippias Major."
Aristophanes:
    "Clouds."
    "Acharnians."
    "Wasps."
    "Frogs."
    "Peace."
    "Knights."
Æschines: "Timarchus."
Aristotle:
    "Politics."
    "Poetics."
Isocrates: "De Bigis."
Demosthenes: "Meidias."
Xenophon:
    "Memorabilia."
    "Hellenica."
    Œconomica."
Athenæus.
Plutarch:
    "Pericles."
    "Alcibiades."
    "Nicias."
    "Lysander."
    "Themistocles."
    "Aristides."
    "Cimon."
    "Alcibiades and Coriolanus."
    "De liberis Educandis."
Dionysius of Halicarnassus.
Diodorus Siculus.
Stesimbrotus.
Eupolis: "Demes."
Ephorus.
Andocides:
    "De Mysteriis."
    "Alcibiades."
Zeno.
Cornelius Nepos:
    "Alcibiades."
Pausanias.

Modern
Foucart: " Les Mystères d'Eleusis."
Jowett, B.:
    "Dialogues of Plato."
    "Thucydides."
Zimmern, A. E.: "The Greek Commonwealth."
Renan: "Marc Auréle."
Grote, G.: "History of Greece."
Bevan, E.: "Later Greek Religion."
Freeman, K. J.: "Schools of Hellas."
Schmidt, A.: "Perikles und sein Zeitalter."
Mahaffy, J. P.: "Social Life in Greece."
Grundy, G. B.: "Thucydides and his Age."
Henley, W. E.: "Views and Reviews."
Glover, T. R.: "From Pericles

to Philip."
Robinson, C. E.: "The Days of Alcibiades."
Henderson, B. W.: "The Great War between Athens and Sparta."
Bury, J. B.: "History of Greece."
Harrison, J. E.: "Mythology and Monuments of Ancient Athens."
Livingstone, R.W.: "The Greek Genius."
Davidson, T.: "Education of the Greek People."
Tucker, T. G.: "Life in Ancient Athens."
Journal of Hellenic Studies.

CHAPTER I

HISTORICAL INTRODUCTION

CHAPTER I

HISTORICAL INTRODUCTION

IF we leave we leave out of consideration the moral wealth bequeathed to the human race by the founders and the prophets of religion, no other spiritual endowment can compare with that which we have inherited from Hellenic culture. The sciences of philosophy and criticism, the arts of literature in all its branches, prose, poetry and drama, of sculpture in all its forms, from minute gem to colossal statue, of painting, of drawing and of architecture, are among the cosmic bounties of that many-sided genius which blazed for a century and a half on the shores of Greece. In some of these manifestations of knowledge and art, subsequent generations and individual creators may claim to have approached that noble illumination, but in none can they claim to have outshone it in beauty or in clarity, and for the most part later ages and renaissances can only measure their achievements beside and far below the standard then set up, which, to our human perception, still seems flawless in temper and in execution. What, above all, characterized this age was its intellectual curiosity, its lucidity of expression and its love of beauty; by these instincts, freely and fearlessly pursued wherever they led, were fashioned those heirlooms which are the chiefest treasures of the human race.

We are apt to think that it was all Greece which, in the noon of the classical age, was aflame with imaginative genius. This is far from being the case: the vast bulk of our debt to Greece is due to Athens, the capital of one small State among its non-cohering peoples. This State in its most populous days numbered not more than a hundred thousand free-men, and its total territory about seven hundred square miles; ingenious chartographers show us how the whole of Attica can be dropped into the interior of

The Life of Alcibiades

Yorkshire without approaching its boundaries. But genius, like the grace of God, bloweth where it listeth, and for a hundred and fifty years, from about B.C. 500 till the middle of the fourth century, the divine gale moved in unceasing magic among its plane-trees and its olives. Homer, to some minds the greatest of all creators, was outside it, being of an earlier epoch and of uncertain nationality; Pindar in the great age came from Bœotia, Aristotle from Eubœa, but apart from these the masters of Greek thought and art are Attic and Athenian.

In this attainment of the peaks up which her noble destiny led her, Athens was spurred on only by her innate intellectual curiosity and her love of beauty, and she pursued her path, not with bleeding feet and painful effort, but, instinctively following that which enchanted her, she mounted with grace and gaiety to the heights towards which we still gaze. For her there was no laborious climbing with exiguous foothold over perilous places; some law of celestial gravitation led her swiftly up the slopes of this Olympus where she is throned for ever, watching with kind and yet faintly satirical eyes the upward efforts of those who struggle to follow her, or seek, owing to their innate love of ugliness, to depose her. Despite the proverb, it is talent, not genius, to which belongs the infinite capacity for taking pains; the spontaneous energy of genius has no need of conscious effort, and it was in the manner of a nation of geniuses that Athens, under the spell of her joyous instincts, became, without struggle or subsequent challenge, the lodestar of all lovers of mental and material beauty.

Religion, as embodied in her current mythology, was but little incentive to her, the legends of gods and goddesses were not the inspiration of her art to anything like the extent that the life of Christ was to the painters of the Italian Renaissance; they were no more to her than magnificent subjects for illustration, and the limbs of young manhood, rather than the divinity of Hermes, were the sculptor's theme in that statue which consecrates anew the holy soil of Olympia. Nor was it primarily for the glory of Athene that the Panathenaic procession wound up the rock-hewn path to the Acropolis, or that inside her temple gleamed the gold raiment and ivory limbs fashioned by Pheidias, in the sense that her glory was the sole end in view, for the gold that decked her had been weighed and valued, and Pericles in one of his Budget speeches reckoned it, as we should say, as bullion at the Bank of Athens if the expenses of the Peloponnesian War required that it should be coined into ships and wages for her sailors; the golden robe of the goddess was, in fact, only lent her, and if Athens needed it she must go naked. Plato, similarly, recommended that, since so much of the received mythology was unsuitable to the minds of the young, it should not be taught in schools, as being of very doubtful edification, which was, indeed, the case. But though the canonical books of Olympus were little to Athens, the sense of beauty was all in all, and it was for the magnificence of the city that on the worship of the high gods was poured forth the full splendour of her peerless art. That thirst for beauty led sculptor and mason to make the house of Athene glorious, to deck her with light and clothe her in majesty and honour, but it was not the fervour of religion which inspired them.

The myths of god and goddess, then, in the fifth century B.C., riddled as they were with adulteries and seductions and rapes and incests, exercised no inspiring force, nor indeed were they considered hallowed by thinking men, or in any way revelations of the divine. But somewhere, secret and sacred in the spirits of the initiated, were certain doctrines of which we know but little, but which were holy to the Greeks in a sense that the amours of Zeus were not. It was in these that the yearnings of the soul of man for the knowledge of what lies outside and beyond the realm of material things found their satisfaction, and chief among them at this period were the Eleusinian mysteries. They were in the keeping of the Eumolpidæ, the Royal Family of the cult, who were their hereditary priests, just as were the Levites in the worship of the Jews, and who, as we shall see in the story of Alcibiades, were a great political force. These mysteries were celebrated every year at Eleusis when, after fasting and purification,[1] initiates witnessed the tableaux of the liturgical dramas[2] in which were embodied certain esoteric revelations, precisely as the central truth of the Christian revelation is dramatically embodied in the Mass. These mysteries, in which the hierophant displayed certain sacred objects to the initiates, just as the priest elevates the holy elements of the Sacrament, were to the Greeks the very core and essence of religion; they were on a different plane of sacredness altogether from that of public worship, and the penalty of death was attached to any initiate who revealed what he had seen at the celebration. Here lay the heart of religion as we understand the word; men looked for spiritual aid not from the fickle roysterers of Olympus, but from the illumination in the Hall of Mysteries which shone "without variableness neither shadow of turning."

But even as the authorized religion of myth as handed down from Homer was to the Athenians more a reference book of hints and suggestions for artistic creation than a magnet to their hearts, so the spirit of such religion manifested itself in superstition rather than in morality: indeed, it was impossible to draw any moral lesson from life on Olympus. Athenian philosophers had not yet formulated any theory of the immanence of God in the material world or in the conduct of life, and not till the middle of the next century did Zeno propound the doctrine that "God is a kind of air or breath, interpenetrating even things ugly or loathsome," or Diogenes Lærtius perceive that "God, Mind, Destiny, Zeus—it is one thing which is called by these and many other names."[3] With regard to conduct, a dissolute habit of living, as Athens saw, tended to unfit her citizens for their service towards the State, for their

---

[1] Foucart, "Les Mystères d'Eleusis," p. 282.
[2] Foucart, "Les Mystères," p. 357.
[3] Edwyn Bevan, "Later Greek Religion," p. 2.

physical efficiency in strength and swiftness which she ever held to be their supreme duty, and for the clear-eyed exercise of their reason, and on this score alone and not from any abstract moral principles she disapproved of excess of wantonness. But except in the minds of a few of her most elevated thinkers there was little that a man could do which was in itself right or wrong, provided that he neglected nothing which could make him a cultured and useful citizen.

The educational system at Athens, as well as her moral code, was entirely devoted to this end, and to making her boys strong and graceful and accomplished in such gentle arts as singing, dancing and recitation. It guarded them from the corruption of their morals while they were still of such tender age as not to know what morals meant, but this supervision ceased when they had the knowledge by which they could choose for themselves. For girls there was provided no education at all, save such as their mothers might chance to give them, and their mothers had learned nothing but sewing, weaving and cooking. But in the city of the maiden-goddess neither wife nor maid had any recognized existence: no respectable woman was ever seen in the streets except at a few festivals; her functions were solely to keep the house and to breed males and their subsidiary wives, and her glory, as Pericles defined it in the great funeral oration, was that she should not be talked about for good or evil among men.

But of the educational system in Athens, and of the aspect which their environment wore to boys beginning to approach manhood, it will be more proper to speak when we come to the influences which surrounded the youth of Alcibiades, and we must first trace, though in sketchiest outline only, the events and political developments of the first half of the fifth century B.C., which had raised Athens to the particular position she occupied at the beginning of his public life. In no other way can we hope to comprehend in its relation to its environment a character which might well be rejected as impossible in the pages of fiction, but

The Life of Alcibiades

which, if we place him in his true setting, may appear in the outcome to be essentially and typically Athenian. Indeed, though the dictum of Archestratus was true, that Greece could not stand more than one Alcibiades,[1] Athens would have lacked the most complete incarnation of her splendour and her shame without him: there must needs have been one Alcibiades, and he Athenian.

The fifth century B.C., which stored for the civilized world the inestimable treasury of Hellenic culture, was for Athens a period of almost continuous warfare; it witnessed the rise of her island Empire, its supremacy and its fall. First came the Persian wars, the events of which it is not necessary to trace, except in so far as they determined the inception of the Athenian Empire, for Athens found therein her capacity for becoming a sea-Power. That change was no less crucial than in the days of Queen Elizabeth was the creation of her Navy by Drake and the great admirals of her age; it forged for Athens her future as the first State in Greece with a dominion of islands and coast-towns, and opened to her the road for her imperial policy.

A huge national crisis under the direction of Themistocles set the wheels of her destiny in motion. After the Greek defeat at Thermopylæ the way was clear for the advance of the Persian armies, and they marched with none to stay them on Athens. Without the aid of Sparta and the Peloponnesian army no resistance was possible, and Sparta, though temporarily allied with Athens, cared nothing for the fate of Northern Greece, if only the invasion of the Peloponnese could be averted. Themistocles therefore urged that the whole population should abandon the doomed city, and embarking on the fleet, seek the safety of the neighbouring islands. To give divine support to this policy, there

---

[1] Plutarch, "Alcibiades," c. xvi. 5.

had come from Delphi, in answer to his delegates, an oracle couched in the true Pythian style. "While all things else," it ran, "are taken within the boundary of Cecrops, Zeus grants to Athens that the wall of wood alone shall remain uncaptured that shall help thee and thy children. Stay not for horsemen and an host of men on foot coming from the mainland; retire, turning thy back. One day thou shalt yet show thy face. O divine Salamis, but thou shalt slay children of women, either at the scattering of Demeter or at the gathering."

The arrival of that oracle was a brave moment for Themistocles's policy, for to what could the dark speech of the oracle allude by "the wooden walls" except to the ships? A small body of dissentients shook their heads over this interpretation, and they built a wooden wall across the west slope of the Acropolis at Athens, which on all other sides is precipitous, and hoped to defend it against the Persian hordes. But for the rest Themistocles's policy, thus endorsed by Delphi, brought conviction, and down to the harbour at Peiræus streamed the citizens of Athens. The wooden wall on the Acropolis was taken, its defenders were massacred and the town was sacked, but the fleet bore away to safety the bulk of the population. The naval victory at Salamis, even as the oracle had said, followed by the battle of Platæa next year, B.C. 479, put an end to the Persian peril.

Such was the first step in the establishment of the Athenian naval Empire, of which Themistocles must be considered architect and originator. Probably his policy, which saved the population of Athens by making them take to their ships, had no other object in view at the moment than their deliverance from certain destruction, but the idea of founding a naval Empire sprang immediately from it; command of the sea on a small scale had saved Athens, what might not command of the sea on a large scale effect? The islands of the Ægean and the Greek coast-towns of Asia Minor were at present scattered and unfederated settlements, at the mercy of raids from Persian and Phœnician ships, and the

The Life of Alcibiades

scheme of welding them into a maritime league under the presidency of Athens began to weave itself in Themistocles's brain. Athens must be born again of wave and sea-wind, and while making herself safe from land attack by means of impregnable fortifications, must transform herself into an island. Her glory and her destiny lay on the water, her might behind the wooden walls which had already saved her from the enemy that had laid her city waste, and founded upon the seas and prepared upon the floods, she could think scorn of all the hoplites of envious Sparta. There lay dominion and destiny.

The rebuilding of Athens, however, was Themistocles's first concern. Phœnix-like, it rose from the ashes of its burning, but the new town was to his imaginative vision the capital of an island Empire and must be fortified against attack by land. This rebuilding of the walls of Athens on a far stronger scale than before roused, as he had foreseen, the jealous mistrust of Sparta, but he out-tricked her opposition, and every man, woman and child wrought in a fever of masonry, while parleyings were in progress.[1] The walls rose apace round Athens and the port of Peiræus, the dockyards were busy, and in a couple of years her navy, now the strongest in Greece, was a tool sharpened and ready in the hand of her two leading statesmen, Themistocles and Aristides, for the fashioning of her naval imperialism. Of this the general idea was, as already stated, to form a confederacy of Ægean islands and Ionic coast-towns, with Athens at their head, for mutual protection against Persian and Phœnician attacks. Thus welded into a league, with the fleet of Athens and the ships of the confederacy at their back, they could conduct, not only defensive, but also offensive operations against the barbarians.[2]

---

[1] Thucydides, I, 90.
[2] Thucydides, I, 96.

The members of the league, duly rated, subscribed to its funds or its equipment in cash or in the furnishing of ships, and most of them, to avoid service, chose the former. This choice was most convenient for the imperialistic purposes of Athens which underlay the league, for the Treasury (though at present situated at Delos) was in Athenian control, and the cash was largely spent in building fresh ships for the Athenian fleet, which, though it was at the service of the league, was certainly at the service of Athens. It was not long before her imperialism emerged into full light; one island, Naxos, seceded from the league and was forced to rejoin, or, as Thucydides pointedly observes, was "enslaved."[1] Thasos similarly was deprived of its fortifications and its fleet handed over to Athens.[2] Athenian colonies were planted on various coasts, Athenian garrisons established in Confederated cities, and step by step the allies became the subjects of the ruling State. Before the middle of the century the bullion at Delos was transferred to Athens, and in payment for its storage there, a sixtieth part of the annual income of the league was credited to the national treasury. Except in name, the confederacy had ceased to exist; in substance it was the Athenian Empire.

Themistocles did not live to see the full harvest, rapidly as it ripened, of his sowing. In B.C. 472, eighteen years before the Treasury of Delos was transferred to Athens, he was exiled by the process called ostracism. This curious institution, so illogical and exuberant, was peculiarly Athenian. Just before the annual election of the ten "Generals" who formed, as we should say, the Cabinet, the question was put to the Assembly, which consisted of all free-born citizens, as to whether they wished to ostracize any of their leaders. If the vote was in favour of an ostracism, a special

---

[1] Thucydides, I, 98.
[2] Thucydides, I, 101.

The Life of Alcibiades

assembly was held, and every citizen wrote on a potsherd the name of the man he desired to see banished. Six thousand votes at the least had to be recorded for any action to be taken, but if that number was reached the man whose name was inscribed on a majority of them was exiled from Attic soil for a period of ten years. There was no disgrace attached to the sentence, for the exile maintained his status as an Athenian citizen; indeed it was a distinction, for no insignificant person was worth ostracizing, but only those who had grown too powerful, or of whose continued pre-eminence the people were tired. It was thus an institution intensely Athenian, for they were, of all people, the most fickle to their great men and the most eager for novelty. They always wearied of those under whose guidance their city had prospered most, and they thus rid themselves of the oppressive presence. Themistocles was ostracized, but was summoned back to Athens to stand his trial on the charge of treasonable correspondence with Persia. Thither he fled, and offered his services to King Artaxerxes against Greece. The King warmly welcomed him and made him Governor of Magnesia, where he died soon after. The traitorous conclusion of the career of this great Empire-builder is not only of melancholy interest in itself, but also because, as we shall see, another accusation, never proved and probably unfounded, similarly drove Alcibiades into conspiracy with his country's enemies to the disastrous undoing of Athens.

. . . .

After the exile of Themistocles a reactionary policy set in for a while at Athens under the leadership of Cimon. His failure to cultivate friendly relations with Sparta caused the balance to swing back again, and in B.C. 461 Pericles came into power. For thirty years the guidance of Athens was in his hands, and neither before him nor after did any leader retain the confidence of that fickle people so long. The two principles of his policy from which he never swerved were the broadest democracy for the citizens and naval imperialism for the State. His constitutional reforms put it within the reach of the poorest and humblest citizen to attain to the highest office, and removed every bar to political eminence.[1] The spirit of his imperialism in extending and strengthening Athenian maritime power was that of Themistocles, and though in this his statesmanship was not original, he developed it on lines that were entirely new. Themistocles, as we have seen, fortified Athens and the Peiræus against attack from the land, but Pericles conceived and executed the amazing idea of connecting the two by enclosing a strip of the plain of Attica in defensive walls four miles long, which ran down from Athens to the sea, thus joining the city to its port, and containing them both within the fortified area. As long as these walls were untaken, it could never be cut off from the sea, and should Attica be invaded, Athens and the seat of Government could not, while her fleet was in being, be severed from her ships or from her subject States.

These long walls, the design of which was to turn Athens into an island, were finished in the year B.C. 458, but close at hand to the port of Peiræus, and constituting a standing menace to its security, lay the island of Ægina with its powerful fleet, which, as Pericles termed it, was "the eyesore of the Peiræus."[2] Ægina had watched with distrust and hatred the rise of the new sea-Power, whose fleet now surpassed her own, and Athens could not tolerate so formidable an enemy at her very doors. She therefore attacked her on no specific quarrel, and after nearly a year's blockade Ægina surrendered, was forced to give up her entire fleet and was enrolled among the island States which were now no longer the allies of Athens but her subjects. Simultaneously, with incredible swiftness of expansion, Athens had two hundred of her ships engaged off

---

[1] Thucydides, II, 37.
[2] Plutarch, "Pericles," VII.

The Life of Alcibiades

Egypt, and had sent expeditions to Cyprus and Halieis; she established herself also at Naupactus, a port on the Corinthian gulf, and thereby checked the freedom of the navy of Corinth. This hold over the sea-power of Corinth opened up a fresh field, and Athens looked westwards to Sicily, which had previously been in the sphere of Corinthian influence, as a new territory for maritime colonization. She founded New Sybaris, and a few years later Thurii, and this idea of adding Sicily to her Empire, though dormant for a while, had taken root in her imperial programme. No dreams of power just then seemed outside the sphere of accomplishment; the vigour of Athens was that of April and its effortless miracles.

So far Pericles had only been extending and amplifying the maritime programme of Themistocles, but in other directions Athens under his guidance made expansions which were directly contrary to the spirit of the original policy. She conquered Bœotia on her northern frontier, and, under the guise of alliance, annexed Megara on the west. The Peloponnesian League, headed by Sparta, though profoundly jealous of Athens' naval supremacy, had been powerless to prevent it, but annexation of States of continental Greece was a grave political error, for it could not be supposed that the Peloponnesian League, far more powerful than Athens by land, would acquiesce in encroachments that it had the means to prevent. To attempt to establish dominion over these States was a reversal, not an extension, of Themistocles's policy, and it strained to breaking point Athenian relations with the Peloponnesian League. Nor was Athens left long in possession of her injudicious conquests; Bœotia revolted in B.C. 447 and the Athenian expedition sent out to reduce it was defeated. The revolt of Bœotia was followed by that of Megara, and Megara, backed up by troops of the Peloponnesian League, invaded Attica. Pericles at once saw the mistake he had made in attempting to extend the dominion of Athens on land, and, though war had never been definitely declared, concluded a thirty-years' peace with Sparta and her allies, giving up the lately-acquired territories, and thus returning to the policy and programme of Themistocles. Such terms, though humiliating to projects of wider imperialism, still left Athens the most powerful of the Greek States. On continental Greece her dominion was again limited to Attica, but the isles of the Ægean, with the exception of Melos, and many coast towns of the Thracian Chersonese, were hers; two hundred dependencies, originally allies, paid tribute to the coffers of Athene. There was no power, either abroad or among the bitter brotherhood of Hellenic States, which could seriously menace her fleet: Athens was an island, the original vision of Themistocles had realized itself more vividly than in the colours of his very dreams, and all that had been lost was the fruit of an ambition directly opposed to his policy. Though the peace lasted only for fourteen years out of the inscribed period of thirty, it is surprising that it lasted so long, for Athens was regarded with the keenest and most watchful enmity by Sparta and the whole Peloponnesian League, and her naval empire of tributary island States was recognized to be no alliance, but a supremacy of naval might.

For these fourteen years from B.C. 445 to B.C. 431, years in which the dominion of Athens declined not a degree from its zenith, and which saw the flower of her artistic splendour supremely blossoming, the hand that controlled her and led her along the path of her eternal destiny was that of Pericles. Apart from the revolt of Samos from the so-called Athenian confederacy, which was followed by its capitulation and the surrender of its entire fleet, Athens was at peace for the last time before her fall. No cloud of serious menace dimmed that unique noon, and Pericles, while continuing to add to the strength of her navy, turned to the work which was infinitely nearer his heart than any political autocracy, and set himself to make the city a palace worthy of the virgin goddess by whose power the might of Persia had been repelled. In this pause of peace before the outbreak of the Peloponnesian War every year saw some new miracle of art

The Life of Alcibiades

divinely manifest. First Athene herself, who had led her children to victory at Marathon and Salamis, must be visibly installed as their ever-present protector, and her image of bronze, forty feet high, rose colossal on her hill beholding Salamis. She carried a huge spear upright in her hand, and the sunlight striking the tip of it shone like a beacon star to her ships at sea while yet the coasts of Attica were veiled and dim. Then next she must be housed in a palace worthy of her splendour, and from Pentelicus, the mountain of her "violet crown," came the hewn blocks of white marble for its building and its decoration. The architects were Ictinus and Callicrates, and on the great marble platform laid with the soft flow of a carpet on the rock there rose the noblest monument of the world. Solemn and solid and of Doric style, it springs like some gracious living growth from the rock, so subtly calculated are the curves of its seemingly rectangular fashioning. It is formed of two chambers facing east and west, surrounded by a colonnade of pillars; of these the eastern was the actual shrine, the western the storehouse for the treasures of the temple and the vestry of its ministers. Incomparably noble as is the mere wreck of the actual structure, it was but the casket and the frame for the sculptures that adorned it, and this work of decoration was entrusted to Pheidias. Over the encircling Doric columns ran the frieze, representing in panels of very deep relief the battles of Centaurs and Lapiths, and on the walls of the two chambers inside the colonnade was the continuous Ionic frieze on which was carved the Panathenaic procession which on the Goddess's birthday wound up the hill to her shrine. At the East end sat the assembled gods, and along the sides starting from the western end marched the great marble pageant. The maidens of Athens carried the vessels for the feast, the oxen and sheep for sacrifice were driven to the altar, and, superbest of all, the youth of the city, mounted on horses, streamed along to do honour to the lady of their manhood. In the triangular pediments over each end of the temple gleamed the company of divine presences; in one was set the birth of the goddess from the brain of her father Zeus, and in the other her contest with Poseidon for the realm of Attica.

How many of these reliefs and statues came to life under the actual chisel of Pheidias himself, we cannot certainly know. In conception, in composition and in technique they are the unchallenged princes of sculptural art, and they certainly owe their inspiration to him. But it seems quite impossible that any one man could have executed them all, and though they were made in the workshops he set up for the decoration of the Parthenon, they cannot be regarded as authentically his. Probably he made the terracotta sketches for them, and left the execution of them in marble (though no doubt with many touches of his own) to his school of apprentice-sculptors, for he was personally employed on the chryselephantine image of Athene that stood in her shrine within. The core of it was of carved wood, colossal in size, and represented her standing, helmeted, with a figure of winged Victory in one hand while the other rested on her shield. But of this core no minutest atom appeared, for the robe of the goddess which covered it was of gold, and of gold her helmet and of gold her sculptured shield and the figure of Victory that she bore; the flesh of her sandalled feet, of her arms and hands and face and neck, was all of ivory, and her eyes were of coloured stones.[1] What these chryselephantine statues were like, and what their effect and splendour, we cannot judge, since no fragment of them has survived, but they were considered as the crown and masterpieces of Greek sculpture.

For ten years masons and sculptors, architects and engineers worked at the building and the embellishing of the house of Athene, and in B.C. 438 it stood complete. Noble, too, must be the gateway into her precinct, that holy hill of the Acropolis, on which

---

[1] Plato, "Hippias Major," 290 B.

The Life of Alcibiades

was her dwelling, and after that was done, for five years more, on the designs of Mnesicles, the colonnade and gateway of the Propylæa rose on the western edge of the hill, and on the bastion beside it the little Ionic temple of Wingless Victory, for Victory had come to abide for ever in Athens, and she stripped off her wings, which she would never need more. Below in the town Pericles built the Odeum for assembly and for the musical contests held at the Panathenaic festival, and at Eleusis a huge hall for the celebration of the sacred Mysteries. All these, if we may judge from the Parthenon and the Propylæa and the reconstructed temple of Nike which alone remain, were of perfect and consummate design, and Plutarch, in a passage of most discerning art criticism, the truth of which is self-evident, tells us that "Each of these works was instantly antique, but in the freshness of its vigour it is, even to the present day, recent and newly-wrought. Such is this bloom of perpetual freshness, as it were, upon these works of his, which makes them ever to look untouched by time, as though the ever-blowing breath of an ageless spirit had been inspired into them."[1] For fourteen years the revenues of Athens were poured out on these immortal splendours, of which the Propylæa was not yet complete when, in B.C. 431, the Peloponnesian War broke out. In these years 8000 talents or nearly £2,000,000 in actual gold were spent on them, which was just about equivalent to the rate of expenditure on the war itself.[2]

The outflow of these huge sums on the adornment of the city was not made without opposition. A consider-able part of them was drawn from the tribute paid by the allied subject-States of Athens, and a political party, headed by Thucydides, made a protest in the Council against the dishonesty of using the money of

---

[1] Plutarch, "Pericles," XIV, 1, 2.
[2] Zimmern, "The Greek Commonwealth," p. 410.

the allies for such purposes. Pericles replied that, in return for their tribute, the allies bargained that they should be afforded protection from attacks of the Persian navy, and that if Athens, who, after all, spent very large sums on her fleet, scrupulously performed her side of the contract, it concerned nobody but her how she spent these moneys. That reply was logical enough; it satisfied the Council, and Pericles could have left the matter there. But, like the political athlete that he was,[1] he chose to take it further, and his manner of so doing shows us how well he had earned his Athenian nick-name of the "Olympian." Instead of contenting himself with the approval of the Council, he summoned an Assembly of the citizens, and asked them if they considered him too lavish in making Athens beautiful. Thucydides, a notable demagogue, had a large party at his back, who would have preferred that these great sums should be spent on State doles for the idle instead of on wages for workers, and the Assembly voted that this expenditure was excessive; they passed, in fact, a vote of censure. "So be it," said Pericles, "I have there-fore done wrong. But now you must consider that not one penny has been spent on these buildings out of public funds. I will bear the whole cost myself, and I shall, of course, dedicate them to the goddess in my own name, and inscribe it there." Truly an Olympian gesture, and it had precisely the effect he had no doubt anticipated, for though he was a rich man we cannot suppose that he had two million pounds to pay for the Parthenon and Propylæa. But he knew that Athens was as proud of her magnificence as he, as the event proved. The Assembly instantly cancelled its vote of censure, and by acclamation bade him spend whatever he liked out of the revenues of the State on this noble embellishment of the town. Though we may be morally shocked at this stupendous misappropriation of

---

[1] Plutarch, "Pericles," IV, 1.

The Life of Alcibiades

funds which were supposed to be devoted to the military and naval operations of the league, our æsthetic sense must rejoice that it produced for all subsequent ages a deathless inheritance of beauty.

CHAPTER II

THE BOYHOOD OF ALCIBIADES

CHAPTER II

THE BOYHOOD OF ALCIBIADES

THE exact date of the birth of Alcibiades is nowhere expressly stated, nor can it be inferred with absolute certainty, but two passages in Plato's dialogues give us enough accuracy for all practical purposes of biography. The first of these occurs in "Alcibiades I," where Socrates reminds him that he is "not yet twenty."[1] Pericles is still alive, but died in B.C. 429, and assuming that the phrase "not yet twenty" meant that Alcibiades was nineteen, it follows that he cannot have been born later than B.C. 448.[2] He appears, however, to have been born a year or two before that, for in the "Symposium" Alcibiades states that he served in the campaign at Potidæa, and mentions events which happened during his service there in summer and in winter.[3] We infer therefrom that he must have been there for the best part of a year, and the campaign at Potidæa came to an end in B.C. 430. Alcibiades would not normally have been employed on active service until he was twenty, for military training at Athens began when a boy was eighteen and lasted for two years, after which he was liable to be called on for service in the field. Since, then, he served for a year at Potidæa, it looks as if he was born not later than B.C. 451. But owing to special circumstances, as we shall see, boys who would

---

[1] Plato, "Alcibiades I," 123.
[2] It is hard to see why Dr. Jowett, who takes B.C. 448 as being the year of Alcibiades's birth, should accuse Plato of an anachronism in making him "about twenty" during the lifetime of Pericles, for this is perfectly correct. ("Dialogues of Plato," II, 446).
[3] Plato, "Symposium," 219.

The Life of Alcibiades

have entered their second year of training in B.C. 430 may have been employed on active service during this year. We can therefore put the date of his birth as being within a twelvemonth of B.C. 450.

His father was Cleinias, a wealthy and patriotic man of noble birth, who in the Persian wars furnished a trireme at his own expense and commanded it at the naval fight of Artemisium in the year B.C. 480.[1] His mother's name was Deinomache, of the Alcmæonid tribe, and she was probably first cousin to Pericles. Diodorus, it is true, tells us that Alcibiades was Pericles's nephew, being the son of his sister,[2] but this certainly cannot have been the case, since Deinomache was of the Alcmæonid tribe,[3] while Pericles (and therefore his sister) was of the Acamantis.[4] But Pericles had Alcmæonid blood from his mother's side,[5] and the simplest solution, which satisfies all requirements, is that Pericles's mother was sister of Deinomache's father. Alcibiades's father, Cleinias, was killed in B.C. 447 at the battle of Coronea,[6] which lost Athens her newly-acquired subject-State of Bœotia, and Alcibiades, aged three, and his younger brother, who was named after his father, were placed under the guardianship of Pericles, his mother's first cousin, and lived in his house. Never, surely, was guardian in charge of so incongruous a ward.

Plato, anticipating Freud, tells us that the early associations of children, the example of their elders, and the environment of their tender years are of the very highest importance in determining and forming their characters. But in the case of Alcibiades, this *milieu* of

---

[1] Plutarch, "Alcibiades," I, 1.
[2] Diodorus Siculus, XII, 7 (followed by Dr. Jowett).
[3] Plutarch, "Alcibiades," I, 1.
[4] Plutarch, "Pericles," III, 1.
[5] Thucydides, I, 127.
[6] Plato, "Alcibiades I," 112.

his boyhood in the house of his illustrious kinsman seems, if it produced any effect at all, to have given rise to a result precisely the opposite to such psychological deduction, and we must fall back on the theory that there is no quality in the world less malleable than genius; for Pericles at the time of his cousin's earliest memories, when the soft wax of childhood should have been receiving indelible impressions, was (though more absolute master of Athens than any king or tyrant could have been)[1] the very pattern of personal sobriety, economy, and high-minded moderation in the conduct of his private life. Had he followed the natural bent of his lofty and aloof mind he would have been a philosopher: his life would have been passed in the shade of academic groves, and it was certainly through no lure of personal ambition that he climbed to his long and dizzy pre-eminence in Athenian politics. Power never intoxicated him; never would he use display or forensic glamour of speech to attract the mob, though he was the most brilliant of orators and though picturesque speech and noble gesture were a sure appeal to his dramatic countrymen. He used, indeed, before making a speech to pray God that he might not say a single word that was not directly to the point, and his speeches as given by Thucydides, though not a literal report of what he said, confirm this account of their fashioning. They were, like himself, perfectly simple and unadorned, "bread dipped in Attic salt"; he relied only on reason and sober fact in his advocacy, and sought for no triumph of eloquence or tribute to his own achievement, because at heart he despised human nature,[2] and its undisciplined adoration and applause were empty chaff to him. The splendour and supremacy of Athens, the welfare and worthiness of her citizens were the lodestar from which his course

---

[1] Plutarch, "Pericles," XVI, 1.
[2] Plutarch, "Pericles," V, 3.

The Life of Alcibiades

never deflected, and once only in all the years of his pre-eminence did he ask a personal boon. It was enough for the Prince of Athens to serve her.

Wealth meant nothing to him; with all his continual opportunities for taking bribes, he never enriched himself, and at the end of his life, in spite of his ascetic and economical modes, his property was no greater than what his father had left him. Mob-worship meant no more to him than wealth, and like Marcus Aurelius, whom in many points he resembled, he never made the smallest bid for the popularity which was showered on him.[1] A stern and austere simplicity characterized his private life; his housekeeping, under the charge of his steward Evangelus, was conducted with the most parsimonious economy, and the receipts from the sale of the country produce of his estates, and the bills for expenditure on food and upkeep, were rigidly scrutinized.[2] He neither accepted nor gave invitations to those gatherings of wit and wine which were so conspicuous a social feature in the day of an Athenian gentleman, and during all the years in which he was head of the State he only once went out to dinner. That was on the occasion of the marriage of his kinsman Euryptolemus, and even then he left before the drinking began.[3]

Such economical seclusion in the head of a great and wealthy house was almost inhuman, and was held up to public ridicule by his spendthrift son, Xanthippus.[4] He was never known to laugh, an un-Athenian and indeed an unamiable trait, his manner was of an aloof suavity, and his self-control equal to that of Socrates himself. One day a rude lout of a fellow had been continually pestering him in the publicity of the market-place, and bawling out insults to

---

[1] Renan, "Marc Auréle," p. 20.
[2] Plutarch, "Pericles," XVI, 4.
[3] Plutarch, "Pericles," VII, 4.
[4] Plutarch, "Pericles," XXXVI, 2.

which Pericles was deaf. As he walked home the man followed him, shouting abuse. It was already dark when he arrived at his house, and still without deigning to reply, he directed a servant to kindle a torch and light the blackguard on his home-ward way. Athens, always on the alert for satirical amusement, saw in this high forbearance a thirst for the reputation of self-control, but the whole conduct of Pericles's life was of a piece with it, and we must regard it as a perfectly sincere expression of his indifference. In any case, so lofty a craze, as the philosopher Zeno remarked, would be highly beneficial to most people if it resulted in a similar nobility of life.[1]

It was no wonder that Athens, who found a nick-name for everybody, christened him "Olympian" Pericles. The epithet was a perfect fit, and if there was a tang of ironical contempt in the name for one who never laughed or drank or relaxed into gossip, it was primarily a tribute of profound respect. That the ferment of power should never have gone to his head, nor any taunt have stung him, would be incredible if we did not remember that he was philosopher and savant by nature, and Prince of Athens only through a sense of duty, and that as politician his sole aim, without a glance at himself, was the establishment of Athens as the imperial and supreme power in Greece, and as leader in the beauteous ways of art and thought. But to the most clubbable people in the world there was some-thing inhuman in this Olympian quality, for after such a triumph as his over the expenditure of public funds, he never loitered in the market-place to receive congratulations, but hurried home, for Anaxagoras was waiting for him to continue that exalted discussion on the origin of the Universe. Some eternal mind, they had just agreed, had set it going, and it was under that impulse that it pursued its inscrutable way. Such topics were alone

---

[1] Plutarch, "Pericles," V, 3.

The Life of Alcibiades.

worthy of study; loftier thoughts arose from the discussion of the sublime truths of nature[1] than from the trifling management of these childish disputes, and they freed the mind from the fetters of passion and superstition. Athens was profoundly superstitious; she found terrifying omens and warnings in every dream and chance happening, and the eternal Verities were the medicine for such ailments. Mind, not Man, was the true study of man, for it purged man from senseless instincts. ... Or Pythoclides was waiting to give him his lesson in music, or Damon, who was his later master.[2] Such, briefly, was the temperament and such the private tastes of the guardian of Alcibiades. It will at once be evident how idle it is to attempt to derive from the influence of so noble a mind and so austere an environment one single trait in his character.

We have far more information about the boyhood and youth of Alcibiades (most of it highly picturesque and unedifying) than about that of any other famous or infamous personage in the whole of history. From his earliest years, long before he took part in political life, he was one of those rare and fascinating individuals whose smallest actions and whose lightest words provoke eager interest, and involuntarily excite strong disapproval and passionate devotion. As a boy, as a youth, as a man, he had a unique charm and distinction which continually earned him forgiveness for his most outrageous escapades. Athens always pardoned him and yearned for him even when he had brought on her storms of ruin and disaster. "In him," as Nepos tells us,[3] "nature seems to have tried what she could do," and it must be confessed that she brought off a masterpiece of splendour and devilry. Vicious, insolent, adorable, detestable, brilliant and fickle, with the face and

---

[1] Plato, "Phædrus," 270.
[2] Plato, "Alcibiades I," 118.
[3] Cornelius Nepos "Alcibiades," I.

body of a god and the wit of Aristophanes, he was the very incarnation of the spirit of Athens.

At the age of three, then, now fatherless, he came with his baby brother Cleinias to the guardianship of Pericles. Pericles's first wife was still living with him, and his two young sons, Xanthippus and Paralus. The wards had, as nurse, a woman from Sparta, named Amycla,[1] for Spartan nurses were much sought after throughout Greece as being rigid and successful disciplinarians. But Amycla made a singularly poor job in her present situation, for never did any boy emerge from a nurse's care so completely undisciplined as Alcibiades. Of Cleinias we learn little, and that little casts a lurid light on his brother, for presently he was sent away by Pericles to be brought up by his brother Ariphron, for fear that Alcibiades should corrupt him. Shortly afterwards Ariphron sent the boy back, as he could do nothing with him,[2] upon which Pericles seems to have resigned himself to the corruption of Cleinias. He was, in fact, no example of a conscientious guardian, for now he appointed as tutor to Alcibiades a Thracian slave of his called Zopyrus, whom, being past all other work,[3] he turned on to manage the most unmanageable boy. The tutor in Athenian households was a mixture of footman, guardian and attendant with the power of corporal punishment. When a boy came to the age of six or seven and went to school it was the tutor's duty to accompany him, and see that he did not loiter or talk to undesirable folk. He sat with him, as we see from the paintings on Attic vases,[4] when he was at his class, and brought him home again. He remained with him certainly till he left his elementary school at the age of fourteen,

---

[1] Plutarch, "Alcibiades," I, 2.
[2] Plato, "Protagoras," 320.
[3] Plato, "Alcibiades I," 122.
[4] For admirable reproductions of these vases depicting school-life in Athens see "Schools of Hellas," K. J. Freeman.

The Life of Alcibiades

and possibly till, when he was eighteen, his military training began.[1] Zopyrus appears to have been quite as unsuccessful with his charge as nurse Amycla had been.

Up till this age of six or seven Alcibiades had lived in the women's quarters of the house. Pericles seldom came there, for he was on bad terms with his wife, whom, about this time, he divorced. Now the boy went off to school with the aged Zopyrus tottering after him, and was weaned from the society of the sex which Athens held to be infinitely inferior, indeed hardly human at all, except for the office of motherhood. Education at Athens was conducted on the most agreeable lines, and, as is right and proper, everything was done to make lessons as amusing as possible, and thus to identify learning with entertainment. There was a little drudgery, perhaps, in the first steps of reading and writing, but even those cannot have been very tedious owing to the jolly spelling games which familiarized the young Athenian with the shapes of his letters, and, as soon as he could tackle words, he gained facility in them by reading Homer. The principles of arithmetic were divertingly acquired by a scholastic application of the game of knuckle-bones, and the boys were furnished with wooden boards intersected by grooves in which were rows of pebbles: there were grooves for units and tens and hundreds and thousands.[2] There were no foreign languages to be learned nor barbarous dialects as mouthed at Sparta or Thebes, for the boy who spoke good Attic had no need to express himself in any other medium. But he must learn dancing, he must learn music and be able to sing and play the lyre and the flute, for these were the accomplishments of gentlemen, and to make boys into gentlemen was the main object of Athenian education. For this reason there

---

[1] Æschines, "Timarchus," 35, 10.
[2] K. J. Freedman, "Schools of Hellas," p. 104

was no technical training of any kind. Trade and commerce and shopkeeping were no part of the ideal equipment: better by far that a boy should learn to speak and sing and hold himself well than that he should acquire the undecorative trade of money-making. In fact, Athenian schools were very like the public schools of England a generation or two ago, where no knowledge that could be of the smallest use in later life formed a subject of tuition; of the two, perhaps the schools of Athens were the more liberal and useful, for there boys learned to speak and to write their own language, and to read the masterpieces of their own tongue, which did not form part of the English curriculum. Most like of all were they in the fact that when the books were closed the most important lessons of the day began in athletic exercises in gymnasium and playground. No one at Athens ever questioned the prime importance of these; it was one of the first duties of every boy to be fit and swift, and brown of body from healthful exposure to the sun, and elastic of skin from copious perspiration, for had not the canonical Hesiod said, "Sweat is the threshold of many virtues"?[1] They returned home for dinner, promoted now from the women's quarters to mess with their fathers, and books and games and bath filled up the hours till sunset, when all schools closed.

Alcibiades showed a precocious originality; he entirely refused to learn to play the flute, for puffed cheeks and pursed mouth were ugly, and ugliness was the devil. Besides, you could neither talk nor sing while you played the flute, as you could while you plucked the lyre. "Flutes, then," said he, "are for the sons of Thebes: they know not how to converse."[2] He had divine precedent in support of this excellent reasoning, for had not Athene herself thrown away the brutalizing whistle when, one day, as she played it, she caught sight

---

[1] Hesiod, "Work and Days," 289.
[2] Plutarch, "Alcibiades," II, 5.

The Life of Alcibiades

of her distorted countenance in a pool of water? This æsthetic refusal of Alcibiades instantly produced among the boys a general strike against flute-playing. He would not play the flute because it made him ugly, so they all refused to play the flute, and, amazing as it sounds, their strike was successful, and flute-playing ceased to figure in polite education. Less æsthetically creditable was an exploit of his in the playground. He was wrestling with another boy, and apparently was getting the worst of it. So he bit him, which was strictly against the rules. The agonized victim dropped his hold, and indignantly told him that he bit like a woman. "No," said Alcibiades, "I bite like a lion."

That was characteristic of his vanity, which grew to truly monstrous proportions; he must always be a lion. A pleasanter trait was his complete fearlessness, for one day, when he was still quite a small boy, he and some friends, in spite of the expostulations of the futile Zopyrus, sat down in the middle of the street for a game of knuckle-bones. A wagon came lumbering along, and Alcibiades shouted out to the driver to stop, for his "throw" was in danger of being run over, and traffic must be suspended. The driver took no notice of this peremptory urchin, and came on, whereupon Alcibiades, while the others escaped to the side of the street, lay flat down in front of the horses, and told him to go ahead. ... What could you do with a boy like that? Zopyrus did not know, nor did Pericles.

But side by side with this fearlessness there grew a trait of lawless insolence,[1] as shown in an escapade of his more mature boyhood. He saw coming up the street the figure of the richest man, not in Athens alone, but of all who spoke the Greek language,[2] the elderly, the highly respected Hipponicus, whose

---

[1] Thucydides, VI, 15.
[2] Cornelius Nepos, "Alcibiades," II.

divorced wife had married his guardian Pericles. So, out of sheer insolence (or perhaps for a bet), he went up to him and smacked his face. We may figure Hipponicus as a pompous, self-important person, and Alcibiades wanted to know what on earth would happen next. But for a boy to assault an elder was always considered most outrageous,[1] and (whatever Alcibiades did being already a topic of excited gossip) it was felt that he had really disgraced himself. But next morning—and here we see a touch of his irresistible charm—he went of his own accord to Hipponicus's house, and asked to see him. He was taken in, and he stripped off his tunic, and invited Hipponicus to give him a sound flogging. It is much to be regretted that Hipponicus did not do so; instead, like everybody else, he forgave him.[2]

Side by side again with this insolence and this charm blossomed the wit and quickness which Athens adored. One morning Alcibiades asked to see his guardian, but Pericles was busy with his Budget, and the boy was told he could not be disturbed, for he was looking into the financial statement which he had to render to the Athenian Assembly. This, as Alcibiades was aware, would include some of those huge expenditures over public buildings about which Thucydides made trouble. So he laughed (unlike Pericles, he was always laughing). "He had better be looking into how *not* to render accounts to the Assembly," he said. ... On another occasion this irresistible boy lured his guardian into a discussion on the true nature of law, putting to him a series of questions in the manner of Socrates, whom, as we shall presently see, he had heard taking part in highbrow debates in his guardian's house. Pericles seems at first to have welcomed this sudden interest in law as a sign of a growing seriousness of mind, but

---

[1] Plato, "Laws," IX, 879.
[2] Plutarch, "Alcibiades," VIII, 1.

The Life of Alcibiades

presently to have suspected that he was being "ragged," which was no doubt the case. So he tried to snub Alcibiades by telling him that when he was a boy he used to be wonderfully clever too, and talk in just that manner. That was unwise; nobody then or thereafter ever snubbed Alcibiades with impunity. "A pity that I couldn't have known you when your brain was at its best," he said.[1] It is no wonder that Pericles, the grave, the Olympian, the truly serious, did not appreciate such humour. He considered him incorrigible, no reverence, no steadiness, nothing but downright impertinence. Alcibiades continued to give him solid grounds for this melancholy view.

We must not, however, take Alcibiades as being the only thoroughly incorrigible boy in Athens (though it may be willingly conceded that he was the worst and most attractive), for, if we can trust contemporary evidence, there seems to have been a new generation springing up which asserted its unruly independence to an extent that its fathers had never done. Aristophanes, that thoroughgoing Tory, bitterly contrasts with the good and modest boys of his youth the effeminate, ill-mannered and immoral young people of the day. If he stood alone we should be right in discounting what he said, for he hated change, and always thought that Athens was going to the dogs, but Plato and Xenophon were of his mind, and Plato certainly was no Tory. Probably the same complaint is made in every generation that the young are abandoned wretches, but Aristophanes's indictment is given with such lurid detail[2] that he can hardly have invented or indeed have much exaggerated his evidence, for the audience would not have seen the point. Let us then concede that Alcibiades's

---

[1] Xenophon, "Memorabilia," I, 2, 46.
[2] Aristophanes, "Clouds," 960.

contemporaries were a shocking lot, and that he was the worst of them.

As this brilliant and precocious boy grew up in the care of a guardian who, from the inevitable defects of his inhuman nobility of character, had no sympathy with any variety of wild oats or animal spirits, Alcibiades must have learned the one isthmus of contact between this island of Olympian austerity and the appetites and affections of the usual man. Pericles, for all his wisdom, had made no domestic success of his marriage with the divorced wife of Hipponicus (whose face Alcibiades had smacked, and whose daughter he was subsequently to wed) and having had two sons by her, divorced her again, leaving her free to marry for the third time, and himself free to be joined, though not in legal wedlock, to the woman who was already his mistress and now became his inseparable companion and helpmate. Aloof and detached as he was, there existed for him, apart from his intellectual cronies, his philosophers and music-masters and great artists, this one deep devotion to Aspasia. She was a Milesian by birth, but legal marriage was impossible, for he himself had passed a law in B.C. 450 that no free-born Athenian man could wed any but a free-born Athenian woman.[1] The offspring of any other union was illegitimate and could be sold as slaves. The law had been in force some five years when he divorced his first wife, and already disfranchisements consequent on it had taken place by the thousand.[2] His cohabitation with Aspasia therefore, though a union of love with a woman who was intellectually his peer, was not a legal marriage, and his son, the younger Pericles, born in B.C. 444 (or thereabouts),[3] was technically illegitimate.

---

[1] Plutarch, "Pericles," XXXVII, 2.
[2] Plutarch, "Pericles," XXXVII, 3.
[3] Schmidt, "Perikles und sein Zeitalter," p. 91.

The Life of Alcibiades

Aspasia's profession, according to every known authority, had been that of a courtesan. She kept an establishment of this kind,[1] and had imported large numbers of beautiful women into Greece.[2] This has seemed so very terrible to many learned apologists that they have decided to disregard all the evidence on the subject as being a scandalous invention of later centuries, and have argued that since Plato speaks with the greatest admiration of Aspasia's intellectual powers, and does not state that she had been a courtesan, she could not have been one. But since Aristophanes is among these authorities, it is not possible to dismiss the evidence as being a later scandal, and the fact that the comic poets are our chief authorities merely shows that such was the belief of the day, else the audience would not have appreciated their allusions. Herr Adolph Schmidt, the most distinguished of these apologists, is at pains to show that since her father's name, Axiochus, is recorded by Plutarch, she could not have been a courtesan (for such were politely supposed to have been of nameless parentage), forgetful that Plutarch in the same chapter gives us the parentage of another of these ladies. He also accounts for her presence in Athens, which would otherwise be that of a young unattached woman, by the gratuitous suggestion that she travelled there with her countryman Hippodamus, who was laying out the streets of Peiræus, under the direction of Pericles, and lest this should not be respectable enough, reminds us that Hippodamus's wife was also of the party: he provides Aspasia with a chaperone in this imaginary situation. Aspasia may have travelled thus, for it is impossible to prove that she did not; on the other hand, there is not the slightest reason to suppose that she did, and Herr Schmidt's wish is the only father to his thought. Whitewash indeed has done its best for Aspasia, just

---

[1] Aristophanes, "Acharnians," 524. See also Cratinus, "Cheiron," Plutarch, "Pericles," XXXIV, 3, Eupolis, "Demes," Hermippus, etc.
[2] Athenæus, XIII, 26.

as it has done for Sappho, and as we are now bidden to believe that Sappho was a schoolmistress with a chaste tutorial affection for her pupils, so this passion for Aspasia's respectability represents her, in direct defiance of all evidence, as a species of Hannah More, blameless and blue-stocking.

But the apologists have been unduly alarmed; they have combated a notion that no one but themselves ever thought of, namely, that Aspasia pursued her calling while she was living in the house and under the protection of Pericles, and took with her there her establishment of the daughters of joy. One of them, indignantly repudiating all the evidence on the subject, tells us that if the charges against her were true it would give us such a picture of Athenian life in the house of Pericles, the greatest of Greeks, that we ought to shut our Greek books and refuse further intercourse with people whose best society was worse than the lowest stratum of modern life.[1] Such indignation is misplaced, for no one ever suggested that she continued her calling under his roof. But there can be no reason to doubt that before that she had been a courtesan, and that she was not legally married to Pericles. There can be no doubt, either, that her union with him (we may call it morganatic if we wish) was one of the noblest matings in history, and of unique intellectual splendour. Emotionally also they were devotedly attached to each other; Pericles never left the house nor returned to it without giving her a loving kiss.[2] In a city where women for the most part had no share in a man's intellectual life, or in his chronicles of romance, such a union of hearts and heads was unique.

Athens, that city of free speech and of intense human interest, was, of course, immensely excited over this domestic event in the

---

[1] J. P. Mahaffy, "Social Life in Greece," p. 20.
[2] Plutarch, "Pericles," XXIV, 5. Athenæus, XIII, 56 (quoting Antisthenes, a pupil of Socrates).

The Life of Alcibiades

house of the Olympian, and naturally it gave the comic poets a grand opportunity for pointed allusions and edged comment; Athens enjoyed her laugh. But to suppose that her sense of propriety suffered any shock when her pinnacled and aloof Prime Minister divorced his wife and took Aspasia into his house would imply a complete failure on our part to understand Athenian mentality or morality. His private life, to begin with, had nothing whatever to do with his public ministry, nor even in his private capacity did the fact that he lived with a woman who could not legally be his wife or bear him legitimate children touch the authenticity of his Olympian quality. In the merry days of Charles II of England a bishop might say a sharp word to the King on such a subject, and thereby earn promotion as being an honest man, but no Athenian high priest could have dreamed of even thinking sharply about Pericles and Aspasia; their relations in no way contravened any religious code or moral decorum. Indeed Pericles's devotion to Aspasia was, even to the most high-principled, a saving touch of humanity in one who otherwise seemed outside the wholesome sphere of kindliness and pleasure; he lost nothing of his genuine Olympian nobility, nor forfeited their respect: indeed it was all to the good that he cared for somebody. He still never drank or went out to dinner, he was still rarely seen in the streets of Athens, save on his way to the Council or the Assembly, nor in the barbers' shops, nor in social conference in the market-place, nor in the Gymnasia, where the adorable youth of Athens wrestled and ran; he had no sympathy, but only contempt, for men who resorted there.[1] It was a strange life; Athens could never understand one so lacking in social instincts, who spent his leisure so much at home, and studied philosophy when he had any time to spare, and it was even

---

[1] Plutarch, "Pericles," VIII, 5.

stranger that he made so close a companion of a woman. For women, as intellectual or emotional consorts, never entered into the lives of most Athenians at all; a flute-girl supplied occasional amusement, a wife supplied sons, and Athens in all the friendships and romantic companionships of life was a city of men. And now Pericles was seen even less than before; he hurried out to meetings of the Cabinet, he hurried home again to Aspasia. But it was his business, and so Athens talked and gossiped about it. Naturally there were jokes on the subject, and naturally everybody laughed, but Pericles was just as Olympian as ever. So, for the first and only time in Athens, a woman took part and more than held her own in the society of men. Never had anything like it been known, for Aspasia held a *salon* in the house of Pericles, to which all the intelligentsia flocked. Socrates was an assiduous *habitué* there; he avowed himself to be a pupil of this remarkable woman, and recounts how he had listened to a speech she had made composed of fragments of Pericles's noble funeral oration, of which he believed that Aspasia was the author.[1] He used to bring his pupils, the high-born youth of Athens, to hear her talk, and in her salon no doubt he first got to know Alcibiades. Aspasia saw how intensely Socrates admired the boy, and mistaking the quality of his adoration, wittily counselled him in verse on the art of love,[2] which Hannah More would surely never have done. She held private classes for rhetoric, sophists used to sit round her and pick up hints in dialectic, Pericles had the highest opinion of her political wisdom.[3] The ægis of his Olympian respectability was on her now, and the citizens of Athens used even to bring their wives, those carefully guarded and secluded folk, to these conferences; Anaxagoras was there, and the great sculptor Pheidias. They

---

[1] Plato, "Menexenus," 236.
[2] Athenæus, V, 61 (quoted from Herodicus the Cratetian).
[3] Plutarch, "Pericles," XXIV, 3.

The Life of Alcibiades

debated on subjects of high moral import, on philosophy, on music, on statesmanship, but most of all on origins and first causes, and of how the world came to be, and by what power it was sustained. We may suppose that the tenets of popular religion and the canon of Olympus were not regarded with much reverence by the speakers, for the accusations subsequently brought against Aspasia and Anaxagoras for impiety had their foundation in what was said at these debates and discussions. Dismal and devastating and interminable must they have seemed to Alcibiades when he returned home from the far more attractive instruction at his school; Pericles and Protagoras argued for a whole day, when an athlete accidentally killed a spectator with a javelin, as to whether he or the javelin or the judges of the games was, according to the strictest logic, the most responsible for the casualty.[1] Perhaps it was reaction against such an existence as that of his guardian, who spent his leisure thus, rather than emulation to mould himself on his example, that was the weightier factor in influencing the character of the ward, for to him these high-brow discussions, their earnestness, their calm balance, their academic precision must have been the last word in boredom. But he was extraordinarily sharp, and, as we have seen, picked up for parody the Socratic manner he had heard in these debates, and tried it on his guardian. There was something human, he thought, about Socrates, and Socrates evidently admired him, even as did the men he passed in the street on his way from school, to whom Zopyrus forbade him to speak. Pericles just as evidently did not.

Alcibiades was beginning to grow up; the years of his early boyhood were past, and from the stories already recounted of his younger days we can easily understand how Pericles failed to find anything akin to his own lofty ideals in that most unruly boy. But

---

[1] Plutarch, "Pericles," XXXVI, 3.

in order to understand Alcibiades we must try to realize, not by the standards and decencies of our own day but by those of Athens, on what amazing and incredible pinnacle he found himself when he came to the age of sixteen or thereabouts. To put it quite bluntly, the whole town was in love with him. Never had even Athens seen a boy of such amazing beauty.[1] He had wit and charm, high breeding (for all his escapades) and wealth, and Athens was mad about him, and did her utmost, with conspicuous success, to spoil him. In the city of the maiden-goddess every good-looking youth had a man who was in love with him (indeed it was a reproach to him if he had not)[2], and Alcibiades had lovers by the score. It is no use to scold the Athenians for their morals or to draw a veil over them: a traveller, when writing of his explorations among a cannibal tribe, might as well draw a veil over its distinguishing habits because its degraded members killed and ate each other, which is a very shocking and immoral thing to do. Shocking also to our codes is the idea that a handsome Athenian boy of this age had always some man devotedly attached to him, but it would be absurd, in attempting to depict a portrait of one of the wayward geniuses of the world, to omit mention of the morals of the day, which, repugnant as they are to our habit of mind, so nearly proved to have been, not the ruin of Alcibiades, but his redemption, for the love of Socrates was the most spiritual influence that ever affected him. In all probability, as we shall see, it nearly overcame the effect of that indiscriminate adoration which made him a monster of vanity and self-centredness. It is also

---

[1] Enthusiasts have encouraged us to see in one of the youths on the Ionic frieze of the Parthenon a portrait of the young Alcibiades, but as the frieze was finished and in place when he was not more than twelve years old, the search for him among young men of eighteen or twenty cannot be fruitful.
[2] Cicero, "de Rep.," fragm. IV.

The Life of Alcibiades

important, in rendering his environment, to try to dissipate the erroneous view of Athenian love which is current.

This Athenian love was by no means as wholly bestial as we are prone to think it. It would, of course, be quite idle to deny that it was accompanied by a vast deal of unnatural vice, but it would be equally idle to deny that it also gave rise to blameless and noble friendships, untainted by physical indulgence. Emotionally, in that age, women had very little existence. Apart from the prostitute class, their lives were simply those of housekeepers and breeders of children. No girl at Athens had any education at all, and could not possibly be a companion to a man except for one purpose. She was usually married at an early age, she had probably never seen her husband before she met him at her marriage feast and she became henceforth a prisoner in his house, intermittently pregnant, with no occupation except to sew and paint her face; if she wanted exercise, the most indulgent and enlightened husband could only suggest that she should fold up and arrange the clothes in her linen cupboards.[1] Her respectability was measured by the rareness with which she was ever spoken of either in praise or blame. Boys similarly, after the age of six or seven, when they were weaned to school from the women's quarters, where they lived with their mothers and sisters, saw nothing whatever of the other sex. Socially they never mixed at all, neither at games nor meals nor dances; women were invisible, and if we want to arrive at the social truth about the sexes at Athens, we must get out of our heads altogether such unreal pictures as Mr. W. E. Henley[2] has prettily sketched for us of how "the youths went by to the gymnasium and the girls near watched them as they went." These fond, admiring glances never passed between boys and girls of the citizen class,

---

[1] Xenophon, "Œconomica," X, ii.
[2] W. E. Henley, "Views and Reviews," p. 94.

but only between boys and men; neither boys nor girls had the slightest chance of looking at each other.

The absence of the culture and of the mental and moral development of women which now make them the natural comrades and companions of men, together with the segregation of the sexes, was no doubt one of the causes of this abnormality which was the normal condition in nearly all Greek States of this century. It is more intelligible when we consider that, as physiologists have shown, both boys and girls usually manifest their first strong affection towards one of their own sex, and that growth and the free mingling of the sexes, in the case of the vast majority, turn these immature passions into natural channels. But we must remember that at Athens this free mingling of the sexes never existed; men and boys lived together, women and girls, and not till the fourth century B.C. do we find the beauty of the nude female form a subject for sculptors.

The social life, then, of Athens did not concern women and girls at all unless they were of the class to which Aspasia originally belonged or until they became wives, and henceforth ceased to exist for anyone but their husbands, and even then they could never, owing to their total lack of education, be the intellectual companions of this quick-witted people; the man who stayed at home much and enjoyed the society of his wife was, to the most clubbable folk in the world, something of a crank. But the Athenian lover, as defined by Plato, was no carnalist, but one who filled the mind of his beloved with all manliness and noble aspirations.[1] He was not, as Socrates the arch-lover of youth is never tired of insisting, the lover of the beauty of his body, but of the beauty of his soul, which he discerned and adored through the fair veil of the flesh. The whole instinct, largely the result of the

---

[1] Plato, "Symposium," 179.

The Life of Alcibiades

social non-existence of women at Athens, was not considered shameful or secret: it was in no sense a hidden moral cancer, nor could it possibly have been, since, as far as we can judge, there was as much cancer as healthy tissue, and many, probably the majority, of the most high-minded of intellectual Athenians, Socrates and Plato, Themistocles and Sophocles, accepted and shared it as a normal instinct, and saw in it an elevating influence.[1] It was not denied that this spiritual love could exist between a man and a woman, but, as Phædrus says in the "Symposium," it was between a man and a youth that it was most manifest: "Love will make a man dare to die for his beloved, love alone; and women as well as men. Alcestis was one."[2] He gives an instance of it from Homer, the Bible of the Athenians, in the story of how Achilles, who had been divinely told that he would return safe home and live to a good old age if he did not slay Hector, forfeited the future in order to avenge his lover Patroclus.[3] Socrates similarly defines his avowed devotion to Alcibiades, telling him that "He who loves your soul is the true lover; the lover of the body goes away when the flower of youth fades; not so the lover of the soul as long as it follows after virtue."[4]

In the light of such passages the Athenian conception of what we call a wholly odious and unnatural instinct wears a somewhat different aspect. There was an ideal affection behind it; it did not result in the promiscuous and abnormal immorality with which it is usually credited, and the friendship between Alcibiades and Socrates will illustrate this further. Indeed the greatest disgrace that even Alcibiades (who, it may be at once confessed, had the morals of a Satyr) ever experienced during his youth was when he ran

---

[1] Plutarch, "De liberis Educandis," II. E.
[2] Plato, "Symposium," 197.
[3] Plato, "Symposium," 180.
[4] Plato, "Alcibiades I," 131.

away from the house of his guardian and spent the night at that of one of his numerous lovers.

Such a prank was held to be wholly abominable and unspeakable, and Ariphron, Pericles's brother, advised that the town crier should go round Athens and proclaim him a castaway. The philosophical Pericles did not consider it yet certain that he was guilty of such a horror; he thought that the missing boy might be dead. "If he is dead," said he, "we shall only know it a day sooner for the proclamation; whereas if he is alive, he will in consequence of this be as good as dead for the rest of his life."[1] Plutarch, who quotes this sad story, does not wholly credit it, though from Alcibiades's further adventures and confessions it sounds extremely likely, as far as his part in it was concerned, while that of his guardian seems equally typical of Pericles. It gives us a true whiff of that frozen and rarefied Olympian air; though he was the boy's guardian, and though he must have known how Athens flattered and swarmed about him, he viewed his fate, whatever it was, with complete unconcern. He seems to have had no sense at all of his own responsibilities, past or present; no touch of regret or pity blurred as with a breath the hard mirror of his incorruptible mind. As for his prognostication, that after such an escapade (if it was true) Alcibiades was as good as dead, nothing could better illustrate to what faulty conclusions a man without weaknesses himself or indulgence for those of others may be led by such philosophical detachment. No one was ever less dead than Alcibiades. It seems quite likely that Pericles did then and there disown him, for there are certain indications in the "Symposium"

---

[1] Plutarch, "Alcibiades," III, 1.

The Life of Alcibiades

and elsewhere[1] that Alcibiades had a house of his own while he was still quite a boy.

With such a guardian, then, we must make allowance for a lad whom Athens was doing her very best to spoil and corrupt. She was crazy about him: whatever he did, as the preservation of these innumerable adventures of his youth shows, was the subject of laughter and gossip. As a boy and a young man he provoked all the social interest which is now shown in the doings of some high-bred, daring, witty and wonderfully beautiful girl; if Athens had had daily papers they would have been full of paragraphs about Alcibiades. Every madcap insolence was forgiven him by the adoring city for his amazing charm and his beauty at an age when, in modern life, he would still have been in the fifth form of a public school and liable to be set down to write five hundred lines of Homer or to be birched. But we find him in his school-class asking his master for a Homer, and, because he had not got one, smacking his face. He was forgiven; nothing happened.

One night, again, an admirer of his had asked him to dine, but he declined, and had some friends in to drink. Then he thought he would go to see poor Anytus after all, and set out with the tipsy boys who had been his companions. Looking in at the door, he saw a quantity of gold and silver tankards laid out ready for Anytus's guests, and he told a slave to pop in and take half of them away, and they all scuttled back again with this agreeable booty. He had been seen, however, and Anytus's guests, learning the reason for the shortage of drinking vessels, were most indignant at this gross insult to their host. But Anytus took a very different view: "I think he has behaved very thoughtfully and kindly," he said, "for

---

[1] Plato, "Symposium," 217. Plutarch, "Alcibiades," IV, 5. In both of these passages Alcibiades is clearly a boy still.

he could have taken all my tankards, and he has left me half."[1] Such pranks were freely forgiven him; even allowing for Athenian morals, we are driven to suppose (as Alcibiades's subsequent life showed) that there was something irresistible about him, for it was not Anytus alone who was made crazy with his charm. The story illustrates, no less, the hopeless inefficiency of Amycla, Zopyrus and Pericles as educational influences.

But among all these adorers whose flattery and admiration might have corrupted a Galahad, there was one (and he loved Alcibiades more truly than them all) who saw that beneath the viciousness and the devilries which had caused his Olympian guardian to give him up as incorrigible, there was a potential beauty of soul which more than rivalled the fair body whose charm was so manifest. Socrates, at the time when Alcibiades was passing from boyhood into early manhood, was a man of nearly forty. He was married to a woman called Xanthippe, who has been canonized as the typical shrew, but indeed it must have been most trying to the temper to be the wife of Socrates. He was very poor; he went about the streets of Athens shabby and barefoot (to see Socrates with shoes on was a sure sign that he was going to a party).[2] He took no part in politics, and spent his entire time, as far as we can judge, in talking, for he was as clubbable as Dr. Johnson, who so rightly preferred conversation to any other form of mental activity. Wherever youth was congregated, in market-place or gymnasium, there was Socrates, fabulously ugly and without any flatteries for the young beauties, and yet they would crowd round him, just for the joy of being sternly catechized by this elderly Silenus, and having it proved to them that they were very ignorant and stupid fellows. He seems to have attained without effort that complete

---

[1] Plutarch, "Alcibiades," IV, 5.
[2] Plato, "symposium," 174.

The Life of Alcibiades

independence of material joys and pleasures at which the ascetic arrives only after years of discipline and struggling self-denial; to Socrates such indifference was natural. But he was no ascetic at all; if he was at a party and drinking was the order of the feast-master, he would drink twice as much as anybody, and while they got tipsy and somnolent, he would continue talking with unclouded logic and clarity. In the immortal "Symposium" described by Plato, the narrator recounts how he was awakened, towards daybreak after a nap, by the crowing of cocks, and found that all the rest of the party, who had been holding a parliament in praise of Love, had gone away or were sleeping off their cups, with the exception of Agathon (who was giving the feast to commemorate the prize he had won with his first tragedy), the comic poet Aristophanes and Socrates. These three were still drinking, and Socrates had just got them into a tight place in his eternal catechisms, and was making them confess that, on their own showing, the true artist in tragedy was an artist in comedy also; Agathon and Aristophanes, in fact, were the same sort of playwrights. This, of course, was absurd, but the two were very drowsy, and so they assented. Finally they went fast asleep, and Socrates (there being nobody left to talk to) finished the wine, went away and had a bath, and then spent the day as usual.[1] But, if the evening was to be passed in talk with no drinking to speak of, that made no abatement in Socrates's pleasure; he did not care whether he drank or not.

Knowledge and the fair beauty of youth were the twin passions of his life—knowledge for its own sake, beauty, not because its physical aspect aroused in him the smallest sensual impulse, but because in it he saw an outward symbol of the eternal and unfading beauty of the soul; sensuality to him, as he told Critias with

---

[1] Plato, "Symposium," 223.

uncompromising directness, was merely piggish.[1] Never did he cease to insist on that to the boys and young men who formed his constant companions. The flesh, so ran his most Christian gospel, warred against the spirit; the two were like a pair of ill-mated horses harnessed to a chariot which was driven by the lover of beauty, and the wicked black horse of the flesh had to be tamed, and its wanton desires beaten out of it, till at length it learned its lesson, and no longer lusted after the fair form, but with awe and holy reverence discerned through it the eternal beauty of God. Thus the struggle between the higher nature and the lower instincts, now purged of fleshly desire, was won, and the whole man became harmonious. It is in this spirit that, at the end of his dialogue with the young Phædrus under the plane trees of the Ilyssus, he offered the prayer which, but for the paganism of its invocation, might have been that of some enlightened Christian mystic after the realization of Him who is altogether lovely. "Beloved Pan," he says, "and all ye other gods who haunt this place, give me inward beauty of soul, and may the outward and inward man be at one."[2]

It was with this gospel of beauty and in this spirit that Socrates pursued Alcibiades as his devoted lover.

In the "Symposium" Alcibiades recounts, with a unique frankness of confession, how this wooing of his began when he was quite a boy. Being very drunk he says he can tell the guests what he would not have dared to mention if he had been sober, and he challenges Socrates to deny the truth of it. With a wealth of detail which it would be indelicate to quote he describes the ghastly humiliation he underwent when he thought that it was his physical attractions that had enslaved Socrates. Socrates convinced him of

---

[1] Xenophon, "Memorabilia," I, ii, 30.
[2] Plato, "Phædrus," 253, 254.

his error with remarkable unconcern, and, though furious, Alcibiades could not help admiring his self-control. Satyr-faced as Socrates was, the boy began to see the "inward beauty" of his lover and the nobility of his teaching. His words became to him a spell that both maddened and charmed him, and listening to him he realized how infamous was his own careless and vicious life, and he longed to unfetter himself from so base a bond.[1] His eyes rained with tears when he listened to him: Socrates made him ashamed of himself, though no one would believe he was ever ashamed of himself. He could find no answers to his arguments, he knew that he ought to do as Socrates told him, but when he was parted from him, his passion for popularity got the better of him again, and he was at his wits' end. Personal beauty, wealth, honour were of no account to Socrates; he despised them all, there was nothing worth having but that inward beauty of soul. Indeed, according to Plutarch,[2] this perception of Socrates's nature wrought a reformation in him, and he snubbed all the rich and famous men who wooed and pursued him[3] for the sake of this ill-favoured lover whose sole desire was to make him despise his egoism and foolish pride and grow to live more nobly. Unfortunately, Alcibiades's career does not bear out any notion of effective reformation. In certain directions Socrates's influence may have kept him straight, or perhaps he sloughed off abnormality with adolescence, but that demoniac passion for popularity of which he accuses himself was certainly not cured. He remained to the end of his life enamoured of the limelight, undisciplined and without the self-control to choose the worthier course if the other was the pleasanter, the more popular or the more picturesquely devilish.

---

[1] Plato, "Alcibiades I," 135.
[2] Plutarch, "Alcibiades," IV, 2.
[3] Plato, "Alcibiades," I, 104.

E. F. Benson

The reader must assign to each of these stories about the youth of Alcibiades such dates as, making allowance for the boy's appalling precocity, best befit their internal evidence. The tale concerning his æsthetic objection to learning the flute belongs to his earlier schooldays, for, as we see from those priceless peeps we get into Athenian life from the scenes on Attic ware, quite young boys of the age of ten to twelve were taught the flute. His pilfering of Anytus's plate, his assault on Hipponicus and his friendship with Socrates, on the other hand, clearly belong, from the nature of the stories, to the years of his adolescence. Moreover, up to the age of fourteen the boys of Athens were kept under very strict supervision, and though Zopyrus was clearly a most inefficient tutor, the rule that men should not be allowed in the precincts of primary schools or in the boys' gymnasium was very strict, and it cannot have been till he was between the age of fourteen and eighteen that he stepped into this astonishing publicity, which he never quitted till the day of his death. No other boy ever charmed and disgusted his adult countrymen as Alcibiades did, nor had so fine a chance, from his own superb natural gifts, of being a national hero and saviour. All the god-mothers of fairyland besieged his cradle with their gifts, but round his boyhood buzzed every sinister influence of flattery and adulation. He entered the early years of his manhood with princely endowments of mind and body, already press-ganged into the service of his own ambitions. His only chance which he had not lost yet was the spiritual pungency of the noblest of his lovers.

CHAPTER III

ALCIBIADES'S FIRST MILITARY SERVICE

CHAPTER III

ALCIBIADES'S FIRST MILITARY SERVICE

THERE was conscription at Athens, as in all other Greek States at this date; every citizen from the ages of twenty to fifty could be called upon to serve in the army. The fleet, which was now the main branch of the services, was manned, for the rowing of the triremes, mostly by slaves and mercenaries, not citizens, and its fighting force was the army. There were no commissions in it which enabled a boy to enter it with the rank of an officer; promotion and honours had to be earned by merit in this democratic State, whether a man was noble or of plebeian birth, although we gather that even in the Periclean age, as in every age since, the Army Council contained snobs of the first water. Two years of training preceded the call for military service, the first year of which was spent by the young recruits, aged eighteen, in camps at Munychia or the Peiræus, a few miles away, and the second year of their training consisted in garrison duty, scouting and patrol work in the frontier forts of Attica.

Alcibiades, if we adopt the most probable chronology, was eighteen in the year B.C. 432, the end of which saw the virtual opening of the Peloponnesian War, and, together with his entering his training for military service, he passed out of the guardianship of Pericles and came into his father's property. Owing to his long minority (for he was only three years old at the time of Cleinias's death at Coronea), his inheritance, under Pericles's thrifty management, had no doubt consider-ably increased (which it certainly did not do hereafter), and he was a very rich young man.

The Life of Alcibiades

He owned an estate of three hundred acres at Erchise,[1] but owing to the Spartan invasions of Attica which began the next year, and were repeated almost annually, that can have yielded him nothing, and from what source he derived the bulk of his wealth we have no information. The capital of most wealthy Athenians consisted primarily in slaves, who farmed country-produce for the city, or were employed in manufacturing goods; and since Alcibiades's country estate was but small and spoiled by Spartan devastations, he probably owned some factory, or, like Nicias, he may have leased from the State concessions in the silver mines of Laurium. Again and again in the pages of Plato and Plutarch his affluence is alluded to, and in modern language we may term him a millionaire. But Socrates, even when dealing with him most faithfully for his manifold iniquities, allowed that his wealth was never a cause of self-esteem with him.[2]

On coming of age, he had to pass a scrutiny before the district officials of his deme, who inquired into his parentage and his birth,[3] and when that was established to their satisfaction, he came into his property, and proceeded to take an oath that he would obey the laws of the State and uphold the Constitution, that he would not on military service disgrace his arms or desert his comrades and would honour the temples and their religious observances. Most of this oath he habitually broke, but he never disgraced his arms nor deserted his comrades. He then became an Athenian citizen, though he did not yet enjoy some of the privileges of citizenship, such as becoming a member of the Assembly, nor was he subject to some of its burdens, such as paying taxes, till he was twenty. But he became an Ephebe or

---

[1] Plato, "Alcibiades I," 123. Socrates, however, is in ironical vein, and possibly is minimizing the acreage of Alcibiades's property.
[2] Plato, "Alcibiades I," 104.
[3] Aristotle, "Politics," 42.

probationary citizen, and his military training at once began. For a year, till B.C. 431, he was in camp at or near the Peiræus, being instructed in his drill and the use of arms, and, since he was presently to join a cavalry corps, learning also to ride. No saddles or stirrups were used, and the young soldier had really to be able to ride, not merely to superimpose himself precariously on a horse, and he must learn to vault to his seat, first with the aid of a long pole,[1] similar to that used in pole-jumping, and then with only a hand on the crupper. A very strict course of physical training accompanied those tuitions, and we gather that the instructor used the stick pretty freely across the shoulders of lazy or awkward boys. The Ephebes, however, to lighten their toils, took part in many festivals and holidays during the year, notably the annual torch-races from the Peiræus to Athens, in which teams ran in relays. These contests, surely the most thrilling of athletic events, were run at night between the long walls, starting from Peiræus and finishing at the cave of Pan: all Athens used to line the longest straight track ever raced over, and huge was the excitement. The relay runners representing their tribes were posted at intervals of three or four furlongs, each ready to throw down his cloak and, snatching the torch from the bearer, to race with it to the end of his section. From the winning-post nothing could be seen of the runners in the darkness but the stars of fire, which, bunched together like the Pleiades, if the race was well contested, streaked across the plain. Up the final lap they poured, with gleaming limbs and torches held high, and sank breathless at the goal. The Ephebes also, to judge by the frieze on the Parthenon, took part in the Panathenaic procession, for the riders are mere boys, and they wear the broad-brimmed hat which, with the short chlamys, was their uniform.

---

[1] K. J. Freeman, "Schools of Hellas," plate IX. This vase, by Euphronius, gives this action quite unmistakably. The boy is clearly about to vault with the pole on to the horse at the word of command.

The Life of Alcibiades

When this first year's training was over they were given spears and shields of their own from the State armoury, and for a further year were employed, as has been already mentioned, in garrison duty at the frontier forts of Attica and in the patrol stations in the country.

Alcibiades therefore, in the ordinary course of training, would naturally have spent this year B.C. 431 in the garrison duties which completed his military training. But in the spring the first invasion of Attica by the Spartan army took place: garrisoning troops were withdrawn from all the frontier forts but one,[1] and those were on active service, and it is clear that no such training of young recruits could be going on during the occupation and ravaging of Attica by the enemy. The question therefore arises as to what was done with the second-year Ephebes. Athens was in need of the full strength of her army for home defence and for offensive operations at sea, and at the same time the siege of Potidæa, which was one of the main causes of the Peloponnesian War, was in progress. It seems, then, quite possible that the Ephebes who had already received a year's training may have been drafted there, for in the camp of the investing Athenian army they could complete their training and learn about patrol and garrison work, which in times of peace they would have done in home stations. The calling out of boys still in training, if the State was pressed for troops, was not unknown; it had occurred in hostilities against Megara in B.C. 458, when boys below the military age and men above it had been employed with great success.[2] There was a similar need now; moreover, Athens was crowded to suffocation with the influx of the rural population whose farms were in the enemy's hands, and it seems quite likely that Alcibiades's "year" was despatched to the siege of Potidæa during B.C. 431. This suggestion also fits in with the fact that he

---

[1] Thucydides, II, 18.
[2] Thucydides, I, 105

was serving at Potidæa for a considerable time, as he mentions both a summer and a winter passed there,[1] and since the place surrendered to the Athenians in B.C. 430, it looks as if he went there in B.C. 431.

Socrates was in the same draft of troops as he, serving, like Alcibiades, in the ranks (for the latter had not yet entered a cavalry regiment), and the two messed together. So once again, after his year's absence in camp, and now with daily contacts, this strange love story renewed itself, and with irritated admiration the boy saw his friend's robust idealism, his contempt for (or rather unconsciousness of) fatigue and physical discomforts. Sometimes the commissariat department failed to produce supplies, and Socrates did not seem to care whether there was anything to eat or not. The weather that winter was very severe, and the men, when they had to go out of their tents, wrapped themselves up in immense quantities of clothes and swathed their feet in woollen socks, but there was Socrates marching barefooted over the frozen ground, and marching better than any, while the ordinary clothes he wore at Athens were sufficient for him. This exasperated everybody; they resented his contemptuous superiority. He went about unconscious of cold feet and icy air, for he was wrapped in lofty speculations. The winter passed and the summer came, and one morning, when he was off duty, he was pondering some knotty philosophical point which he must unravel, and from dawn till noonday he stood motionless, lost in thought. By now he had become a "character" to the men, and the word ran round that Socrates was thinking. Supper-time came, and still he was thinking, and when night drew on some of the soldiers brought out their bedding from the tents in order to watch him. But neither night nor day, darkness nor light, made any impression on him, and till

---

[1] Plato, "Symposium," 220.

The Life of Alcibiades

dawn the following morning he stood there thinking. Then the knotty point was solved, and he said a prayer to the rising sun and went to his tent. Yet, though impervious to hunger and thirst and fatigue, no one, if there was jollity about, enjoyed himself so much as he. And then he had the gift which all adore, a courage which nothing could shake, and that, too, as well as his catechisms, was at Alcibiades's service. In some skirmish the boy was wounded, but his friend was by him, and saved both his life and his arms, to lose which was indelible disgrace. Alcibiades was awarded the prize of valour for his conduct in this engagement, but he frankly says that the generals wished to bestow it on him partly because of his rank, and that the prize ought to have gone to Socrates. But Socrates was even more keen than the generals that his beloved should have it.

It was with a mixture of rebellious protest against Socrates's influence over him and of a nobler longing to surrender to it that Alcibiades inimitably told in the "Symposium" the story of this most remarkable private in the campaign at Potidæa. Pericles, it is abundantly evident, had roused in him no desire to emulate that inhuman integrity, which was so utterly out of sympathy with frailties, and looked on them with contemptuous repulsion, but Socrates, though no less lofty a spirit, was not of that arctic type; he could revel with the roysterers, and enjoy himself more than anyone. He had no touch of priggishness; the jollities of life he took with gusto, but they were toys, not fetters, and the beauty of the physical world was but a faint gleam, seen in a glass darkly, of the light invisible. It was just this humanity which enabled him to pierce the joints of the boy's armour of vanity which the rest of Athens had combined to forge for him. Again and again Alcibiades nearly succumbed to the arrows of that loving contempt for his worthlessness; if only they had pierced a little deeper we feel that instead of the record of noble gifts turned to evil purposes, and of the magic influence he was to hold over the citizens of Athens used for selfish ends, we might have had the story of a life that thrilled us, not with the dazzle of a perverted brilliance, but with the serene shining of moral splendour. He was only twenty as yet, and though for four or five years he had been consistently spoiled (and in that spoiling we must include his guardian's indifference), his character was not yet formed beyond remoulding. His own beauty and charm were always his greatest enemies, for up to the end his most hideous transgressions of the codes of loyalty and honour were always forgiven him the moment he turned with a smile of reconciliation or regret towards the city on the hill in whose downfall he was to play so relentless a part. For some years yet the balance trembled when he was in touch with Socrates, for, from the fact that his confession in the "Symposium" has a reference to the battle of Delium in B.C. 424 and to Aristophanes's play "The Clouds," first performed in the following year, it is evident that Socrates's influence was still potent with him when he was at least twenty-seven.

This siege of Potidæa was among the main causes of the Peloponnesian War, which broke out a year before the town finally surrendered in B.C. 430. The affairs at Corcyra were no less contributory, but not in so direct a fashion, and these we may omit for the sake of simplification: at the bottom of both was the jealousy of the Peloponnesian States at the soaring sea-power of Athens and her vigorous colonizations. Potidæa, a coast town on the isthmus of Pallene in Chalcidice, was originally a Corinthian colony, but had joined the Athenian alliance in B.C. 434, and now paid tribute to Athens. It became known at Athens that Corinth was meditating reprisals in that region, and in order to make it impossible for Potidæa to revolt and lead a general insurrection of the coast-towns, Pericles sent orders that the walls of the town facing the sea were to be destroyed (thus laying it open to attack by the fleet), hostages to be given, and the Corinthian Civil Magistrates who were annually sent there to be dismissed. On the arrival of these orders, Potidæa sent envoys to Athens, protesting against so stern a sentence, but simultaneously another deputation, with delegates from Corinth, went to Sparta to ask for the promise of help in case Athens insisted. This was just such an opportunity as Sparta desired: for years she had watched with fear and jealousy the growth of the Athenian sea-power which once already, in her subjection of Bœotia, had threatened to rise further yet, as by some strong spring-tide, and flood the mainland. Though she was not yet ready to strike an offensive blow, she promised the Potidæan and Corinthian envoys that if Athens attacked Potidæa, she would invade Attica.

The exact rights of the case can be plausibly argued either this way or that. Potidæa, it is true, had been a Corinthian colony, and by the terms of the Thirty Years' Peace both Athens and the Peloponnesian League had bound themselves not to tamper with the allegiance of each other's allies. On the other hand, assuming that the town had voluntarily joined the Athenian confederation (which seems to have been the case), it was perfectly correct for Athens, since the Corinthians were tampering with her loyalty, to render her incapable, by the destruction of her seaward wall, of revolt. But since both sides knew that war was, sooner or later, inevitable, they were rather manœuvring for position than concerning themselves about equity.

The threat, however, of the invasion of Attica was serious, and Pericles saw that Megara, which, having regained its independence, was now a member of the Peloponnesian League, was a dangerous neighbour on the immediate west frontier of Attica. The easiest way of neutralizing that menace was to cripple Megara before the war broke out, and with a brilliant piece of unscrupulous statesmanship he passed a decree excluding Megarian ships and traders from all markets and harbours within the Athenian dominions. Such an embargo meant swift and certain financial ruin for Megara, and Aristophanes's scene[1] of the Megarian farmer

---

[1] Aristophanes, "Acharnians," I, 530.

disguising his daughters as pigs and smuggling them into an Athenian market was an apt representation of his sorry case. Megara appealed to Sparta, and the islanders of Ægina lodged a further complaint that Athens had robbed them of all independence.

A Congress was at once held at Sparta to examine into these grievances, and the Corinthians, who throughout were the instigators of the war and played jackal to the lions, were spokesmen for the Peloponnesian League, and they soundly trounced the Spartan Government for their continued dilatoriness which had led to the tyranny which Athens had established. There was also at Sparta an embassy from Athens itself, which had come "on other business,"[1] but no doubt the "other business" was merely an excuse for being present at Sparta and watching events. They were allowed to speak in defence of their city; this speech, as reconstructed by Thucydides, gives an admirable summary and justification of the policy which had led to the rise of the Athenian empire, and is worth close attention. As an analysis and defence of Athenian imperialism, it might have been delivered by Pericles himself, and was undoubtedly inspired by him when he sent the envoys "on other business."

The speaker first reminded the Congress of the services rendered by Athens to Greece in the Persian War, notably at Salamis, where the Athenian victory prevented the enemy from attacking the Peloponnese and ravaging it at will. Athenian ships, Athenian generalship, and Athenian altruism in sacrificing their homes and not deserting the cause of Hellas were the three factors which saved the whole country from becoming a Persian satrapy. This preamble had not any particular bearing on the present situation, but it was the invariable custom of advocates in Greece,

---

[1] Thucydides, I, 72.

The Life of Alcibiades

as in England, to call attention to the high character of their clients; a man accused of pilfering would enlarge on his heroism in saving a child from drowning ten years before. Then came the pith of the speech, reasoned and subtle and wholly Periclean.

Empire had been forced on Athens. She had founded her island confederacy to protect scattered Greek colonies from the Persians; she had maintained it because the honourable discharge of her contract with her allies compelled her so to do, and, further, such maintenance of it was essential to her own existence. Had she permitted her dependents to revolt they would have gone over to Sparta and become her enemies, and Sparta herself controlled the cities of the Peloponnese in the upholding of her own supremacy. She acted on land as Athens by sea, and who could blame Athens for keeping the power which was hers? Moreover, she ruled with moderation, disputes between her and her allies were submitted to arbitration, and her imperial sword was not wantonly unsheathed.

A serious decision was now before them all; when once war began who could foretell the inscrutable end? To be in a hurry to deal out blows and if reverses came then to have recourse to deliberation was a disastrous procedure. The treaty had provided that differences should be settled by arbitration, and if the Spartans refused that, the responsibility for the war would be theirs. Sparta would find Athens ready.[1]

The Spartans then deliberated alone, and in spite of the counsel of King Archidamus, who urged that since the Athenians had accepted the principle of arbitration with regard to Potidæa and other disputed questions it was wise to take that as a basis for negotiations, but to prepare for war, a large majority of his Council voted for its immediate declaration. The Delphic oracle was then consulted, and the god very prudently answered that if they did

---

[1] Thucydides, I, 73-78.

their best they would win. This reply could never be assailed, for if they lost the god could always retort that they had not done their best.

The Spartans, however, in spite of the vote of the Council, were not ready for war, and were in no hurry, though their allies, notably the Corinthians, who were afraid that Potidæa would fall unless some attack on Attica forced the Athenians to withdraw their troops, urged them to immediate action. But they were in no sort of peril themselves, and with the dilatoriness which was as characteristic of Sparta as swiftness was of the Athenians, they refused to be hustled, and spent the rest of the year B.C. 432 in diplomatic embassies of incredible futility. They sent to Athens to demand that the "curse of the goddess" should be driven out, which was an iniquity some three hundred years old; it was as if England were now on the brink of war with Spain, and the Escurial, which was not ready, asked her to restore some piratical seizure made by Drake in the time of Queen Elizabeth. This curse, however, when elucidated by Athenian antiquarians, was seen to have some bearing on the present situation, for it rested on the Alcmæonidæ, to which tribe Pericles belonged on his mother's side, and Thucydides supposes that Sparta thus hoped to discredit him with the citizens. Athens, too, was in no hurry, though not from dilatoriness, but because she had other pressing business on hand. She had troops at Potidæa, and hoped to capture it before war broke out, the boycotting decree against Megara was in force, and she hoped to cripple Megara, and she was engaged in pourparlers with certain Sicilian colonies. So with a pleasant smile she replied to these antiquarian demands by asking Sparta to drive out the "curse of Tænarus," which was quite unconnected with the present state of tension, but constituted a fair *tu quoque*.

Thereupon Sparta, still unwilling and unready, dropped the curse of the goddess, and sent embassy after embassy to Athens, the upshot of whose message was "The Spartans desire to maintain peace, and peace there may be if you will restore independence to

The Life of Alcibiades

the Hellenes." In detail this included the raising of the siege of Potidæa, the freedom of Ægina and the rescision of the decree against Megara. This was tantamount to yielding every point in dispute without arbitration. An Assembly was held, and there was a strong party in favour of giving way. Had Athens done so, the dismemberment of her Empire must at once have followed; every subject city would have appealed to Sparta for the restoration of its independence.

But Pericles was absolutely firm; he saw that war was inevitable, and no concessions, small or great, could avert it. According to his invariable custom, he did not attempt to minimize the trouble that lay ahead; he warned the Assembly that Attica would be invaded, and that their harvests, their farms and their stock would be destroyed. But Athens itself had impregnable fortifications, and with its long walls down to the Peiræus, was virtually an island. This was the policy inaugurated by Themistocles and perfected by himself, and he maintained that it would stand the test of war. He recommended that a final answer should be given to these unending embassies, to say that Athens was still ready to submit all these points of dispute to arbitration according to the treaty made at the Thirty Years' Peace; that she would admit the Megarians again to her markets and harbours if Sparta would admit foreign States to trade in Laconia, and that she would give independence to all her subject cities which were independent at the time of the treaty if Sparta would give a similar independence to her allied States.

His view carried the voting, and war was now inevitable, for Sparta would not conceivably accept such proposals. She was just as imperialistic on land as Athens was by sea, and ruling States cannot give up their dominions by mutual consent any more than they can agree to total disarmament. The end of the year B.C. 432 saw the existing treaty in fragments.

CHAPTER IV

HISTORICAL INTERLUDE

CHAPTER IV

HISTORICAL INTERLUDE

IT was in May, B.C. 431, when the crops were ripe, that King Archidamus with a large Peloponnesian army made the first of his invasions into Attica. In a last effort to induce Athens to give up all for which she was going to war, while Sparta gave up nothing, he sent an envoy to the town from his camp on the Isthmus of Corinth, but he was sent away unheard, and must cross the frontier before sunset, for Athens could not parley while her enemy was mobilized and on the march. The danger was now at the doors, and the first and most pressing necessity was to bring the inhabitants of the villages and farms of Attica within the protection of the fortifications and long walls which had been built for this express purpose in case of invasion. They streamed in, laden with such property as they could take with them, and there was ample time for this, for Archidamus, entering Attica across the Bœotia frontier, wasted some days in vainly trying to take the fort of Œnoe, which was still garrisoned. He then advanced, and ravaged the plain of Eleusis and the district of Acharnæ. He seems to have hoped that the sight of burning crops and felled fruit trees would have tempted the Athenians to give battle,[1] but it was scarcely likely that an integral part of the policy which for fifty years had been moulding Athens into a naval Empire would be abandoned at the very first turn of the screw. These troops had been left in Œnoe with the express purpose of delaying the invasion, owing to the unwillingness of an advancing army to leave an untaken fortress in their rear, but all the other frontier forts of Attica had

---

[1] Thucydides, II, 11.

The Life of Alcibiades

been abandoned, since Pericles, not agreeing with subsequent scholar-strategists who blame him for not holding them, saw the folly of keeping troops in isolated posts and in danger of capture. His strategy, strictly consistent with this fifty years' policy, so far from being "the art of bringing the enemy to battle," was, indeed, the exact contrary; it was to make it impossible for the enemy to give battle at all. But it occurred to him that possibly Archidamus might spare his country estates, either from friendly motives or because such a favour would create an unpleasant and treasonable suspicion against him, and he promised the people that if they were spared he would present them to the city. There indeed was the quick Athenian foresight; Agis had baited the trap, exactly as Pericles anticipated, and spared Pericles's estates. The result was that the Olympian's honour stood higher than ever.[1]

Themistocles's dream, of which Pericles had been the interpreter, had come true; Athens linked up to the Peiræus was an island, as befitted the Queen of the Seas, and within the coasts of her fortifications the population of Athens was as safe as when originally the wooden walls, spoken of by the Delphic oracle, had been its refuge. But it remained to be seen if the vision was substantial. It had been a sore uprooting for the people who had for so many generations been dwellers in the country and who had lately repaired the damage done to their houses and estates by the Persians;[2] sore also it was for them to behold the smoke of burning crops and homesteads, but Athens had command of the sea, and during these successive invasions there was never any lack of provisions in the town. At first the refugees had swarmed into the city itself, and those who lacked friends to house them had bivouacked in any empty space, in the shrines of heroes and even

---

[1] Justin, III, 7.
[2] Thucydides, II, 16.

on the Pelasgic area which was taboo for human occupation. Presently the congestion of this overcrowding was relieved, and the expatriated flowed into the Peiræus and the broad space, from the town to the port, enclosed between the long walls. But the loss of so much property, and the sight of the destruction of crops right up to the walls of Athens, caused a strong feeling against Pericles, and there was a great outcry when, in pursuance of the "isle of Athens" policy, he refused to allow any sortie to be made against the invader. Here again he has been blamed by subsequent critics, just as he was by the farmers of Attica then. But such a course would have been infinitely unwise: no success in small skirmishing against so large an army could have resulted in any solid advantage, and to have permitted it would have been to reverse the whole policy for which the long walls had been built and the destinies of Athens fashioned for the last fifty years. His adherence to it, and the fact that his decision, though unpopular, was obeyed, give us the measure of his strength and of the confidence he inspired. It has also been urged by a modern critic that on the threat of the Spartan invasion, Pericles ought, among other offensives, "to have hurled a hundred thousand men against Megara," and for not doing so he has been labelled "a timid and respectable Bürgermeister."[1] That is surely a harsh judgment, for since the total army of Athens did not approach that figure, it is difficult to see where the most intrepid Bürgermeister could have obtained the troops. Even if he could have, Athens and the Peiræus would have been left without a single soldier, and the entire navy of a sea-power unmanned. The sea, not the land, was the theatre for Athenian attack, and important operations were effected. The hostile population of Ægina was expelled from the island, which was colonized from Athens; this had the very desirable effect of

---

[1] B. W. Henderson, "The Great War between Athens and Sparta," pp. 59, 60.

The Life of Alcibiades

decreasing the overcrowding. A fleet of a hundred ships was sent to the island of Cephallonia, which joined the Athenian Confederacy on the mere sight of them, and, after the retiring of the Peloponnesian army, Pericles allowed the troops to ravage the Megarian territory. This they did every year as a reprisal for the invasion of Attica until they took the port of Nisæa, which was the object of these raids.

During the winter the public funeral of those who had fallen in the war was held in Athens. The bones of the dead, according to the national usage, were collected and placed in biers, and Thucydides tells us that women were allowed to be present; the fact that he records this shows how complete the seclusion of women in Athens was. A curious feature of the ceremony was that an empty bier was also carried to the cemetery in memory of those whose bodies had not been recovered.[1] A somewhat similar custom survives ecclesiastically in Greece to this day, for on the evening of Good Friday an empty bier is carried in procession round every town. Pericles was chosen to deliver the funeral oration, and his speech, as rendered by Thucydides, who was probably present, is of the utmost interest for the picture he draws of the Athenian spirit and temper. This, though perhaps idealized and showing Athens as he would have it, throws a most vivid light on that eager and genial community.

"There is no exclusiveness in our public life, and in our private intercourse we are not suspicious of one another, nor angry with our neighbour if he does what he likes; we do not put on sour looks at him, which, though harmless, are not pleasant. And we have not forgotten to provide for our spirits when weary many relaxations from toil; we have regular games and sacrifices during the year, our homes are beautiful and elegant, and the delight

---

[1] Thucydides, III, 34.

which we daily feel in these things helps us to banish melancholy. ... For we are lovers of the beautiful, yet simple in our tastes; we cultivate the mind without loss of manliness. Wealth we employ not for talk and ostentation, but when there is a real use for it. With us to avow poverty is no disgrace ; the true disgrace is in doing nothing to avoid it. ... To sum up, I say that Athens is the school of Hellas, and that the individual Athenian in his own person seems to have the power of adapting himself to the most varied forms of action with the utmost versatility and grace."[1]

This sketch of the Athenian character well defines the charm which inspires all Athenian art from the fragment of a painted potsherd to the noblest of its marbles; whatever they produced was instinct with that "versatility and grace" which distinguished them as individuals. But to subtle exquisiteness of touch was joined the defect of its adorable quality, and they lacked the steadfastness which marks the nation which, grimly and doggedly, and unshaken by veering fortune, pursues its task to the end; in Pericles's words we can read the unspoken fear in his mind that he addressed a community in which grace was harnessed with fickleness. They had borne, though not without reaction and resentment, the destruction of their homes and the ruin of their crops; and the policy of abandoning Attica to the invaders while the fleet ranged freely at sea had justified itself. But when next year, in the summer of B.C. 430, the Peloponnesian army again invaded Attica, their steadfastness was subjected to a more crucial test. The plague broke out in the over-crowded town, and in the frightful suffering and mortality which it caused the grit and courage of Athens, both physical and moral, collapsed. Neither the skill of human physicians nor sacrifices and supplications to the aloof gods were of avail, and the demoralization of the people was more ruinous to

---

[1] Thucydides, II, 35-41 (Jowett's translation).

the State than the scythes of death. The gods would not hearken, and the fear of them as a controlling force withered; honourable and upright men died as helplessly as the rest, and conduct was ruled only by the instinct of snatching at any pleasure. Why should a man respect either divine or human law when the gods were drowsy and when he would probably not live long enough to suffer punishment for legal transgressions? Appalling was the death-roll: during that summer certainly twenty-five per cent, of the population perished.

Fear of the plague had caused the Peloponnesian armies to retire from Athens sooner than they had intended, but the invasion had lasted forty days, and they ravaged the southern and eastern coasts of Attica as far as Laurium and the State silver mines. But it was the plague far more than the invasion that now, though only temporarily, broke the moral of Athens, and in spite of strong opposition from the war party, delegates were sent to Sparta asking for peace. Sparta refused to listen to any discussion of terms, hoping for an unconditional surrender, and, in order to hasten matters, dispatched an embassy of Spartan, Corinthian and Argive delegates to Asia to propose an alliance between Persia and the Peloponnesian States against Athens. Nothing could more vividly show with what intensity of fear and hatred Athens was regarded. It so effectually extinguished all pan-Hellenic sentiment that the aid of Persia, who fifty years ago had been the national enemy of Greece, could be invoked against the State which had been the chief means of saving her, and we doubt whether "pan-Hellenic sentiment" was ever more than a phrase, rhetorically employed when one Greek State desired the help of another. The projected Persian alliance, however, quite miscarried, for the envoys at a preliminary conference in Thrace with a view to the relief of Potidæa were handed over to an Athenian ship and taken to Athens. They were executed without trial, as a reprisal for the treatment of traders by the Spartans, who, whenever they made a capture at sea, whether of neutrals or Athenians, instantly killed their prisoners.

So the Athenian embassy to Sparta asking for peace was fruitless, and the fickle people turned on Pericles as being the author of the war and the cause of all the suffering, which need never have come to them if he had consented to rescind the Megarian boycott.[1] Twice had their harvests been destroyed, and that was due to his policy; pestilence had reaped the fields of their manhood, and that again was laid to his charge for having caused the overcrowding of the city. Scurrilous rhymes were shouted after him in the street; his refusal to allow a sortie against the marauding troops was denounced as cowardice. The leader in these attacks on him was Cleon,[2] the noisy but very able leather-merchant, who achieved the first steps in his political career by his assiduous propaganda against the older statesman. Not only Pericles but also his associates were the objects of promiscuous persecution. The sculptor Pheidias was accused of having stolen some of the gold which was entrusted to him for the fashioning of the robe of the chryselephantine statue of Athene; scandals were invented or revived that he had made his workshops a place of assignation where Pericles could seduce free-born Athenian women who had come there ostensibly to see the sculptures for the Parthenon.[3] On a charge raked up from so antique a muck-heap nothing could be proved or disproved, but the accusation of his having stolen the gold was instantly refuted, for the metal given to Pheidias had been weighed and recorded, and had been applied to the statue in such a way that it was detachable. So now it was taken off and weighed anew, and the tally was correct. That having failed, Pheidias was further accused of having executed on the embossed shield of

---

[1] Plutarch, "Pericles," XXIX, 5.
[2] Plutarch, "Pericles," XXIII, 7.
[3] Plutarch, "Pericles," XXIII, 9.

The Life of Alcibiades

Athene a portrait of himself and of Pericles. Two of the figures there were held to resemble their supposed originals, and it is very likely that they did. Pheidias was convicted on this charge of blasphemy, was thrown into prison and died there. Athens had made an end of the most gifted sculptor of all ages because he was a friend of Pericles.

The mob next turned on Aspasia. She was accused of impiety of some sort, and, more definitely, of having procured free-born Athenian women for the pleasure of Pericles. He appeared and spoke at her trial, and secured her acquittal. A similar accusation of impiety was brought against his old friend and instructor Anaxagoras, who was fined five talents, and thereupon left Athens for ever. Finally Pericles was directly attacked, and on his return from the attempted capture of Epidaurus, where he had conducted an expedition which failed to take it, he was deposed by a ballot vote from office, and the correctness of his accounts was called in question. Cleon prosecuted him, and he was found guilty of embezzlement to the extent of fifteen talents, and fined fifty talents. That a man who had handled huge public funds for so long could have been guilty of so paltry a theft appears hardly possible, but the verdict certainly went against him.

Domestic troubles crowded in upon him; his spendthrift son Xanthippus borrowed money in his name, which Pericles very properly refused to pay, and, with that callous, inhuman uprightness which was characteristic of him, brought a suit against his own son. In revenge for this, Xanthippus publicly asserted that his father had committed adultery with his daughter-in-law, and this quarrel remained un-reconciled till the death of Xanthippus, who died of the plague, which had already carried off Pericles's sister and many of his friends.[1] But, still unbroken by the malicious attacks of his enemies and the visitation of the gods, he maintained that calm and detached composure which had earned him the title of Olympian. Then came the final stroke; Paralus, the only legitimate son remaining to him, fell a victim to the pestilence, and as his father laid his wreath upon the dead, he broke down for the first time and wept.

The siege of Potidæa was over; after incredible privations the city surrendered, and Alcibiades, now fully of age, with the fresh glamour of his prize for valour, returned to Athens, to find his guardian broken down by his sorrows, impoverished by the very heavy fine inflicted on him and deposed from the political office he had held so long. For thirty years he had been the supreme figure in Athenian politics, under him Athens had attained Empire, her temples and public buildings erected by him had made her the Zion of art, and now he was a private citizen again, who had a vote in the Assembly but no more. The solaces of private life were gone, for both his sons were dead, Anaxagoras had fled from Athens and Pheidias was in prison.

Athens, meantime, having broken, in a fit of childish temper, him who had been the architect of her greatness and the creator of her splendours, was making trial of other leaders and finding them noisy self-seekers, without a shred of the authority which Pericles's lofty and detached abilities had always commanded. Fickle as the wind, she veered round again and began to long for the leadership she had rejected and for the direction of the man who, in pursuance of what he believed was wise policy in the interests of her welfare, had never shrunk from unpopular measures. Her tantrum was over, she was eager to reinstate him, and Alcibiades

---

[1] Athenæus, XIII, 56 (quoted from Stesimbrotus, who was a contemporary of Pericles). Plutarch., "Pericles," XXXVI.

The Life of Alcibiades

was among those who urged him, though reluctant, to forgive the insults that, with blows direct and indirect, had been showered on him and to return to public life. Pericles was, above all, one who practised the counsel he had enunciated in his funeral oration: "day by day to fix your eyes on the greatness of Athens, until you become filled with the love of her," and in the spirit of those noble words he once again, though old and broken, took the helm of state. In all the years of his service he had never asked any boon for himself, but now he longed for one piece of human consolation for his sorrows. He proposed the abrogation of the law he had himself introduced which limited the citizenship of Athens to those who were of Athenian parentage on both sides. In consequence of it several thousand citizens had been disfranchised. But he himself now had only one son left, the child of Aspasia, who by Pericles's own law was illegitimate. So with the human yearning that his legal line should not come to an end, he asked for the abrogation of his own law and the legitimatization of his son. It was granted him.

That was his last public measure; it is a thing that touches the heart of humanity to see his austerity and aloofness dissolved for once in this most natural yearning. He fell ill, as it was thought, of some form of the plague, not violent and sudden as the seizure usually was, which slowly sapped his strength. One day in the autumn of B.C. 429 his friends were round him, waiting for the end, and, thinking he was unconscious, "praised him soft and low" and spoke to each other of his greatness. But he had heard them, and, rousing himself, said that he was surprised that they praised him for deeds which were the mere favours of good fortune, but said nothing of the one merit that he claimed for himself. "No living Athenian," he murmured, "ever put on mourning because of me."

CHAPTER V

ALCIBIADES'S ENTRY INTO POLITICAL LIFE

CHAPTER V

ALCIBIADES'S ENTRY INTO POLITICAL LIFE

ALCIBIADES had returned with his messmate from Potidæa in B.C. 430, and proceeded to astonish, shock and enchant the citizens of Athens. He was the tallest and handsomest of the golden youth, he had a charm which few could resist even when he scandalized them most, he was of noble birth (and the democracy loved that), he was immensely wealthy and open-handed with his riches, he had received the prize for valour in action, and with impulsive generosity he had begged that it should be bestowed on Socrates, to whom it was really due. Brave and witty, wealthy and beautiful, he was possessed of all the qualities which attracted, and he pressed them all into the service of his unbounded ambitions and love of popularity.

He became at once the most marked young man in Athens, just as he had been the most adored boy; whatever he did was the cause of gossip, and he seems to have done a great deal. It fed his vanity that tongues should wag about him, and one day he thought of a pleasing device which should make them wag the more under the excuse of stilling them. He owned a very magnificent dog, which had cost him £280, and the dog had a splendid tail. To the consternation of Athens, it appeared one morning with no tail at all, for its master had cut it off. But when his friends remonstrated with him and told him that all Athens was furious with him for this mutilation of the beautiful, he only laughed and said, "That is just what I did it for; I want Athens to chatter away about this, so that they shan't say anything worse about me." And so, according to plan, they talked the more about him. Then, again, he lisped when he spoke, and Aristophanes made a joke about his lisp in his play, "The Wasps." He appeared in a new cut of shoe, and the shoe was

The Life of Alcibiades

called the "Alcibiades,"[1] and the golden youth of Athens all ordered "Alcibiades" from their shoemakers, and lisped when they spoke. His horse-breeding establishment was the most famous in Greece, so too his equipment of racing chariots. He had an eye for chariots; he was once on a visit to Argos, where a friend of his knew there was a very fine state-chariot for sale, and commissioned him to buy it for him. Alcibiades admired the chariot too, so he bought it and raced with it himself.[2] And his stud was that of a sporting millionaire; a few years later, at the Olympic games of B.C. 420,[3] he sent in seven entries for the chariot race, a larger number than any king or commoner had ever run before, and three of them finished first, second and either third or fourth. This was an absolutely unique record, and was duly celebrated by the poet Euripides in an impassioned ode. Far beyond Athens went the tale of his splendour, and at the games that year the Ephesians sent him a magnificent tent to house him, and Chios sent him forage for his horses and herds of cattle for his sacrifices, and Lesbos sent him barrels of wine for his hospitalities. Insatiable of distinction and popularity, this was all much to his mind, but it was not to him an end in itself, but only the picturesque setting for his more solid ambitions. He wanted to be on the lips of men, not merely for his shoe or his dog's docked tail, or even for the bluest of blue ribands on the turf, but as the wielder of the destinies of Athens. The rest were decorations, pretty, and also calling attention to himself.

During these years, after his return from Potidæa and before his entry into public life, he married, and the house to which he went for his wooing was that of Hipponicus, whose face he had experimentally slapped in the insolence of his boyhood, though he had made amends next day by presenting himself for a flogging. It

---

[1] Athenæus, XII, 47.
[2] Plutarch, "Alcibiades," XII, 2.
[3] Or possibly B.C. 416.

is not certain whether Hipponicus was alive when this marriage took place, and it may have been Hipparete's brother, Callias, who most imprudently gave his consent to it. The bride brought with her a respectable dowry of ten talents, and though, according to Athenian law, the wife's money did not pass into the control of her husband, there was nothing to prevent her giving it to him, or putting it into the common stock,[1] so most likely it went into the racing establishment. She was an affectionate and well-behaved wife, and duly presented him with a son named Axiochus,[2] who, when he grew up, aimed at being exactly like his father, and imitated him in the most ridiculous way, trailing a long robe behind him and grievously overdoing his lisp.[3] As Alcibiades himself died in B.C. 404, it is clear that his son must have been of age to take notice of his father's habits when he was in the heyday of his life at Athens, which came to an end in B.C. 415. We must assume, therefore, that Alcibiades married the hapless Hipparete very soon after his return from Potidæa, and that Axiochus was born as soon as might be.

Alcibiades celebrated the happy advent of an heir by a visit to his brother-in-law Callias, and suggested that he should give him another ten talents, as this was the agreement between them if Hipparete had a child by him. Whether there was such an agreement and whether, if so, Callias performed it, is unknown, but we may get an idea of how he regarded Alcibiades by the fact that he made over to the city of Athens all his property, if he should himself die without children, so that Alcibiades should not get hold of it. Alcibiades could not be called a good husband, for, though he seems to have outgrown the abnormalities of his boyhood, such was his susceptibility to the charm of professional ladies, both

---

[1] Xenophon "Œconomica," 14.
[2] Plato, "Euthydemus," 275.
[3] Kock, "Com. Att. Frag.," I. 688.

The Life of Alcibiades

Athenian and foreign, that presently Hipparete could stand his infidelities no longer, and went back to live with her brother. As the sequel showed, she was evidently in love with him still, and hoped that this extreme step would induce him to mend his ways and behave with more decency. But, as it had no effect whatever, for he went on just as usual, she sued for a divorce. High Alcibiadean comedy ensued.

Hipparete had to appear in person before the court to give evidence in support of her case. Even as she stood there her rascally, irresistible husband appeared. He picked her up in his arms and carried her away in insolent and triumphant defiance of the protection of the law court; he took her right through the market-place, which was the centre of Athenian life, ran into his house, past the grinning slaves, and dumped her down in her old quarters. The incident of the dog's tail was nothing to this; if Athens had gabbled, or was still perhaps gabbling about that, here was a new subject for them. Nobody had ever done such a thing before, but then there had never been anybody in the least like Alcibiades. He just picked her up, with a kiss to stop the mouth that was about to recount his naughty ways to the solemn magistrate, and ran off with her. So the magistrate had to go on to the next case, since there was no petitioner. Hipparete loved Alcibiades as so many others did, and perhaps she knew that he was really fond of her, in spite of his infamous infidelities. She preferred to get what she could of him, for the freedom she sought was dust and ashes in her mouth when she thought of his rare and incomparable presence, and she lived with him till the day of her death, and made no further attempt to regain her freedom.

It was soon after the death of Pericles that Alcibiades made his entry into public life and began to speak with that attractive lisp in the Assembly, and took a definite side in politics. His first recorded appearance in the House was thoroughly characteristic. An appeal for money to meet the expenses of the war was being made, and private citizens were asked for patriotic contributions; one after another they announced what they would give, and their promises were hailed with applause, for the Athenian, like everybody else, was pleased with the generosity of other people. Alcibiades was passing outside while this was going on, and it so happened that, being a patron of cock-fighting and quail-fighting (sports forbidden but winked at by the State), he was carrying a champion quail under his cloak. He asked a bystander what the cheering was about, and being told the reason of it, went into the Assembly, and, mounting the platform from which the donors announced their gifts, named his own contribution. He was always open-handed with money, and we may suppose that his promise was a generous one, for the crowd shouted with joy at his munificence. As he bowed his acknowledgments, he forgot about the quail, and the bird, perhaps already fitted with spurs for its combat, flew out from underneath his cloak. Instantly the business before the House was suspended, and the Assembly, with even louder shouts of delight, resolved itself into an harmonious committee to catch Alcibiades's quail. A sea captain, by name Antiochus, secured it, and took it back to its owner. After this sporting interlude, the Assembly, much refreshed, went on with the affairs of state. No more vivid little scene for our realization of how this idol of Athens was worshipped by his contemporaries can be imagined. The cream of it lies in the fact that it was improper to be the owner of a fighting quail; it was almost as if some youthful member of the House of Commons, after his maiden speech, dropped a small roulette-board which bowled away along the floor, while the entire House sprang from their seats to retrieve it for him. But this young member was Alcibiades, and the whole House of Commons jumped up, with roars of delighted laughter, to restore his contraband bird to him.[1]

---

[1] Plutarch, "Alcibiades," X, 1.

The Life of Alcibiades

Whether he held any official position during these years before the Peace of Nicias is doubtful. Plutarch says that he took care of the Spartan prisoners from Sphacteria who had been brought to Athens in B.C. 425, when he was twenty-five years old, and that he was resident Consul for the Spartans. This, however, is unlikely, for Thucydides expressly states that one of his reasons for detesting the Spartans was that his forbears had been consuls, but that his grandfather resigned the post, and that Alcibiades looked after these Spartan prisoners in the hope that he would be reappointed, and was furious because he was not.[1] He had now entered the cavalry, but there is no record of his having been employed on active service till the year B.C. 424, when he fought in the disastrous battle of Delium, which finally put an end to the anti-Periclean scheme of re-annexing Bœotia. The Athenian infantry, among whom was Socrates, serving as a hoplite, broke before the weight of the Bœotian attack, and Alcibiades, who galloped up to stand by him, described in the "Symposium" Socrates's calm and deliberate retreat, contrasting it with the headlong flight of the rest. He stalked along like a pelican, rolling his eyes, and making it very clear that anyone who attacked him would meet a hot reception. Laches, the Athenian general who was with him and who subsequently was killed at the battle of Mantinea in B.C. 418, was markedly his inferior in cool presence of mind.[2] Alcibiades stayed with them and saw them safe back to camp.

This inimitable little record shows that the old devoted friendship between the two had survived those years of licentious living in Athens. Socrates was still the one human being who could make the young man feel that he ought not to live as he did, silencing the truer aspirations of his soul and busying himself with

---

[1] Thucydides, V, 43.
[2] Plato, "Symposium," 221.

vicious trumperies. Socrates still made him ashamed of himself, "but when I am not with him the love of popularity conquers me. Sometimes I wish he was dead," said Alcibiades, "and yet I don't. Bring some more wine."[1]

The war went on without any winning advantage being scored by either side till B.C. 421, in which year Nicias, who had been elected a general year by year since the death of Pericles, brought about the makeshift peace known by his name. Alcibiades, then twenty-nine years old, worshipped by the gay citizens, who adored his insolence and splendour, but looked on with grave head-shakings by balanced and solid folk like Nicias, had already made himself someone to be reckoned with in political life. He had extraordinary quickness and versatility in debate,[2] though he often paused long to get the word that should exactly convey his meaning, and had a high reputation as a brilliant young soldier. The following year he was elected as one of the ten Athenian generals, which gave him, as we should phrase it, Cabinet rank. Probably he had no real political convictions in the sense that Pericles had, for Pericles had a policy definite and consistent, to be pursued in the face of any misunderstandings and unpopularities, whereas Alcibiades's patriotism, though he devoted the utmost of his brilliant abilities to the service of Athens, was inspired more by personal ambition than by love for her, and when she turned against him the very proof-spirit of vengeance was no less potent an inspiration. Thus, though he believed, and quite rightly, that the peace policy of Nicias was a chimerical dream, we cannot leave out as determining factors in his opposition to him that he hated Sparta for personal reasons, and also that to have joined the party of Nicias would have deprived him of any opportunity of

---

[1] Plato, "Symposium," 216.
[2] Demosthenes, "Meidias," 145.

leadership; he would have had no chance whatever, as his supporter, of supplanting him. Nicias, just now, as a successful negotiator of a pie-crust peace for which war-weary Sparta and Athens alike longed, if only for purposes of recuperation, was acclaimed as a national benefactor, and ambition alone would have driven Alcibiades into opposition. Moreover, to him, seething with energy and the desire for action, nothing could have been more alien than a policy which aimed at a humdrum and prosperous tranquillity, such as was to the mind of the timorous and unenterprising Nicias, whose personal Utopia was to draw large profits from his leases in the silver mines of Laurium, to consult his diviners every hour of the day to make sure that he was not offending some malignant demon, and to get cured of that tiresome complaint in his kidneys.

As for the principles of democracy which Alcibiades professed, he had no belief in them whatever. He was a democrat, because popularity with the mob was necessary to advance his own career, and he had no scruple in repudiating them altogether when he turned against Athens and assured Sparta that democracy was an "acknowledged failure."

On the other hand, far quicker in perception and intuition than Nicias, who had a parental pride in this peace, Alcibiades undoubtedly and correctly saw that a treaty which left every smouldering animosity unquenched, and contained so many clauses which neither side attempted to carry out, could not possibly be of long duration. It was a clumsy and self-seeking makeshift, and Thucydides plainly states that Nicias's eagerness for peace was due to his wish to retire with the reputation of a successful general, and to have his name known to posterity as one who never brought disaster to Athenian arms;[1] and his

---

[1] Thucydides, V, 16

unwillingness to command in the Sicilian expedition five years later, with his continued requests to be relieved of his post, fairly bear this out. Thucydides, indeed, refuses to consider this Peace of Nicias as a peace at all, and continues to base his dates in the history of the war (directing attention to his method of chronology) on the assumption that since B.C. 431, when the war broke out, there was never any interruption to it till the collapse of Athens, after the loss of her fleet at Ægospotami, in B.C. 405.

This estimate of Thucydides as to the utter unreality of the peace is testimony in favour of Alcibiades's antagonism to Nicias and to all his words and works being genuine and sincere. Thucydides is the most impartial of all historians; no one holds the balance with such scrupulous steadiness, and in his opinion the so called peace made no break in the war, which lasted continuously for a period of twenty-seven years from B.C. 431. He atheistically reminds his readers that its duration was the only accurate prophecy ever made by the Delphic oracle, which had foretold that it would last for "thrice nine years."[1] Thucydides had been banished from Athens for twenty years after the fall of Amphipolis, for which he was held, in part at least, responsible, and lived among Peloponnesian as much as among Athenian settlers in other States. His claim, therefore, that he had unique opportunities for impartial observation is a very good one. Unlike Themistocles, and, later, Alcibiades, he seems to have borne no grudge against his countrymen for his exile, and his record is one of bleak neutrality, which is the true attitude for the historian. He had the contempt of the keen observer for Nicias, who was so short-sighted as not to see that the peace for which he received so much credit was nothing more than a fake; he had also an obvious admiration for the abilities of Alcibiades, and never sought to bring

---

[1] Thucydides, V, 26.

The Life of Alcibiades

discredit on his public record by loading the scale against him with the irregularities of his private life. His witness therefore as to the flimsiness of the peace supports Alcibiades's sincerity in opposing Nicias for sound and not selfish reasons.

The event justified him, for the chippings of the stone-cutters who inscribed the interminable clauses of the treaty had hardly ceased to fly when causes of dispute arose. The envoys of Corinth, whose statesmen were always famous fishers in troubled waters, did not even go straight home from its ratification at Sparta, but turned aside to intrigue at Argos, which, having taken no part hitherto in the war, was undrained of man-power and resources, and, next to Sparta, was far the most potent State in the Peloponnese. They put their point with extreme cleverness; the war, which had been nominally undertaken to win the liberty of Greek towns and islands from their subjection to Athens, had ended in an alliance, for it was no less than that, between the oppressor and the so-called liberator. This looked very ominous; it pointed to a design on the part of these two sovereign States to enslave the whole Hellenic world. The Corinthians therefore advised Argos to issue a manifesto to all other States of the Peloponnese that she would welcome them as allies in a counter league for the maintenance of Hellenic liberty. Hatred of Sparta would induce many States to join it, and the idea of becoming leaders of this confederacy naturally flattered the Argives. They responded to the suggestion, and Mantinea and Elis, which had a quarrel with Sparta, at once joined. Four States, including Corinth, were thus allied, and there seemed a fair prospect of Sparta being soon isolated in the Peloponnese. But Tegea, whose adherence would have put the balance of power into the hands of the new league, refused, and so too, in North Greece, did Megara and

Bœotia,[1] though there was a strong party in favour of the alliance.[2] No advances, of course, were made to Athens, for this Argive League was directed against her and Sparta alike.

In the meantime, causes of dispute had been growing up like tares among the wheat between the two principals. Athens discovered that Sparta had concluded a private treaty with Bœotia, which lay on the northern frontier of Attica, and made a strong and reasonable protest; such an alliance secretly concluded with a State with whom Athens had been twice at war during the last twenty years had a sinister aspect. Simultaneously, Argos, finding that the new league was not gaining the adherents she hoped for, began to apprehend that she would be isolated and find Sparta, Athens, Tegea and Bœotia all combined against her. She therefore thought it wiser to play for safety and to abandon her anti-Spartan alliance, and instead she entered into negotiations for a treaty with Sparta, against whom, so lately, she had been forming her own combination. This Argive League had been a serious challenge to Spartan hegemony, and she was delighted to welcome these advances.[3] Corinth meantime, as usual, sat on the wall.

From this brief summary (which omits many minor points of intrigue) it will be seen that the peace of Nicias, far from securing tranquillity, had only given rise to a series of feverish surreptitious shufflings of the cards; never had the States of Hellas been involved in more complicated plots and counter-plots or so riddled with apprehensive jealousies. Indeed their diplomats were like men blindfolded and groping in a delirious darkness; each, as he collided with and clutched another, hoping to have found a friend, discovered that he was more likely to have run into the embrace of an enemy. They turned this way and that with squeals of constern-

---

[1] Thucydides, V, 31.
[2] Thucydides, V, 38.
[3] Thucydides, V, 41.

The Life of Alcibiades

ation, and of them all, Alcibiades alone, sweeping from his mind all these cobwebs of intrigue, had the insight to determine where, for his city, the real danger lay. He decided that the first and foremost of her foes was Sparta, her ally, that Sparta was absolutely untrustworthy, and really desired an Athenian alliance to enable her to crush Argos, after which she would attack Athens herself. It is more than probable that this was her design, and, in any case, any definite and reasoned policy was better than this whirligig of indecisions.

He already, as we have seen, had a private animosity against Sparta, and his political ambitions pulled with his wounded pride, for it was by defeating Nicias, the author of this pro-Spartan peace, that he hoped to make himself the director of Athenian policy; thus all his personal bias was on the side of his public statesmanship. But we must not for that reason conclude that there was no political conviction behind it, nor, just because he was Alcibiades, ferret out a crooked motive in every thought and action of his. Looking at the situation detachedly, and remembering the Spartan alliance with Bœotia, we see that his distrust of Sparta and his divination of her programme were probably quite correct. He framed a consummate counter-stroke, and sent a private message to Argos, asking her instantly to send an embassy to Athens, with representatives of her allies Mantinea and Elis, to invite Athens to join the league against Sparta, which Argos was on the point of abandoning, and promised them his full support. He wisely determined to leave Corinth sitting on the wall.

It was a brilliant idea; all the Argive ambitions revived again, for Athens had been an old ally of hers, and the league, if backed by the unrivalled supremacy of the Athenian fleet at sea, became a most promising proposition. Though the Argive envoys were already in negotiation at Sparta, they at once sent representatives to Athens, as Alcibiades had suggested. This caused consternation, as well it might, at Sparta, for the prospect of Athens, Argos, Mantinea and Elis in alliance was most unpleasant, and Sparta hastily dispatched an embassy of her own to Athens with orders to apologize fully to her for the Bœotian alliance which had caused the quarrel, and to assure her that it was in no way directed against her. Anything more transparently false could hardly be imagined, for this was the only object it could possibly have had, but Sparta always framed her diplomacies on the assumption that everybody would believe the word of so blunt and honest a State. At the same time, her envoys were to insist on the restoration of Pylos, and their credentials gave them full power to settle all disputes that might arise.

For the moment, when this Spartan embassy, most unwelcome to Alcibiades, stated their mission to the Council, it looked as if his policy of alliance with Argos had received its death-blow. There was Nicias, with a considerable peace party at his back, ready to accept this apology for the Bœotian alliance, to believe (with some difficulty) in its innocuous intent, to give back Pylos and to do anything to secure an understanding with Sparta. Worst of all, the envoys had full power to arrange matters. Their proposals seemed very reasonable to the Council, for here was a chance to build a firm alliance instead of that crazy structure which was already showing a hundred cracks and fissures. Their reception was favourable, and an assembly of the citizens was called for next day, when the people would be asked to confirm the views of the Council.

Alcibiades rose to the heights of unscrupulous audacity; he was never so fertile as when he was in a fix. He got the Spartan embassy to meet him privately, and with all his charm of frankness put it to them that though the Council had given them a very encouraging audience, it would be a different matter when they met the Assembly next day. The Athenians were a very peppery and high-handed set of people, and if they heard that the envoys had full power to arrange a treaty, they would assuredly browbeat them and coerce them into giving way to extravagant demands. Surely the right, the tactful thing to do, would be to tell the

The Life of Alcibiades

Assembly they had not got full powers, but must refer their negotiations for sanction to the Government at home. Thus they could discuss terms without fear of being bullied into submission. If they would adopt his suggestion, he promised them all his influence in their favour, and he would get Pylos (over which there would certainly be difficulties) restored to them.

This seemed to the Spartan envoys most excellent tactics. They knew that there was a strong war party at Athens, and that this very able and engaging young man, with his lisp and his power of choosing precisely the right word, was at the head of it. Here indeed was a wonderful method of neutralizing its opposition. They agreed to say on the morrow to the Assembly that they had not come with full powers, they heartily admired his sagacity, and thought him "no ordinary man."[1] That was a very just conclusion.

The Assembly accordingly met next day, and Alcibiades in his suavest manner asked the envoys, as agreed, what powers they had, and they answered, as agreed, that they had not got full powers. At that they learned for certain that he was no ordinary man, for he turned on them with a torrent of violent abuse. They had told the Council yesterday that they had full powers, and now they told the Assembly that they had not. "There is no trusting such people," he cried, and the Assembly roared applause, and was ready to make a treaty with Argos out of hand. A vote would have been taken then and there, but an earthquake occurred at the moment, which caused the Assembly to disperse at once; no God-fearing man in Athens would continue his job when Zeus gave such a direct hint that he had had his eye on them and was growling in his beard. Nicias, above all, was most punctilious in his respect for eclipses and other irregularities of nature, and indeed this earthquake was most convenient, for, philo-Spartan as he was, he had been

---

[1] Plutarch, "Alcibiades," XIV, 8.

astounded at the flagrant falsity of these hapless envoys, and now he had time to think matters over and see if there was any means of saving the situation. It was only too evident that the Assembly would have nothing to do with any proposal the envoys might make. ... Alcibiades's annoyance can easily be imagined; his trap had been brilliantly successful, and he really could not have anticipated an earthquake.

The adjourned Assembly met next day; Nicias made the best of a bad job, and though it was quite useless after what had occurred to ask the people to trust delegates whose lack of good faith had been so glaringly exposed, he persuaded the citizens to let him go to Sparta and test the sincerity of the Government by asking them if they really would give up this Bœotian alliance which was regarded with such suspicion at Athens. Sparta, offended, we may guess, at the refusal of Athens to treat with her envoys, who had specially been given full powers, refused, and Nicias returned to Athens to report his ignominious failure. Alcibiades had arranged that the Argive embassy should attend the Assembly when this announcement was made, and they instantly proposed the quadruple alliance between Athens, Argos, Mantinea and Elis, which was exactly the purpose for which Alcibiades had invited them there. It was agreed to and its terms were arranged. These were of the most comprehensive nature: it was to be binding for a hundred years, none of the allied States should, in any circumstances, attack each other, each if threatened by any enemy could call in the assistance of the rest, no allied State should allow the passage of hostile troops through its territory if such troops were intended to attack other members of the alliance, and, as we shall observe, the sea was held to be Athenian territory.

Had this treaty of Alcibiades's held firm even for a tenth part of the period for which it was concluded, and had it been supported with only moderate activity, it is safe to say that instead of the collapse of the empire of Athens, Greece would have seen the end of the no less tyrannical dominion of Sparta. In spite of the

The Life of Alcibiades

victory she was to win at Mantinea, she could not for long have stood against those three Peloponnesian States backed by the sea-power of Athens. Cythera would have been again occupied, her southern coasts ravaged by the Athenian fleet of the allies, and while her forces were engaged there Argos would have invaded Laconia from the north. She was in a hopeless position; she was cut off from her Corinthian and Bœotian allies by Argos, and could have made no concerted movement with them, and, as long as her enemies used their combined power, she was at their mercy. The inherent instability of any lasting alliance between Greek States broke the treaty down, but, considered in itself, it was a consummate piece of statesmanship, and Alcibiades alone had contrived it. His first appearance as a politician on the statute-book, so to speak, though based on that most unscrupulous device against the Spartan envoys, showed his insight into the situation, and no more effective scheme, sound and subtle, to thwart Sparta's intended programme could have been framed. Simultaneously, he had dealt a staggering blow to the ascendancy of Nicias and the peace party. He was immediately elected a general, and in the next year Nicias was not re-elected. That was a rich sop to Alcibiades's greed for personal distinction, for he had ousted from the Cabinet, in which men of diametrically opposite views could sit, his chief political opponent.

This alliance with Argos was not, as it appears to be on the surface, a reversal of the Periclean policy of confining the scope of the Athenian Empire to the sea. Alcibiades, as the master-spirit for the moment in Athenian politics, had not the faintest idea of trying to annex Argos or the minor allies, but of combining with her to drain the pond, so to speak, and leave Sparta gasping like a stranded fish. That he adhered to the Periclean policy is proved, moreover, by the character of his activities this year. He sailed round to the coast of Achæa with a small force of Athenian troops and contingents from the allies, and persuaded Patræ, an important town a little inland, to attach itself to the sea by the building of long walls to its harbourage, similar to those which joined Athens to the Peiræus. Patræ would thus become, like Athens, an island on the mainland, secured from invasion by land, but linked up with the Athenian Empire by sea. He asked no tribute from it, for a port just outside the Corinthian gulf was a sufficient acquisition in itself, as a check to the navy of Corinth. Its ultimate incorporation, however, in the Athenian Empire was obvious enough, and some Peloponnesian critic said to the Patresians, "Athens will swallow you up." This was a very just observation, but Alcibiades had a masterly response. "That may be so," he said, "but she will swallow you up quietly, feet first. But Sparta would swallow you head first, in one gulp."[1] He was perfectly right; Patras without her long walls was helpless against a gobbling Sparta, and though she might eventually be digested into Athens, she would have a longer lease. To build a fort in connection with the sea on the adjoining promontory of Rhium was Alcibiades's next project, but Corinthian intervention made that impossible.

Patræ, however, was a distinct acquisition, and by way of linking up Argos more closely with Athens, Alcibiades saw how advantageous it would be if the route of communication between the two towns could be shortened. At present, ships from Athens must sail round the long tongue of land ending in the promontory of Scyllsæum to reach Argos, whereas if only Epidaurus, a small pro-Spartan State on the east coast of Argolis, were allied or subjected, the two towns would be in much closer touch. His aim was statesmanlike and on Periclean lines; his method of accomplishing it as unjustifiable as, in the late European War, Germany's treatment of Belgium. "You must pick a quarrel with Epidaurus," was his advice to the Argives. "Anything will do. We want Epidaurus; she is in our way." Most conveniently for this unscrup-

---

[1] Plutarch, "Alcibiades," XV, 3.

The Life of Alcibiades

ulous purpose, Epidaurus had neglected to pay a peppercorn rent for a glebe belonging to a temple of Apollo which was in the "gift" of Argos, and on this excuse and no other Argos prepared to invade the unfortunate little State.[1] An unholier pretext for war cannot be imagined, but if called on to justify such a step in the Assembly at Athens, Alcibiades could shrug his shoulders and point to the treaty. The quarrel between Argos and Epidaurus was the affair of Argos, and Athens was bound to support her ally.

Sparta watched these proceedings with ugly apprehensions; if she had acted at once, she could have stopped this invasion of Epidaurus by threatening Argos. But to move with decision and promptness was as alien to the Spartan character as delay was to the Athenian. She sent an expedition as far as her northern frontier with the clear intention of intervening, and then she recalled it again, as the sacrifices to the gods, from which omens of success or failure were taken, were unpropitious. This piece of piety was a favourite device of hers; twice during the Persian Wars, when the whole future of Hellas was at stake, she had refused to march because the sacrifices were unfavourable, and there can be no reasonable doubt that the inspecting priests were ordered to make a gloomy report of the conditions of the entrails. When once Sparta was forced to fight, she fought with individual and collective heroism, but only sheer necessity drove her to it. Then as the Argives, now joined by a contingent of a thousand Athenian troops under Alcibiades, laid waste a third of the entire Epidaurian State, once more Sparta advanced to the Argive frontier, and once more, owing to the unwholesome appearance of the sacrifices, she went home again. During the winter, however, of this year, B.C. 419-418, as the Argive troops suspended operations, the sacrifices looked much more promising, and as there was no fighting going

---

[1] Thucydides, V, 53.

on, Sparta sent three hundred men to garrison the town of Epidaurus. They went there, it is important to note, by sea.

It would be pleasant to be able to think that this transport of her troops by sea was a piece of well-calculated statecraft, but the temptation to unearth here just one solitary instance of Spartan brains evolving a subtle, an Athenian device must be resisted, for unhappily there was no other route by which to send them without traversing Argive territory. But this shipment of troops led at once to the first discord in the concerted music of the Athenian-Argive alliance, for by the terms of their agreement the confederates were bound to oppose any transit of armed forces of the enemy, and the guardianship of the sea was, of course, in the care of Athens and her fleet.[1] The Argives lodged a complaint at Athens, and demanded that, by way of making good their breach of the rules, they should reinstate Helots at Pylos, and encourage them to ravage Laconia.

This was in flat violation of the Peace of Nicias, and there was strong opposition to so extreme a step at Athens. Even the war party seemed doubtful whether such a challenge to Sparta was wise, and though the Argive demand was carried out, Alcibiades added a footnote to the inscribed treaty of the Peace of Nicias, that the Spartans had been the first to break it. But his party certainly lost support over so provocative a procedure, for next year, B.C. 418, Nicias was re-elected a general and Alcibiades lost his seat.

The failure of the Argive alliance (which was entirely his work) to accomplish anything hitherto, and the signs already manifest of its instability, perhaps accounted for this, but what no doubt also conduced to his rejection was the debauchery of his private life, his drunkenness, his immoderate insolence. In the end Athens always forgave him, but there were reactions, and now a large section of

---

[1] Thucydides, V, 47.

The Life of Alcibiades

her citizens who valued some sort of decency in the conduct of their statesmen seem to have been really disgusted with him.[1] Athenians were notoriously simple in their dress, and there was Alcibiades peacocking through the market-place with a long purple cloak and a golden shield, on which, instead of his own most honourable family arms, was a device of Eros with a thunderbolt, to typify his invincibility in the wars of love. The luxury of his life became effeminate; when at sea he had the deck of his trireme scooped out and his bed slung hammock-wise so that he should sleep more softly, and to his impudent lawlessness there were no bounds. He wanted his house, for instance, decorated with mural paintings, so, to get it done more quickly, he locked up the painter, Agatharchus, and kept him prisoner there till he had finished it;[2] he used the State silver plate of Athens, which, as general, he had the right to employ for official entertainment, for his own private parties. Perhaps the crowning insolence was after his victory in the Nemean games; he commissioned the artist Aristophon to put up on the walls of the public picture gallery in Athens a representation of the nymph Nemea holding him in her arms. And the worst of it was that the mob was delighted and flocked to see it. ...

Nicias therefore was forced to return to public life and military command, from which he would gladly have retired altogether. He was an extremely wealthy man, deriving his income by leasing from the State concessions in the silver mines of Laurium, which he worked with his own slaves, and he spent his money lavishly on public shows and festivals. This was popular with the Athenians as far as it went, but he had none of that personal hold over them which Alcibiades had. He was by no means (what we should call) a magnetic personality; he was nervous and slow in debate, shy and

---

[1] Cf. Thucydides, VI, 15.
[2] Plutarch, "Alcibiades," XVI, 1, 2, 4; Andocides, "Alcibiades," 17.

recluse and hypochondriac, and he would gladly have been left alone to live out, in gentle, private fussiness, the remainder of his days. He was terrified of life generally and of public life particularly, and his days were spent in propitiatory pieties, for he sacrificed to the gods every day, and kept a private diviner, whom, so Plutarch tells us, he constantly consulted, not only on matters of State when he was in office, but also about his health and his domestic affairs and the management of his mining interests; Freud would have diagnosed him as a man of many phobias. He did not in the least wish to be harnessed to the State chariot again, but this eclipse of the war party and his own re-election as general forcibly backed him into the shafts. The peace which he had contrived in B.C. 421 was still technically unbroken, and his party demanded his leadership again as the author of it. He had, too, a strong sense of duty, and, retiring though he was, it cannot fail to have been a gratification to have scored such a triumph over the war party and that disreputable young firebrand Alcibiades, whose mode of life was no less abhorrent to him than his policy. Alcibiades had beaten him once by that unscrupulous trick with regard to the Spartan envoys which had led to the Argive alliance, and to have turned the tables like this must sensibly have sweetened the necessity of getting into harness again. Once there, though he would have been much happier spending quiet mornings with his diviner, he never spared himself; he was at the War Office all day, or, if his presence was required at the Council, he was in his place for the whole of the sitting. Even his bath and his dinner, so his secretary Hiero was for ever saying, could not be enjoyed without interruption: interviewers and despatch cases poured in, and often he was at work all night.[1] But both his industry and his piety were devoted to playing for safety, and this at a moment when a vigorous support of the

---

[1] Plutarch, "Nicias," I-V.

The Life of Alcibiades

Argive alliance might easily have cramped or paralysed the Spartan offensive of the next year. But in pursuit of this policy of safety, Nicias neither supported it nor broke it off.

Sparta, during the summer of B.C. 418, began to realize that unless something more enterprising was done than sending troops to the frontier and recalling them again, the danger of this Argive combination would threaten her very existence. Several cities of the Peloponnese had seceded from alliance with her and others were disaffected, and the trouble would spread.[1] So now she put her whole forces in the field; they were joined by 5000 Bœotian heavy-armed infantry, with 500 cavalry, 2000 Corinthian troops (since unarmed neutrality was a shade hazardous when all Greece was arming) and the full strength of the Phliasian army, Phlius being the rallying-ground for their immense mobilization. Never had so large a Hellenic force been gathered together; it was a match, not for one Argive confederacy, but for two,[2] and only ludicrous want of generalship on the side of Sparta, whose army was under the command of Agis, son of King Archidamus, saved it. After some manœuvring, the Argives were completely surrounded, but, by what we can only describe as imbecile staff-work on both sides, the troops were under the pleasing impression that they held a commanding position, while Agis was unaware that, if he attacked, they were at his mercy. Thrasyllus, the Argive Commander-in-Chief, probably knew better, and by a superb piece of bluff he contrived a meeting with the incompetent Agis, and managed to secure a four months' truce pending arbitration. Agis thereupon withdrew his army, and on returning home he was very severely blamed for letting slip so grand an opportunity of crushing Argos, while the Argives, still firmly convinced that they could have

---

[1] Thucydides, V, 58.
[2] Thucydides, V, 60.

defeated the Spartans, vented their fury on Thrasyllus for having saved them by stoning him. By taking sanctuary, he saved his life, but his property was confiscated. This unintelligible farce of a campaign then terminated.

Athens, under the influence of Nicias, had not assisted her allies in any way at this crisis which might have proved a crushing disaster, either by sending troops to their aid or by making an attack by sea on the coasts of Laconia, but now, on the withdrawal of the Spartan army, Nicias, unwilling, as far as we can follow his vacillating and dangerous policy, to abandon the Argive alliance altogether, dispatched a meagre contingent of a thousand infantry and three hundred cavalry. Alcibiades accompanied them as Ambassador to their allies, though, since he was no longer a general, he held no military command. But that made no difference, and as Ambassador he told the Argive Government that they had no power to make a truce without the consent of Athens, and insisted on military operations starting at once. That persuasive tongue convinced the Mantineans and Eleans, though the Argives were unwilling to break the truce, and an expedition set off to reduce Orchomenus, an Arcadian town allied to Sparta. But endless quarrels broke out, for there was neither unity of command nor of purpose, and after the capture of Orchomenus, the Eleans seceded and went home, while the rest, now joined by the Argives, attacked Tegea, which had always refused to join the league. Her fall would have been a most serious matter for Sparta, and at last she realized that she must do something more than mobilize, make sacrifice and withdraw. She called up her allies again, and before the end of the summer there was fought the battle of Mantinea, in which Argos sustained a complete defeat. In the winter a treaty of peace was made between her and Sparta, and this was followed, on the part of Argos, by a renunciation of her league with Athens. Mantinea followed suit, and thus Athens lost all her Peloponnesian allies.

Never had so brilliant though unscrupulous a piece of states-

The Life of Alcibiades

manship, as the foundation of this quadruple alliance had been, come to so guttering an extinction, and the responsibility for that must certainly be ascribed to Nicias. From the first he had been against it, but when, on Alcibiades losing his seat as general, he had inherited it as part of the existing programme, he neither repudiated it, which would have been highly approved at Sparta, nor supported it in any effective manner. His support, in fact, had merely earned for Athens the acute hostility of the Spartans without benefiting the Argives or demonstrating the potential strength of a close alliance. Indeed Athens was now in a position of greater isolation than before the foundation of the league, for Argos had at any rate been a democracy with a natural bias to Athens; now, in deference to Sparta, an oligarchy was established. Once more, however, the democratic party favourable to the Athenian alliance re-asserted itself, and with the help of carpenters and masons from Athens began building long walls to connect Argos with the sea, and thus link her up with the island Empire. But these were destroyed by the Spartans, and during B.C. 417 the alliance finally flickered out.

It seems probable that in this year Alcibiades was re-elected as general, for in B.C. 416 we find him in command of twenty ships;[1] indeed, a farcical incident in Athenian politics this year seems to prove that this was so. The failure of the Argive alliance, as contrived by him and mismanaged by Nicias, had led to even keener antagonism between the two as the leaders of the peace and the war party, and the device of ostracism was resorted to, so that the people might express by their vote their choice between them, for the ostracism of either would be equivalent to a decision against the party he represented.

Prominent among the noisy members of the war party was a

---

[1] Thucydides, V, 84.

low, blustering man by name Hyperbolus, whom Aristophanes calls the successor of Cleon, and who saw, so he thought, an opportunity for himself to step into the leadership if the vote was declared against Alcibiades. Consequently, though he belonged to the same party, he assiduously canvassed against Alcibiades, thinking that Nicias's party would assuredly vote for his ostracization, and that if a certain contingent from his own joined them, Alcibiades would have to leave Athens for ten years and the way to leadership would be open to himself. This was dirty work, but by all accounts Hyperbolus was a dirty fellow. His scheme, however, magnificently miscarried, for it leaked out and came to Alcibiades's ears, who hit on a peculiarly pleasing device for making an end of Hyperbolus and his tricks. He proposed to Nicias that, just for this one occasion, their parties should make alliance and vote solid against Hyperbolus, of whom everybody would be glad to get rid. This scheme (so simple if you happened to think of it) came off successfully, and to the unbounded delight and amusement of Athens Hyperbolus was banished. It was a "rag," and Athens adored a rag. But on reflection she was vexed to think that the dignity of ostracism had been conferred on such an odious little brat. It was not intended for the riddance of mere vermin, nor had anyone hitherto been ostracised who had not, so to speak, earned the distinction in being a danger to the State by reason of his greatness. But Hyperbolus was not a danger to anybody, and if ostracism was to be employed against such creatures it had better be abolished. Abolished, accordingly, it was, not by legislation, but by being dropped like a worn-out tool or a spoiled toy; the farce of ostracising Hyperbolus was the finish of the institution. That was very like Athens.

The menace of a Peloponnese now united with Sparta beyond hope of reconciliation, together with the failure of the Argive alliance, seems to have convinced Nicias that it was wiser to consolidate the naval Empire of Athens than to waste time over futile diplomacies, though approved of by diviners. Moreover,

The Life of Alcibiades

there are indications that this coalition of Alcibiades's section of the war party with his own for the ostracism of Hyperbolus led to some interchange of views and a partial *rapprochement*, and we find Nicias attempting the recovery of the revolted cities of Chalcidice, which, though not successful, was a return to the Periclean policy. But in B.C. 416 this policy was stretched in a direction which Pericles would never have permitted, and, from the sequel, we trace in it the hand of Alcibiades. An expedition was sent against the island of Melos, which had been colonized from Sparta, and now, almost alone of the islands of the Ægean, stood outside the Empire of Athens. Though the troops made a hostile landing, they did not at once attack the town, but consented to a parley with the Melian Government. This parley is given by Thucydides at great length; his object is to present to his readers what Athenian imperialistic policy had come to be.

Athens frankly states the object of her mission, which is to insist that Melos should become a State subject to her. Melian neutrality could no longer be tolerated, and the argument that she had never injured Athens was unacceptable. In two words, "Justice only enters where there is equal power to enforce it; the powerful extort what they can, and the weak grant what they must." Athens did not desire the destruction of the Melians; she would sooner they yielded, because she would be the richer for their preservation. But neutrality would not do; it was morally more dangerous to Athens than their hostility, for that she should allow them to exist as neutrals would be interpreted to mean that she was afraid of them. Nor was it any use their saying that it would be cowardice or a loss of honour to yield; this was not a question of honour, but of mere prudence. As for talking of divine protection, the gods were just as likely to protect Athens as to protect Melos. It would also be very unwise of them to expect help from Sparta or to make a fetich of that word "honour." Honour is often a will-o'-the-wisp which lures men on into quagmires from which there is no escape. Besides, there could be no disgrace in yielding to a power they were unable to contend against, which would treat them very reasonably.¹

Now this is the unexpurgated language of pirates and highwaymen: no argument is advanced, but merely the threat of force; there is no attempt to persuade by appeals to reason, but only an inexorable ultimatum. This is so curious that it has been argued that Thucydides, who gives in extensive dramatic dialogue (a form never elsewhere employed by him) this debate between Melians and Athenians, invented this bleak truculence in order to hold up to public infamy the savagery of the country which had exiled him.² But this contention will hardly stand, for there is no other sign in all the pages of his history that animosity against her ever melted the arctic frost of his impartiality. His supposed falsification, too, of what was actually said is pure assumption, whereas the sequel shows that Athens, whether or not her envoys spoke with the flinty callousness which he attributes to them, acted in precise accordance with this spirit. Melos refused to yield, and, after a few months of hopeless resistance, surrendered; all men of military age were put to death, the women and children enslaved, and the island was recolonized by five hundred Athenian settlers.

The explanation, then, that Thucydides invented this debate between Melians and Athenians, which was no more a debate than is the squeak of a rabbit in the teeth of a weasel, will not hold water. But the inherent improbability of Athens delivering this savage thunderbolt out of a clear sky remains, for it was quite unlike her not to show reason for insisting that Melos should abandon her neutrality. She had an excellent argument to put forward, which must have occurred to her, namely, that ever since she founded the Confederacy for the protection of the Ægean

---

¹ Thucydides, V, 85-113.
² Dionysius of Halicarnassus, "de Thucydides," 37-42.

The Life of Alcibiades

islands against Persia, Melos had enjoyed, without contributing a drachma to the naval expenses of Athens, the security which the Confederacy had conferred on her. But to deliver this ultimatum without first appealing to reason was wholly unlike Athens, and I venture to suggest that during these years in which Thucydides had been banished (and had therefore had no opportunity of knowing if such an attempt had been made) Athens had, unsuccessfully, put forward to the Melians some such argument.

There is a point in the debate which perhaps bears this out, for the Athenian spokesman explicitly says: "We will not waste time in proving at length that we have the right to rule because we overthrew the Persians; or that we attack you now because we suffer any injury at your hands."[1] The first clause certainly looks as if the argument had been advanced to no purpose before; the overthrow of the Persians (and the consequent security of Melos) had been rejected by the Melian Government as reasonable grounds on which they should join Athens, and there was no use in discussing that topic again. Nor was this the first time that Melos had resisted Athens; she had refused in B.C. 425 to join the alliance, and Nicias had wanted to conquer her then.[2] In the light of this the savage ultimatum wears a different aspect; the appeal to reason had already been made. Melos was now given a second chance, and again refused to take it.

It is true that once before sentence of extermination had been passed by the Assembly at Athens, on the revolt of Mitylene, but there is a wide difference between the two cases, for Mitylene, already a subject State, was in rebellion, whereas Melos was a neutral. Moreover that sentence, passed on the persuasion of Cleon, was not carried out, but revoked next day. We cannot

---

[1] Thucydides, V, 89.
[2] Thucydides, III, 91.

therefore believe that any party in Athens would have ordered this massacre when Melos surrendered, had there not been some previous attempt, as possibly indicated by the envoys, to persuade. Who actually introduced to the Assembly the resolution for the massacre is nowhere stated, but it must be remembered that Nicias had previously wanted to subdue the island. It certainly was not Alcibiades who introduced it, for Plutarch states that he only supported it, though for that reason he considers him responsible for it: we may assume, therefore, that the war party were in favour of it.

It is indeed probable that Alcibiades was at Melos when it took place, for he appropriated one of the Melian women whose husband or father had been among the victims and made her his mistress,[1] and had a son by her. Plutarch, with satirical intention, tells us that the Athenians found an instance of Alcibiades's "kind-heartedness" in rearing this child instead of exposing it. But the gibe is pointless, for his son could not have been born till after he left Athens in the summer of B.C. 415, and he did not return there again for eight years. The rearing of the child therefore had nothing whatever to do with him.

---

[1] Plutarch, "Alcibiades," XVI, 5.

CHAPTER VI

THE SICILIAN EXPEDITION

CHAPTER VI

THE SICILIAN EXPEDITION

THERE came to Athens in the year B.C. 416 a body of delegates from the city of Egesta in Sicily, bringing with them some expatriated citizens of Leontini. They appealed for help in the crisis that threatened their very existence, for Egesta had quarrelled with her neighbour Selinus, and Selinus had called in the aid of Syracuse. Syracuse was the largest and most powerful town in Sicily, and she would have been delighted to swallow and assimilate Egesta. Indeed, Egesta was doomed unless the Mistress of the Seas came to her aid.

Now Athens cared no more for the sad plight of Egesta in itself than she cared for the sad plight of Melos, where the blockade was now in progress, and the envoys from Egesta were quite aware of that. But they were very sound diplomatists (as well as the most remarkable liars, as was subsequently manifest), for they went to the right person and they said the right thing. They did not go to Nicias, who would instantly have turned down any idea of Athens interfering in Sicilian affairs and have brought all his diviners to demonstrate that it was against the will of Heaven, but they went to Alcibiades, and based their appeal, not on his sense of compassion for them, but on far more promising arguments. ... "Consider," they said, "what is going on in Sicily. Syracuse, that colony of Corinth, friend of Sparta and foe of Athens, is swallowing up Sicily. She has already gulped down Leontini (once allied to Athens), as these poor exiles whom we have brought with us will testify, and, unless help is sent to us, Syracuse will gulp us down also, and soon Sicily will be completely in her power; it will be a Dorian federation. Indeed, if she is allowed to go on like this, the day will not be far off when Syracuse will join up with Sparta,

The Life of Alcibiades

and send to Greece troops and triremes for the overthrow of Athens herself. Would it not be far wiser for the Mistress of the Seas to intervene now, and crush, as she so easily can, the growing might of Syracuse? Egesta, with her enormous wealth, of which we can furnish proof, will gladly pay the expenses of such an expedition."[1]

We can imagine how Alcibiades's eye gleamed as he heard this, and as the vision of Athens, mistress not only of the Ægean but also of a new western Empire in Sicily, brightened in his imagination. Now that Melos's fate was sealed, there was no room for further expansion of Athens in the Ægean; she had no more to conquer.

The idea of the conquest of Sicily (with himself as prime mover in it) soared like flame, and it was, too, in harmony with the policy framed by Themistocles, and applied by Pericles, which had now passed into his portfolio as head of the imperialistic war party. For Sicily was an island of maritime towns: Syracuse, Megara, Heraclea, Gela, Camarina were all on the coast, and their position almost predestined them to become the allies (subjects) of Athens. A golden dream, indeed, and behind it glimmered a huge further splendour. Once Sicily was annexed there was Carthage to follow, there were the coasts of Libya, there was the whole of the Mediterranean sea-board. All should be set in the diadem of Athens, and it should be he, Alcibiades, who gave her an Empire, so infinitely greater than was hers now. ... For immediate consideration, it was pleasant to know that Egesta would furnish the costs of this expedition for her succour; thus there would be no money to be voted.

He set about the business of interesting the citizens in this project with all his skill and subtlety. It must not at present be

---

[1] Thucydides, VI, 5.

brought before the Assembly, for there was Nicias to be reckoned with, who would certainly oppose it, and possibly the Assembly might reject it, if they were unprepared for it. It must first be rumoured and discussed—everything was done by talk in Athens—at the barbers' shops, and in the market-place, and at dinner parties. People must be inoculated with the idea, they must have repeated little doses of it; they must be fed, too, with the accounts of Sicily's immense wealth, and begin to smoulder with the dream in which he blazed, of Athens Queen of the great sea as far as the borders of the known world to the West, where stood the Pillars of Hercules. At once he set about this infection; he talked and he made others talk, and presently Athens was thinking of nothing else than Sicily. The Ephebes would sit on the sand at their training-camp at Munychia and draw maps of Sicily there, and the older men traced in the blown dust before their shop doors the chart of her coasts, and those who had been to her cities showed with their sticks the shape of her harbours. And then they went on to speak of what Athens would do next when Sicily was hers. There was Carthage, there was Libya; away into the sunset would stretch her imperial dominions.[1] Even the soberer and staider men who were of Nicias's party got intoxicated with the heady beverage of her new glories: it was like vintage-time, when the fumes rose thick from the must and wine was in the very air. She of the violet crown of mountains would soon be crowned with the violet sea that washed the shores of the world.

The atmosphere being thus created, Alcibiades let the envoys put their appeal before the Assembly, but there were still many who disapproved of the project altogether, and the question of whether an expedition should be sent was debated again and

---

[1] Plutarch, "Nicias," XII, i, 2; "Alcibiades," XVII, 3.

The Life of Alcibiades

again.[1] Eventually, as a preliminary measure, it was decided to send delegates to Egesta to ascertain whether the envoys had been speaking the truth about the enormous wealth of the town and its ability and willingness to pay, as they had promised, for the costs of the expedition.

Off they sailed with the Egesteans, and the latter, as we may be sure, held numerous little conferences, which always terminated on the approach of an Athenian, and they talked about the weather and the glory of Athens. Cordial and convincing was their welcome when the deputation arrived at Egesta. They wanted to know whether the city was capable of paying all expenses? That was easy; let them go and take a look at the treasure-house of the temple of Aphrodite at Eryx. They did so, and found it crammed with bowls and flagons and censers, all of gold. Every night some wealthy citizen of Egesta feasted the crews of the triremes, and every night, to their astonished gaze, the tables groaned under the gold plate and the gold and silver drinking-vessels belonging to the host of the evening. Never had such magnificence been seen; every gentleman of Egesta seemed to own plate worth a king's ransom. Did they want some little guarantee that this wealth would be at the service of the noble Athenian fleet? By all means; let them take sixty talents back to Athens as a small advance. As stupefied as the Queen of Sheba when she saw the splendour of Solomon, the Athenian delegates returned home with the firm conviction that Egesta was El Dorado.[2]

Alas! for their credulity; they were the victims of a series of conjuring tricks. The huge golden treasure in the Temple of Aphrodite was for the most part not gold at all; we must suppose that a few gold pieces were put in front, and the glimmering mass

---

[1] Thucydides, VI, 6.
[2] Thucydides, VI, 46.

behind was silver only.¹ The embassy, no doubt, had come out of the strong sunshine into the dim treasure house; they had handled a few gold vases, and had marvelled at the quantity without paying attention to the quality of the rest. As for the gorgeous plate displayed at the banquets of these hospitable fellows, it was the same plate every night, the hospitable fellows sent it round to the house where the Athenians were being entertained. And not only did they feast their eyes at each of these banquets on the whole of the plate that Egesta contained, but a quantity of it did not belong to Egesta at all; it had been hastily borrowed from neighbouring towns for their express bedazzlement. The sixty talents which the delegates took back to Athens appear to have been real; and that was a clever bait of the Egestean fishermen if it should hook the Athenian navy. That was not much to pay for it; it would furnish pay for the crews of sixty triremes for just one month.

But these conjuring tricks were not exposed yet; they had quite taken in the delegates, whose report, when they returned to Athens, on the authentic wealth of Egesta carried the day with a people already intoxicated (thanks to Alcibiades) with the dreams of a new Empire in the golden West. The Assembly passed a vote that a fleet of sixty triremes should be sent to Sicily under the joint command of Nicias, Alcibiades and Lamachus, of whom the last, though an elderly man, was of the same fiery and impulsive type as his younger colleague. The programme was, first, to give assistance to Egesta; secondly, to restore Leontini, and, when this was done, "to advance Athenian interests in Sicily in any way they thought most desirable."² It is hardly necessary to state that this was really the object of the expedition: the succour of the Egesteans was only the excuse for it, and the reason of it was to found an Athenian

---

[1] Mr. Grote ("History of Greece," VII, 199) thinks that they were silver-gilt. But is not that predating the invention of gilding by almost too many hundred years?
[2] Thucydides, VI, 8.

The Life of Alcibiades

Empire there. The Assembly, after passing this vote, adjourned for five days, when it would meet again to discuss the equipment of the fleet and vote the supplies which the generals might think necessary for the advancement of Athenian interests.

It is easy to imagine the very disagreeable five days that Nicias spent when, by the vote of the people, he found himself a colleague of Alcibiades, whose policy and whose private life were alike abhorrent to him, and his domestic diviner, we may feel sure, was much over-worked. Moreover, Nicias was radically opposed to the whole expedition, and meant to do his best to get the decision revoked. To accomplish that, he was ready to allow that his pet Peace had no real existence, and to take the line that, Sparta being as hostile as ever, it was madness to attempt to establish a new Empire while the old was still so far from secure. As for the menace of which the Egestean envoys spoke, of a Doric Sicily combining with Sparta for the overthrow of Athens, that, in his view, was the veriest bogey, decked out to scare Athens into sending this expedition to save their town. Athens had jumped at the idea; it gave the hot-heads of this dangerous imperialism just the excuse they wanted. Nicias was convinced that the inspiration of the whole excitement and war fever was the ambitions of Alcibiades, now his colleague, a young man thirty-five years old, profligate and debauched and unscrupulous, who was simply playing for his own hand, with Athens for a pawn in his game of illimitable egoism. No one could deny that he was a brilliant soldier, but what of his principles? There was some far-reaching purpose in all he did,[1] and that purpose always proved to be his own advancement. "An arrogant, lawless young fellow," thought Nicias. "What a colleague for me! But colleague of mine though he is, I shall attack him personally before the Assembly."

---

[1] Thucydides, VI, 15.

It was the greatest mistake to do anything of the kind, though Nicias was held in great respect at Athens, for throughout a long public service he had been a uniformly honourable man and a successful general. But he proposed now to ask the Assembly to revoke the decision it had made five days before and abandon the Sicilian expedition altogether, or, failing that, to get it to cancel the appointment of Alcibiades by making a personal attack on him. Either attempt was, probably, in the present temper of Athens, doomed to failure, but he might, on the merits of his case, have produced some reaction by just such a sober and reasoned speech on the imprudence of the project as he actually delivered. But to follow this up, as he did, by a direct attack on the man who had produced this wild enthusiasm for it was a great error. Nicias's opposition to the expedition was sound enough and clearly inspired by sincere patriotism, but personal animosity took the place of patriotism when he dealt with his colleague, and the manner of his attack was highly unfortunate. He did not allude to him by name, but said that "there may be some young man here who is delighted at holding a command, and the more so because he is too young for his post."[1] But the Assembly had just elected him as general, with the knowledge that he was no grey-beard, while Nicias's further opinion that "a mere youth cannot plan and execute off-hand such a serious business" was not likely to carry much weight, since the Assembly had elected him only a few days before just because they thought he could. Even more injudicious was the sneer that "this youth may be one who is much admired for his stud of horses," for Alcibiades had the popularity of the owner of a Derby winner, and the Assembly was not likely to admire him the less for that. And then Nicias's dislike of him got the upper hand altogether, and he told the Assembly that

---

[1] Thucydides, VI, 12 (Jowett).

The Life of Alcibiades

Alcibiades wanted to make money out of his command to recoup him for his extravagance: "such fellows defraud the public."

The Assembly, which always adored "scenes," must have waited in delighted suspense to see how their idol would meet these rude and irrelevant attacks, and in the frank and ingenuous good humour of his reply we catch a glimpse of the quality of his charm. This unprovoked abuse from a colleague with whom during the last week he must have been in daily conference did not dim for a moment the sunny boyishness of his answer. Besides, its blundering folly made it easy to forgive, for Nicias (the silly old man!) had attacked him for just those qualities—his youth, his magnificence, his gaiety—for which Athens adored him. ... He spoke at once in reply, and said that since Nicias had attacked him he was compelled to praise himself. If he was just an extravagant boy admired for his stud of horses, he really must remind them that in the last Olympic games he had entered, at his own expense, seven racing chariots, which nobody had ever done before, and that they had come in first, second and fourth. Was not that good for Athens? Of course it was: Greece thought that she had been exhausted by ten years of war, and he had taught Greece that there was still some life in her. Surely there is some use in the "folly" of a man who at his own cost benefits, not only himself, but also the State. Who, also, but this mere boy, had made the quadruple alliance with Argos and forced Sparta to risk everything on the battle of Mantinea? They won, it is true, but they had hardly recovered their courage yet. ... And then, instead of making any counter-attack on Nicias, or urging that he should be deposed, he most charmingly said that Nicias had a great and well-deserved reputation. That, however, was no reason why Athens should be afraid of himself because he was young; let Athens employ both, for age and youth have no power unless united.

That was all he had to say on the personal question; he had been gay and good-humoured, answering the snarling rancour of his elder colleague who detested him, not with a gibe at senility in reply to the contemptuous allusion to his own comparative youth, but with a hand held out in welcome. Had he followed Nicias's example, and sneered at the greybeards sitting by him, as Nicias had sneered at the young men who supported himself, he would, perhaps, have scored a popular triumph, for Athens was crazy about this illimitable Western Empire, but he was far wiser than that. Nicias was honoured and respected in Athens, and where was the use of ridiculing Nicias's supporters, if by this disarming desire to co-operate with the "old lot" he could attain the immediate object, and launch the ships of Athens *en route* to Sicily? He might easily have retorted to the very offensive expressions which Nicias had used about him by jeering at old age, even as Nicias had jeered at youth. He might, with complete justice, have pressed the question as to why Nicias had not supported (or disowned) the Argive alliance, or have ironically congratulated the author of the "Peace of Nicias" on his rather tardy discovery that Sparta was as hostile as ever. He could also have reminded him that the Assembly, only five days before, had voted for the Sicilian expedition, and that it was entirely out of order (which was quite true) to reopen the question. He could have scored heavily on all these points, but he scored far more by refusing to do so. Perhaps indeed he had no desire to score on such topics, nor any temptation to be otherwise than sunny and genial. Certainly that was his *métier* in Athens, and he was not such a fool as to alienate further a portion of his audience by such gibes as Nicias had so stupidly launched. "Let us pull together, old and young," said Alcibiades. That was certainly consummately clever, but cleverness is not necessarily a negation of sincerity. Probably Alcibiades was perfectly willing to have Nicias for a colleague, for thus all parties in the Assembly would be backing the expedition.

We may omit his reasoned defence of the expedition as being Thucydidean rather than Alcibiadean, and, having given to Thucydides all the credit for the masterly analysis of the needs and conditions of Empire, picture Alcibiades sitting down again, all

The Life of Alcibiades

smiles and candour, scarcely even caring to look at Nicias in order to see how he had taken it. He had the Assembly with him now, which was all he wanted; the people were more resolved on the expedition than ever, and it must have been hardly necessary for him to bring forward the Egestean envoys to remind Athens of her promise of aid. Nicias saw that the sense of the meeting was against him, and not yet giving up hope of getting the expedition abandoned, cleverly shifted his ground. The Assembly, he said, was clearly resolved on it, and he hoped all would go well. But this equipment of sixty triremes, already voted, was, in his opinion as General, altogether inadequate. They must have far more ships, and secure an overwhelming superiority at sea, and a larger body of troops, native and mercenary. If they were not prepared to furnish these, he would resign his command. This was an able stroke, for Athens, as he rightly judged, trusted him, and would not willingly let the expedition sail without him; also so large a vote would squeeze the pockets of those who had imagined that Egesta was to pay all costs. But this attempt was as complete a failure as his attack on Alcibiades had been. The Assembly cordially agreed with him, and was more enthusiastic than ever. Nicias should have his tremendous armada, which would put success out of the hazards of luck and crystallize it into certainty. What vote did he suggest?

Nicias must have known that he was beaten, and he said he must consult his colleagues. But that would not suit the Assembly; it wanted his definite personal answer, and Demostratus,[1] one of Alcibiades's supporters, insisted that there should be an end of these excuses and hedgings; the Assembly asked for his estimate. Nicias was unable to avoid a definite answer, and he could not resign when Athens was prepared to grant all he asked. He then said he must have a hundred ships, instead of the sixty originally

---

[1] Plutarch, "Nicias," XII, 4.

voted, and five thousand heavy-armed troops; he clearly hoped that the Assembly would demur to such a demand. Instead it passed a vote of unlimited credit to the three Generals for all that they thought needful. In fact, Nicias's opposition and his attack on Alcibiades had only resulted in the very thing he had been most anxious to avoid, for now the expedition was to be on a scale nearly twice as large as had been originally intended; Athens was staking far more heavily on it than she would have done had not he opposed it.

Preparations for the most magnificent armament that had ever left Hellenic shores were instantly set on foot; war-fever raged and the whole populace was delirious with it. There was no need for census-lists or press-gangs to rout out men liable for service, for they presented themselves in crowds, eager to be chosen to serve under Alcibiades, even as the West Country flocked to Drake when he hoisted his flag on the "Revenge" and invited volunteers to serve against the Spanish Armada. Both had the power of inspiring confidence which is the hall-mark of leadership; English and Athenians alike hailed them as super-men on whom success must attend. Sophists and professional orators were eloquent on the dawning of new glories for the city, soothsayers proclaimed the protection of the High Gods and the conquest of Sicily.[1] Alcibiades had his private diviners, and they naturally were most encouraging, and he hunted up from a collection of supposedly ancient oracles one that promised great fame for Athens to be won there. It was very pleasant also that envoys who had been sent to the shrine of Ammon in the Libyan desert now returned with a most sumptuous pronouncement which promised to Athens the capture of the entire population of Syracuse.[2] Alcibiades himself was now more

---

[1] Thucydides, VIII, I.
[2] Plutarch, " Nicias," XIII, i.

The Life of Alcibiades

than ever the idol of the people; it was he whose insight had set on foot the movement to help Egesta, but that now had dwindled into a minor operation under his expanding schemes. Athens was to add all Sicily with its fabulous wealth to her Empire, and that was but a stepping-stone across to Carthage and to the conquest of all the coasts of the great sea. The people were drunk with the strong wine of imperialism, and Alcibiades was the god of its grapes. But as this popular apotheosis grew more fervent, the more implacable grew the hatred of his enemies, waiting for their opportunity.

Now the rummaging up or the invention of oracles and divine pronouncements in favour of a great political programme was no new thing; Themistocles, as we have seen, produced a Delphic utterance to induce the citizens to take to their ships in the Persian peril and set religious machinery to work, and no doubt Alcibiades was doing the same when now he wound up his private diviners. But two could play at that game; other people (especially Nicias) had private diviners as well, and diviners were naturally loyal to their employers, for entrails were ambiguous things and capable of more than one reading. So now a reactionary crop of discouraging auguries began to sprout; there was a gold Palladium, or image of Athene, for instance, at Delphi, perched in a bronze palm-tree, which Athens had dedicated out of her spoils in the Persian War. News came from Delphi that day after day ravens of ill omen hopped about this image and pecked it; they also stripped the gold dates off the palm tree and scattered them on the ground. Of course the war party affirmed that Syracuse had bribed the Delphic priests to invent this disconcerting tale. Then someone discovered an oracle which commanded Athens to send for the priestess of Athene's temple at Clazomenæ; this was done, and when the lady arrived it was found that her name was Peace. ... Again, there was an astrologer called Meton, who was possessed, and who set fire to his house, thereby portending the destruction of Athens. The war party laughed that to scorn, for Meton, it appeared, when his house was a pile of ashes, came before the magistrates and begged remission of service for his son, in view of this calamity, there was method in Meton's madness. But perhaps Alcibiades was not so merry when he heard how his old lover Socrates had foretold disaster. Socrates was no idle fabricator of omens, and his divine guide had told him that ruin was coming to Athens from Syracuse. Again, the festival of Adonis occurred at this season of the Spring, and, according to the usage of it, images of the boy beloved of Aphrodite were laid out as for burial in street and market-place, and the women held mock rites of funeral over them, beating their breasts and chanting dirges. Though precisely the same thing happened every year, this was held to be an ominous coincidence; who knew whether before long Athens would not be mourning for her dead in square and at street corner?

But all is grist to the mills of superstition, and this way and that were bandied these warnings and these encouragements without any interruption of the preparations, for the gods themselves seemed far from unanimous. Daily, in the eyes of the multitude, Alcibiades soared into the empyrean of his power and popularity, and daily, in secret, his enemies and detractors, those who sincerely disapproved of him and his policy, and perhaps even more those who were only eager to leap into his place if he could be thrown down, worked against him. Then one morning, when the resplendent fleet was almost ready to sail, Athens awoke to find that during the night an outrage had occurred which shocked the lightest-hearted and the least superstitious.

Athens was remarkable for the number of its temples; there was hardly an open space in the town from which there could not be seen the house of some protecting god or hero, and certainly there was not a street in the town, however mean, from which could not be seen, not one, but many representations of the god Hermes. These were busts, bearded or youthful, with the head and shoulders made in a piece with the pedestal on which they stood, armless, legless and bodiless, but with the carved index of sex. They stood everywhere, outside temples, at cross-roads, in the

The Life of Alcibiades

gymnasia, in front of all public buildings, and many private houses had also their Herm by the side of the front door to guard and protect the home. And now, when Athens woke that morning for one of the final days of preparation before the great Armada put to sea, it was to find that these tutelary images had been mutilated; noses and ears and marks of sex had been struck off. The most monstrous sacrilege had been committed; it was as if in some mediæval Italian town every image of the Madonna in shrine and at street-corner had been foully violated. According to one account, only the majority of the Herms had been disfigured;[1] according to another[2] there were very few that had escaped, and this outrage could not be the work of one hand, but of some conspired action.[3] But one important image had been spared, which stood outside the house of Andocides the orator, a man of noted oligarchical and anti-democratic politics. He was instantly clapped into prison to await trial as being the author of the outrage. Nothing could have been really more improbable than that he was the culprit, for no criminal, of whatever views, could have been so insane as to mutilate every Herm in Athens except the one outside his own house, unless he positively wished to attract popular suspicion. It instantly fastened on him, though of all men he was really the most likely to be innocent, and gaol was considered the best place for him pending inquiries. Otherwise, there was not the faintest clue as to who had committed this outrage.

But theories abounded; one ingenious solution was that some Corinthians belonging to the alien merchant population of Athens had done it, for Syracuse, against which the expedition was so soon to sail, was a colony of Corinth, and the supposed design was to stop its sailing, for no city in which so great a profanation had been

---

[1] Thucydides, VI, 27.
[2] Plutarch, "Alcibiades," XXI, i.
[3] Cornelius Nepos, "Alcibiades," III.

committed would be likely to embark on such an undertaking, with the wrath of heaven eager for vengeance. Others thought it was the work of some wild young scamps, who had committed this sacrilege in the mere wantonness of a drunken orgy. And the name of Alcibiades began to be whispered. There was no particle of evidence against him, but who in Athens could fail to remember a hundred lawless escapades of his, at which respectable folk had shaken their heads? Just whispers; even his enemies, when they heard such, said, "Oh, impossible!" but they told others what a ludicrous suggestion they had heard, and fanned the scandal. No public accusation was made; there was only bated talk. But it seems quite incredible that, on the eve of the starting of the great expedition of which he was in command, he should have been guilty, however drunk, of an act of so ill-omened a nature, which might even have stopped the expedition altogether.

The Council of the Assembly took this unpropitious incident very seriously. They met many times within a few days and investigated, but without result, any clues that were brought forward. Large rewards were offered for information that might lead to discovery, and then, with a wider sweep of the net, they made the announcement that anyone, citizen, foreigner or slave, who could produce evidence, not only with regard to the mutilation of the Herms, but as to any other profanation, would not be proceeded against, even if he had been personally concerned in it. And then the whispers about Alcibiades rose into tumult of open speech, for Pythonicus and Androcles, democratic leaders of some position, appeared before the Assembly and (under the head of "other profanations") laid before it the evidence of certain foreigners and slaves that Alcibiades and a party of his friends had enacted a parody of the most holy Eleusinian Mysteries. The evidence was detailed and circumstantial; Theodoras had played the part of Herald, Pulytion of Torch bearer, and Alcibiades of the High Priest, while the rest of the tipsy company had impersonated the initiates. The President of the

The Life of Alcibiades

Council then ordered all members of the Assembly who were not initiates to leave the court, so that the knowledge of the secret rites should not be revealed to them, and a slave described what he had seen at this orgy. The initiates, who remained, could thus judge whether the Holy Mysteries had been blasphemously parodied. After hearing what the slave averred that he had seen, they found (in our modern terminology) a true bill against Alcibiades, and he was impeached on the charge of sacrilege for having revealed and made mock of the sacred rites into which he had been initiated.

Now whether Alcibiades was guilty or not was never certainly established, for he was never brought to trial. But subsequent events, some of which did not occur for years later, furnish a probability amounting to certainty that he was innocent, and that the charge was a false but most capably-planned attack, invented by political opponents and by those of his own party, such as Androcles, who saw in his hoped-for downfall a chance for their own ambitions. Moreover, the evidence of one slave (for no other witnesses were produced) as to what he had seen was no proof that Alcibiades was guilty. Androcles (on the supposition that the story was a fabrication) could have obtained that evidence by instructing this slave under threat of torture what to say; he could, as an initiate, have invented a scene which was clearly a parody of the Mysteries, and drilled the slave into describing it as having taken place in his presence. But, if a plot, it could not have been more skilfully timed, for the mutilation of the Herms, in itself a very grave matter, had just occurred, Alcibiades's name had been whispered as the author of the outrage, and now, when this far more serious charge was made directly against him, the hinted suspicion in the other case linked itself up with this. He was notoriously lawless and given to drunken freaks, and though such escapades amused and delighted the mob, they would certainly be prejudicial to him on his trial. Again, these two outrages were of the same nature: both were contemptuous of those beliefs on which (though they did not enter into the conduct of life) the stability of the State was founded; both, to a city anxious and unnerved and on the eve of a tremendous undertaking, seemed items in a revolutionary programme to upset the Constitution.[1] The tutelary deities of Athens had been insulted and mocked at in the first, and now the veil of the holiest places in the sanctuaries of the gods had been rent and its most secret mysteries parodied before the eyes of the profane. If the outrage on the Herms may be compared to the disfigurement of images of the Madonna, this charge now brought against Alcibiades was as if he had been accused in some country of burning Catholic faith, of celebrating the Black Mass. The insult to what was but a material symbol of a god was far less than this direct sacrilege towards the spiritual truth that lay behind symbol; this, in Christian phrase, was sheer blasphemy against the Holy Ghost.

Alcibiades fully realized the extreme peril in which he stood, and he adopted the only line consistent with innocence. Well aware that the mutilation of the Herms was being engineered to his prejudice on this other charge, he asked to stand his trial at once, so that if he was guilty he might be punished (and the punishment would almost certainly have been death), and that, if he was acquitted, he might set out in joint command of the expedition without this charge hanging over his head. This was a just and reasonable demand, but it did not suit Androcles, for he knew that if Alcibiades was tried now he would have the support of the army, which was devoted to him, both personally and as being the real inspirer and leader of the expedition. Moreover, a large contingent of Argive and Mantinean troops who were serving as mercenaries declared that if anything untoward happened to him they would break their engagement. Alcibiades knew this as well as Androcles, and thus his petition to be tried at once, which was what no guilty

---

[1] Thucydides, VI, 27.

The Life of Alcibiades

man, who had the chance of getting away, would have made, wears a rather different aspect, for he, too, was sure that the vote of the army would acquit him.

Androcles could hardly advocate in person the postponement of the trial, for he had brought the charge himself, and he therefore suborned other spokesmen to represent to the Assembly that the expedition was now ready to sail, but that it could not start without the Generals in command of it, and a long and disastrous delay would be therefore caused if the trial took place now. Let Alcibiades stand his trial when the war was over, or, if it was unduly prolonged, some future date could be appointed for which he would be recalled. The laws of Athens would not change in the interval.

Alcibiades strongly protested, for he correctly saw the intention behind this, namely, that in his absence his enemies could work up a more bitter feeling against him and fabricate fresh evidence. The accusation had been made, and in common justice he demanded to be allowed to clear himself now and take up his command without fear of fresh mischief brewing against him in his absence. But the Assembly decided against him, and he was ordered to start at once. Neither Thucydides[1] nor Plutarch,[2] from whom the above account is mainly compiled, express any view as to his guilt or innocence, but both are agreed that this conspiracy lay behind the accusation, and that his downfall rather than the execution of justice was its object. Athens paid dearly for the decision; it is not too much to say that the disasters of the next five years were the direct consequence of it.

Orders were therefore given for immediate embarkation, and almost the entire population of Athens, citizens and foreigners

---

[1] Thucydides, VI, 28, 29.
[2] Plutarch, "Alcibiades," 19, 20.

alike, went down to the Peiræus to speed the departure of the most splendid armament that had ever left Greek shores. All told, the fleet numbered nearly a hundred and forty ships of war, and their captains had lavishly spent their own money in addition to that supplied by the Treasury on the decoration and efficiency of their vessels. Four thousand heavy-armed soldiers, all citizens of Athens, were the main fighting force, there were also three hundred cavalry, and due complement of archers and slingers of allied troops. When all were aboard, a trumpet proclaimed silence, and prayers for the blessing of the gods were recited by the herald, and the responses were chanted by the entire force and by the huge crowds which lined the piers. Then from the ships rose the great shout of the paean, or national war-cry; libations from gold and silver drinking-cups were made on every deck, and the fleet put to sea in single file. Once clear of the harbour, the sails were spread, and with wind and oar they raced across to Ægina. There were many who had been filled with fear and forebodings at the hazards ahead, but so gallant a sight of youth and vigour, so brave a company of triremes, restored their courage. Yet, had they known it, not a single ship out of that supreme Armada would ever come back into the Peiræus again; of the flower of the youth that manned them no more than a few broken fugitives, and of their three Generals one only, round whose head now hung the suspicion of an unspeakable infamy. A Pentecost of calamity had swept over Athens before the crowded quays welcomed home him who had brought incredible disaster on her, but whom she was to hail with heroic honours as the only man who could save her.

The orders for the fleet were to sail to Corcyra, where victualling ships would be gathered to join her, and from Corcyra three vessels would be sent on ahead to notify to Egesta that the Armada was on its way, and to ascertain what sort of reception it might expect from neighbouring cities ; the main fleet was then to proceed across the Ionian Sea in three squadrons. But powerful as was this armament, never had there sailed one under so

The Life of Alcibiades

inharmonious a command. Nicias alone was sufficient to damp the spirits of the most eager; he disapproved of the expedition altogether, and had done his best to stop its sailing, and now, instead of making the best of what he had been unable to prevent and inspiring his men with pride and confidence in the great enterprise, he was full of despondency. As the ships foamed out to sea, he looked back at the dimming shores of Attica,[1] with headshakes and sad glances and copious expressions of regret that the Assembly had not listened to him.

Perhaps Alcibiades looked homeward too, grimly conjecturing what poisonous brew would surely be concocted for him by the enemies whom he had not been permitted to face, and who now, in his absence, were already busy with fresh fabrications. It had been he who, above all others, had been responsible for this voyage, and he believed that the armament might accomplish his design, and return triumphant to Athens bearing to the Virgin Goddess the diadem of a new and splendid Empire. If he returned with it, its victorious general, there was little to fear for himself, for the troops would see to his safety and the citizens acclaim him their hero. But it might be otherwise, for it had been intimated that he might be sent for to stand his trial before the campaign was over; in that case there would be no devoted legions to support him and in his hands no imperial gift. Hitherto every lawlessness and arrogance had been forgiven him, because he had been there in Athens, with his beauty and his wit and his irresistible charm to turn away wrath. But now he was no longer there, his enemies had the field for calumnious sowings to themselves, and the Athenians were fickle folk; had they not turned against Themistocles and Pericles, those two builders of Empire? He had sworn that he was guiltless, and his protest at not being allowed to stand his trial at

---

[1] Plutarch, "Nicias," XIV, 2.

once makes it probable that he was; but what an opportunity his enemies had now of forging such chains of evidence as would fetter the most innocent! Supposing he were sent for and must go back alone to Athens before the expedition had accomplished anything?

The evils of the divided command were quick to manifest themselves, for no three men could have been less fitted jointly to plan a campaign. There was Nicias, who fervently wished they were all safe back in Athens again; once a reasonably bold and successful general, though never a strategist, he was now old and he was ill, and these handicaps to enterprise, combined with his radical disapproval of his mission, led him to propose a policy of fatal hesitancy and caution to which he doggedly adhered till he landed the expedition in irretrievable ruin. At the moment Syracuse was quite unprepared, many of its leading men did not believe that the Athenian fleet would come at all, far less that it was already on its way, and had he counselled that an attack should be made without loss of time, it is probable that Syracuse would have been captured, after which the fall of Sicily into the hands of Athens must have followed. Instead, Nicias's proposal was that the fleet should first sail to Selinus (for the ostensible object of the expedition was to assist Egesta), and, having induced it to yield, should circumnavigate Sicily, making a demonstration in force opposite the coast towns to show them the might of Athens, and then go home again.[1] He proposed, in fact, to abandon altogether the real object for which this great fleet had sailed, which was, as every Athenian knew, the conquest of Sicily and its incorporation into the Empire. The sixty ships originally voted would have been sufficient for the succour of Egesta, and Nicias knew as well as Alcibiades that they had not been sent out for that reason, but only on that excuse. His

---

[1] Thucydides, VI, 47. II

The Life of Alcibiades

plan of campaign, in a word, was not in accordance with the declared will and intention of the voters who had appointed him general, but with his own dissentient inclination. Lamachus, an honest and robust soldier, was for making an attack on Syracuse out of hand; Alcibiades for first demonstrating in front of the coast towns allied to Syracuse, with the object of detaching their allegiance and then attacking.

Lamachus's proposal was sound enough, but that of Alcibiades, if we examine it more closely, was strategically sounder. For at present the Athenian fleet had no friendly harbourage in Sicilian waters, and in case of an initial repulse or even a failure to take Syracuse at the first attempt, it would be highly inconvenient, if not dangerous, to have no neighbouring base for repairs and revictualling. Any repulse, even if negligible in itself, would certainly stiffen the loyalty of cities allied to Syracuse, whereas it would be an effective solvent of that loyalty if the Athenian fleet was at a friendly base in the port of some city which had seceded from Syracuse. Subsequent historians have condemned Alcibiades's scheme, forgetting that Athens had no base in these waters, and this proposed provision for one seems not only a prudent but a necessary measure, with which, when Alcibiades advanced it, Lamachus at once concurred. The only matter for our surprise is that Alcibiades, with his hot-headed impulsiveness, should not have voted for Lamachus's proposal to strike a sudden and unexpected blow, and it is not fanciful to see in his wiser and more prudent proposal some personal reluctance to run any risk. His own future and probably his own life would have been forfeit if the first news to arrive at Athens were that of some repulse. But both he and Lamachus were agreed that Nicias's programme, dictated by his own disapproval of the object for which the expedition had sailed, was imbecile.

The Athenian fleet had arrived at Rhegium when this debate of the High Command took place, and news of it reached Syracuse. Instantly the Syracusans set to work to garrison the forts in the neighbourhood and, anticipating the Athenian plan of action, sent troops to strengthen the resistance of their allied towns. Rhegium had given the fleet a very lukewarm welcome and now the three ships sent on to Egesta had rejoined with the depressing news of the hoax which had been played on the Athenian envoys. The wealth of the town was a mere fable, and instead of providing the whole cost of the expedition, all that Egesta could do was to promise thirty talents, which would provide the costs of the fleet for exactly eight days. Nicias's comment, not very helpful, was merely, "I always thought so," but though this was a disappointment, it must be remembered that the fleet had not really come out here to help Egesta, but to annex Sicily.

So in pursuance of Alcibiades's plan of campaign various visits were made to the coast-towns; at Messana there was again but a tepid welcome, and Catana was chilly. Then a demonstration in force of the entire fleet was made at Syracuse,[1] and ten ships rowed into the harbour to see if any naval preparations were in hand. There was no activity in that direction, for Syracuse was still occupied in making herself safe against attacks by land, and from the deck of one of their ships an Athenian herald proclaimed that they had come to restore Leontini, and that any Leontinians in the town had better join them. The only capture they made was of one vessel which had on board the census list of Syracusan citizens which had been sent for from the temple of Zeus along the coast in order to organize the conscription of those of military age; Athens thus learned how many men would take the field against her. But this capture much perturbed Nicias's soothsayers, for had not one of the most promising oracles said that "Athens shall capture all the Syracusans"? It would be a very sorry practical joke,

---

[1] Thucydides and Plutarch differ in their accounts here. The former seems correct, as best fitting the plan which had been adopted.

The Life of Alcibiades

they thought, on the part of Delphic Apollo if he meant that they should capture just a list of the Syracusans, and in very bad taste.

Nothing, then, was astir at Syracuse, and the fleet sailed back to Catana. The sight of the Athenian ships had caused the Government to reconsider their chilly welcome, and now they invited the generals to come and make an official statement of their case. Alcibiades was the spokesman, and he went into the town alone to address the Assembly, for Catana had not yet decided whether or not to admit the troops. While he was speaking (and quite certainly by his contrivance) some Athenian soldiers broke in through a postern gate and began strolling about the market-place, where the meeting was in progress. Alcibiades took no notice and went on speaking, but those of his audience who were of Syracusan sympathies did not like this at all; they thought that Catana was in the hands of the Athenians, and judged it more prudent to slip away. With their opposition removed, the Assembly voted solid for alliance with Athens, and Alcibiades's squadron took up its quarters in the harbour, and had now a base in Sicily. He put out again to bring the rest of the ships in here from Rhegium, and on his way back with the whole fleet, now about to establish itself at Catana, news reached him that Camarina was also ready to join the Athenian alliance; his policy of detaching the allies of Syracuse before making the attack on the town itself was evidently being justified. Before reaching Camarina there came a further rumour that Syracuse was manning its navy, and the entire fleet sailed there, evidently intending to give battle at once. But there was no truth in the report, and, after an ineffective visit to Camarina, where revolt was not yet ripe, the entire Athenian fleet returned to its base at Catana. There for the present we leave the theatre of war, with all going according to the policy which Alcibiades had initiated, and return to Athens.

Events there, since the departure of the fleet, had moved in a direction that fulfilled his forebodings when he was refused an immediate trial. The absorbing topic was no longer the great expedition which had sailed for Sicily on that morning of May, for the whole town was in a delirium of detective fever about the mutilation of the Herms and the sacrilege with regard to the Eleusinian Mysteries for which Alcibiades had already been impeached. In its determination to discover all the culprits who had been concerned in both these outrages, Scotland Yard of Athens invited any information, and paid no heed to the character of the informants. The lowest and most disreputable wretches made accusations against highly respectable citizens, who were instantly clapped in gaol till the evidence had been examined. Large rewards were offered; the first prize, so to speak, for the solution of either of these puzzles was 10,000 drachmas, so it was no wonder that Scotland Yard was busy taking down depositions. Some of these were the most blatant perjuries; one informer, for instance, said he could give the names of those who had mutilated the Herms, for he swore that he had seen them actually engaged in their sacrilegious work. When he was asked how he could have recognized them (for the outrage had taken place at night), he thoughtlessly gave the glib answer, "By the moonlight." But there had been no moon that night, so the great prize was not for him.

The prisons were full of suspects, among whom was still Andocides the orator, who had been the first to be arrested, on grounds, as we have seen, that proved him either an idiot or innocent. In prison, however, he languished until a fellow-captive, Timæus, also arrested on suspicion, put it into his head that he might turn king's evidence, confess that he was guilty, and name a few other culprits. "You will be given your pardon for turning king's evidence," said the artful Timæus "and it is surely more comfortable to save your life by a false confession than to lose it on a false charge. As for the others you will inform against, though they, poor fellows, are innocent, it is the duty of a loyal citizen to sacrifice a few shady characters—choose the shady by all means—in order to save a quantity of excellent men who are now suspect."

The Life of Alcibiades

This diabolical counsel was duly acted on by Andocides; he confessed his own guilt, and informed against a number of other men (among whom, we may devoutly hope, he included Timæus) and thus secured his own pardon. All these, with some slaves of his own whom he callously added to his list for the sake of verisimilitude, were executed, with the exception of some few who escaped, and all those who were in prison under suspicion were released.

Athens felt more comfortable now that she believed that the mutilators of the Herms had been brought to justice, but there was still the profanation of the Mysteries to be investigated. Androcles, who had produced the evidence to implicate Alcibiades, fanned the suspicions of the town against him to a blaze by insisting that he was also implicated in the mutilation, and that these two outrages were part of his conspiracy to upset the democracy and all established institutions, and set up an oligarchy or tyranny, with himself as tyrant. It was thus part of the fast-ripening plot against him that he was the instigator of both these outrages, his object being, like that of the Bolshevists, first to produce chaos out of existing order, and then a new order, with himself at the head, out of chaos. Evidence, though of the most suspect sort, multiplied; a foreigner named Teucer had fled to Megara on the night of the mutilation, and now, from the safety of another State, he sent word to Athens to say that he had been concerned in both outrages, but that on promise of pardon he would come back and lay his evidence before the Council. This was granted him, and he informed against eleven persons, including Alcibiades, as having been concerned in the parody of the Mysteries; another informant, a woman called Agariste, also accused Alcibiades of giving a second performance of the sacrilegious service, not at the house of Pulytion, but at that of Charmides. Whether any of this fresh evidence was genuine, or as perjured as that of Andocides, we cannot tell, but it was tainted by the fact of its being organized by Alcibiades's avowed enemies in his absence. It served their purpose of blackening his case, and black indeed it was now, for Athens believed in his guilt and in the design that underlay it. As to that there was no evidence of any sort, but the populace had been induced to think that he was the head of a great conspiracy to overthrow the Constitution. To such a fever of fear and excitement had they been worked up that when it was known that a small Spartan force was at the Isthmus of Corinth, it was believed that they were connected with his schemes, and were marching on Athens, where his fellow-conspirators were ready to co-operate with them. Panic seized the city, and for a whole night all the troops in Athens stood under arms, until next day it was known that this Spartan force was on its way to Bœotia, where it duly proceeded. The ferment now had penetrated the whole mass of the people, and the Assembly ordered that the State-galley, the "Salaminia," should be sent out to Sicily to bring Alcibiades home to be tried, with certain others who were supposed to be implicated. It set forth, and learned at Rhegium that the whole Athenian fleet was at Catana and sailed thither. But the harbour was still empty, for, as we have seen, the fleet had gone to Syracuse, and had not yet returned. The "Salaminia" anchored to wait for it.

CHAPTER VII

ALCIBIADES AT SPARTA

CHAPTER VII

ALCIBIADES AT SPARTA

ALCIBIADES leading the fleet in his flagship, was returning to the harbour at Catana. His policy with regard to the detaching of the allies of Syracuse before the attack on the city itself was bearing fruit. Of these Sicilian cities Catana had joined Athens, so, too, had Sicilian Naxos, and Camarina promised well, though not yet ripe, while Messana, which at his first visit from Rhegium had been lukewarm, was, so he had just heard, rapidly coming round. A party still favoured Syracuse, but the faction in favour of Athens had prospered and was eager to surrender the city to the Athenians. Naxos, Catana, Camerina and Messana, all hostile a few months ago, were detached or wavering from their old allegiance. Lamachus was quite converted to his strategy, and with Lamachus in his pocket, Nicias could always be outvoted—feeble and upright old Nicias, with his diviners and his incessant pain in his back from kidney trouble. If Nicias had had his way, the fleet would by now have terrorized Selinus into submission (what a wheel for the breaking of a butterfly!) and be sailing back to Athens. That would have been a risky return for Alcibiades; who knew what devilries Androcles might not have brewed? Nothing of the dream for the accomplishment of which the fleet had set forth would have been realized; all that it would have done was to have succoured Egesta, at staggering expense. There would have been little enthusiasm over the return of the generals.

But now his own great scheme for the annexation of Sicily was ripening fast; soon, very soon, when Syracuse was isolated, it would be time to make the attack, and then—what news for Athens, and what a home-coming for himself! Syracuse, with none to aid her, must fall, and Sicily must follow, and it was he who

The Life of Alcibiades

would have directed the whole campaign, which would ripen into the doubling and more than doubling of the dominion of the Athenian Empire. The quays at the Peiræus would be thronged again to meet the victorious Armada, as they had been thronged to see it depart, and he would step ashore, lightly carrying Sicily in his hands, as a gift to his adoring citizens. Sicily, with all her wealth and her vast tribute money, would be an Athenian island, and it would be he to whom Athens owed this great gem in her imperial crown.

That was splendid enough, but it was only the first act in the drama which he had dreamed, though alone it would be sufficient to make him master of Athens in a way that his guardian Pericles had never been. An upright, honest man, thought he, was Pericles, much respected, but little loved. He never understood Athens as Alcibiades did, nor knew the value of gaiety and personal splendour. Alcibiades had been through uncomfortable moments when that matter of his supposed sacrilege had been before the Assembly. Athens had been genuinely shocked, but though he had implored to be tried then and there, he would not now, with this marvellous return in prospect, have chosen otherwise. No trial now would be possible when he came back in this superb triumph, for the army would be with him, the people acclaiming him; he felt much safer now than he would have done even if he had been tried at once. Perhaps he had been very tipsy one night at Pulytion's house—or was it at the house of that delightful young Charmides?—and perhaps he had dressed up and imitated the solemnity of the High Priest at Eleusis with his box of sacred symbols. He really did not know, and emphatically he did not care. Nor would Athens care, when he foamed back into Peiræus in his flagship, bearing another little box, which he would present to the beloved city, and which contained the insignia of her new Empire. Thirty-five years old, and to have done that!

He lay soft in his hammock on deck and watched the shores flitting by; there was a good wind, and they would soon reach

Catana. There was a girl there, extremely attractive ... or should he tonight work away with Lamachus at the development of the campaign? A good soldier was Lamachus, but comic; he sent in bills to the Athenian Treasury for his clothes and his boots when he was on service,[1] whereas Alcibiades entered seven chariots for the Olympic contest and never sent in any bill at all. What manner of splendour, he wondered, should he display at the next games ; beat his own record? ... But now the sailors were tramping about, taking in the sails, and his ship, leading the rest, was rounding the last rocky promontory into the bay of Catana. He would tie up at the quay, choosing his own berth, for the harbour would be empty but for a few fisher-boats.

His vessel rounded the promontory and opened the harbour, and he saw that a Greek ship rode there. He recognized her at once, for she was Very familiar, and indeed he had sailed in her when he took the decree of massacre to Melos last year. But the "Salaminia" could only have come here on one errand, and he knew what that must be. Fear was an emotion to which, as all historians are agreed, Alcibiades was a complete stranger, but we may search history in vain to find a man who was so capable of hate. His own glory and the glory of Athens had been his adoration ... and now the "Salaminia" had come for him.

Her officers came on board; there was no mistaking his ship, for on the prow was his swaggering shield of gold and ivory, bearing the device of the young God of Love wielding a thunderbolt, which had been so deep an offence to the staid old Puritans of Athens. Their orders were brief; Alcibiades was summoned to return to Athens, in his own ship, to stand his trial for sacrilege. But he was not to be arrested (such were their orders), nor must any violence be used, for fear that open mutiny

---

[1] Plutarch, "Nicias," XV, 1.

The Life of Alcibiades

might break out among the troops; the Mantinean and Argive regiments, for instance, had already sworn that if any harm came to him they would not sail with the expedition at all, and they would no doubt do any bidding of his. Mutiny might be more widespread than that; the whole expedition would flock to the beckon of his finger, for every man knew that in his absence the command would revert to the dilatory, half-hearted Nicias.[1] But he made no such gesture, though it was easily within his power to refuse to obey the summons and to leave the "Salaminia" to remain at Catana or go impotently home, while he pursued the campaign he had planned, which was working well, and would, so he had every reason to believe, give Athens the Empire she sought and himself the very Acropolis for his footstool. The fleet was streaming into the harbour now, following his flagship with the sign of the invincible Eros, and with that at his back he could snap his fingers at the "Salaminia." Yet he said he would go, and he shook off, like a man springing lightly from his bed in the morning of a new day, all the golden dreams he had been devising. It seems almost inexplicable that he, the most ambitious and, at that moment, the most powerful man in all Greece, should have done so, for no one could have made him leave the fleet if he had said "Stand by me, soldiers and sailors of Athens, for the 'Salaminia' has come to fetch me home, where they will kill me," and there was only one possible motive that could have made him sacrifice all his dizzy desires for the new passion that burned hotter than they, and it was revenge.

Though Alcibiades instantly professed himself the obedient servant of the sovereign will of the people, he had not the smallest intention of going to Athens at all, but to appear to obey was the only means whereby he could carry out the terrible purpose which he had perhaps already thought over, in case of the "Salaminia's"

---

[1] Plutarch, "Alcibiades," XXI, 6.

appearance. He must have smiled to himself when he said he would go and when he saw that the officers of the "Salaminia" believed him; did those slow wits at home think that they had really got him? It was clever of them to use no force, else surely the whole fleet would have risen to protect him, but he was cleverer in yielding. So seemingly sincere was his acquiescence, so joyful even the prospect of being brought to trial and being given his opportunity of proving his innocence, that the bearer of the warrant must have thought him pathetically ignorant of all that had been going on in Athens. So in actual fact he was, but his imagination had vividly pictured it. Their orders, he now understood, were that he should be allowed to sail his own ship home, with others on board who had been implicated by the evidence which had been elaborated during his absence. Quite so; he was ready, but—would they excuse him?—there were a few brief businesses to be done first: he must, for instance, tell his fellow-commanders, Nicias and Lamachus, of this summons, and we may be sure that to them he was all smiles and certainties for his swift return when cleared from this monstrous accusation; and then he gave to some confidential agent a despatch which must be delivered without delay at Messana. At Messana, he knew, there was a plot to surrender the town to Athens, but there was a strong Syracusan party in the city, at present ignorant of it, and this despatch of his gave them full information. There would be time for them to nip it in the bud, and it would never flower. That was the first and least of the forfeits that Athens paid for sending the "Salaminia" to Catana, and from the moment of its arrival there the history of the Peloponnesian War is the history of Alcibiades.

He made then no melodramatic gesture; the vengeance of a clever man always goes quietly about its work, and never sacrifices its chance by any premature explosion. The officers on the "Salaminia" were no doubt pleased with the tactful way in which they had done their errand; perhaps they had told the poor devil that the feeling in Athens ran high in his favour. Now, once they

The Life of Alcibiades

had left the harbour, they congratulated themselves on having detached him from the fleet, with which there might have been serious trouble, and here he was coming gently and quietly home, all unconscious that Athens was for him nothing more than a butcher's shop. The two ships touched at Thurii, and then a very curious thing happened: Alcibiades, with the others who were coming so willingly back to Athens, disappeared. He was not on his ship, and they could get no news of him in the town; there was no Alcibiades at all. Search was made and search was fruitless, and there was nothing for it but to conclude that he had changed his mind about coming home. A rather dejected "Salaminia" pursued its course across the Ionian Sea, and on its way it doubtless overhauled and passed a trading vessel which had put out from Thurii while search was being made for Alcibiades, and was now steering for Greece, though most emphatically not for Athens. From its deck Alcibiades watched the great ship sweep by, and presently he stepped ashore at the port of Cyllene in Elis.

At this point there is some discrepancy (though of no great importance) between the various accounts of his movements. Thucydides[1] says that he went straight to Sparta on the invitation of the Government, Plutarch[2] that he went first to Argos and there offered his services to Sparta himself, Cornelius Nepos that he went first to Thebes.[3] In any case, he now learned the sequel to the arrival of the "Salaminia" at Athens, namely, that he, with the others who had escaped from Thurii with him, had been condemned to death, that his property had been confiscated, and that he had been excommunicated. All priests and priestesses were, ordered publicly to curse his name, and this curse for his eternal

---

[1] Thucydides, VI, 88.
[2] Plutarch, "Alcibiades," XXIII, 1.
[3] Cornelius Nepos, "Alcibiades," IV.

damnation was engraved on lead tablets and stone pillars,[1] by order of the sacred family of Eleusis.[2] When he heard this, he pronounced his own epitaph, which was a model of truth and accuracy, "I will show them that I am alive," he said. He at once proceeded to do so, and (now following Plutarch) he opened negotiations with Sparta, promising, if she would give him safe conduct, to lay his services at her disposal. Greatly had he been her foe during the war (she might remember that little matter of her envoys whom he had checkmated in so pleasing manner), but even more greatly could he be her friend. Sparta said she would be very glad to see him.

There arrived at Sparta simultaneously with him envoys from Syracuse, who had appealed to Corinth, as being their mother-city, for aid against this immense Athenian fleet. Corinth passed a vote to support Syracuse with all energy, and true to her invariable policy of enlisting the energies of others, had sent them, with representatives of her own, to Sparta. These envoys and Alcibiades were therefore both there on the same business, and so they were summoned to appear together before the Assembly, and he was called upon to speak first. Sparta was already intending to urge the Syracusans not to make terms with Athens, though she did not propose to give them any practical assistance, but, after Alcibiades's speech, there was no need either for Syracusan or Corinthian to address the Assembly at all. His words had roused to action the energies of Sparta, always slow to move, according to his advice, and from that day till he left Sparta again it was his programme which directed the course of the war against his own country. Athens had confiscated his property, she had excommunicated him, she had publicly cursed him and she had condemned

---

[1] Cornelius Nepos, "Alcibiades," IV and VI.
[2] Plutarch, "Alcibiades," XXXIII, 3.

The Life of Alcibiades

him to death for an offence of which, as we shall see later, he was almost certainly innocent. Whatever his private life was, whatever his devouring egomania, he had hitherto devoted his wealth to her splendour and his dazzling abilities to her service. Now she had cursed his name, and he cursed hers; she had declared his life forfeit, and he wrote MENE, MENE, on the wall of the Spartan Assembly-hall: "God hath numbered thy kingdom and finished it." Against our moral condemnation of a man who for the next two years used all his magnificent abilities to bring ruin on his country must be weighed our appreciation of the death-warrant she had signed against him.

His speech was a marvel of forensic dexterity, and though it is very unlikely (though possible[1]) that Thucydides actually heard it, his account of it has the true Alcibiades touch in its arrogance, its naïve unscrupulousness, its amazing surprises and its limpid lucidity. He was speaking, he told them, to an oligarchical and a monarchical people, and he appeared before them as a democrat. But democracy, in his sense of the word, was only a power opposed to tyranny, and as such he had upheld it. But he utterly repudiated such a type of democracy as now governed Athens; its follies were universally admitted, and the worst of them was that it had passed sentence of death on himself. ... This brief political exordium had an immediate purpose in dispelling the prejudice his listeners would have against one who had been in Athens a leading democrat; its ultimate purpose will appear in his peroration. ... Let them then listen impartially to the practical suggestions he had to make.

He said that they must excuse him for seeming to instruct them, but he knew the policy of Athens in a way they could not, for it was his creation, and he outlined the objects of her Sicilian

---

[1] Grundy, "Thucydides and his Age," p. 19.

expedition. The first of these was to conquer Sicily, and then the Greek settlements in Italy; after that they meant to attempt to subjugate Carthage. Then, with the whole resources of Hellenic Sicily and Italy (possibly Carthage as well) incorporated in their Empire, and with barbarian mercenaries from Iberia, they intended to attack the Peloponnese. They would have built another fleet in Italy, and with this huge Armada blockading the coast, and raiding cities as it willed, they would crush the Peloponnese into submission, and rule the entire Hellenic world. He could assure them of that, for the scheme was his own. Now, unless Greece (and especially Sparta) interfered, this imperial programme would certainly be carried out. Syracuse could not stand against the fleet, which was there now, and the conquest of Sicily must inevitably follow on her fall. Then indeed the stormy wind and tempest would burst on Sparta and the other States of Greece. If Greece was to remain free, they must act at once and on two lines.

(1) They must send out to Sicily a force of troops who could man the ships and take the field on arrival. It was most important that they should be commanded by a Spartan general, who would organize the Syracusan troops and give them the practical assurance that Sparta was with them.

(2) They must prosecute the war, not in Sicily alone, but also in Greece, and in particular in Attica, by fortifying and occupying Decelea. (This was a position on high ground between the mountains Pentelicus and Parnes and about equidistant from Athens and the Bœotian frontier.) Athens had always (he could tell them) feared this, and with good reason. With Decelea in permanent occupation of the enemy the whole stock of Attica would fall into their hands; slaves would desert, and the silver mines at Laurium could no longer be worked. Above all, the island allies of Athens would be disaffected when they saw Sparta vigorously prosecuting the war, and they would cease to pay tribute. That, with the cessation of work in the silver mines at Laurium, would mean complete financial ruin.

The Life of Alcibiades

Such was Alcibiades's advice, lucid and convincing, and he rounded off his speech with a peroration so surprising that we may be perfectly sure it is genuine, and no reflection of what Thucydides thought he would be likely to say,[1] for no one but Alcibiades could possibly have thought of it. After giving Athens's bitterest foes the most brilliant scheme for her complete ruin, he declared that he loved her. "The true patriot," he amazingly told them, "is not he who when unjustly banished refrains from attacking his country, but he who in the warmth of his affection seeks to recover her *without regard to the means*." This sentence, I venture to suggest, is not in the least cryptic, and has only one possible meaning, namely, that having, with Sparta's help, brought Athens to her knees, he hoped to go back to her, and once more stand at her helm. But now we see the true point of that political digression with which he began his speech. Democrat he had been, but only as the upholder of freedom and the foe of tyranny; the democracy, as now understood at Athens, was "admittedly foolish and mistaken," and to him personally as detestable as it was to Sparta. His country, for the present, was lost to him, but he sought, with Sparta's help in return for the help he was now giving her, to regain it. He looks forward, in fact, to his return to Athens, when he had proved to Sparta the right way to conquer her, as the head of the State, but as foe to such insane democratic principles as now ruled her. Looked at in this light, not only does this peroration pick up the thread of the exordium and make the whole lucid and intelligible, but we shall find that Alcibiades acted in a manner quite consistent with it, for he always intended to return to Athens, and when first he began to lay his plans for so doing he made it an essential condition of his return that the democratic government

---

[1] Thucydides tells us that in his reports of speeches he often gives "the sentiments proper to the occasion." Thucydides, I, 22.

should be strongly modified. ... For the present, addressing this oligarchical Assembly, he outlines political views which would be highly acceptable to them, confesses that he means to return to Athens, and thus knits together the beginning and the end of his speech. The immediate business, however, was these schemes for her downfall which he had outlined.[1]

This speech of Alcibiades in which he persuaded the Spartan Assembly to send out a Spartan commander to take in hand the defence of Syracuse, and to fortify Decelea, was a disaster more potentially momentous for Athens than anything she had yet suffered during the war. Sparta at once dispatched an extremely efficient officer called Gylippus to Sicily, whose strategy eventually caused the capture of the entire Athenian fleet. Nominally the peace of Nicias was still in force as between Sparta and Athens, but this did not technically violate it. Sparta and Athens were not at war, Sparta only sent troops to Syracuse, a colony of her ally. But she did not at once establish herself at Decelea, for this occupation of Attic soil would have been an act of war, and she waited till, during the summer of B.C. 414, the Athenians violated the peace themselves by landing troops, at the instance of Argos, on Spartan territory. This left Sparta free to retaliate in any manner she pleased. Early in B.C. 413 she invaded Attica and began with all speed to build the fortress at Decelea, and Alcibiades's programme for the ruin of Athens was completely adopted. From that time till the end of the war Sparta occupied Decelea permanently.

For two years Alcibiades lived at Sparta. The wisdom of the advice he gave the Assembly on his arrival there justified itself from the very first, and the news from Sicily as soon as Gylippus began to get to work there endorsed and re-endorsed his devilish sagacity. Gylippus was a brilliant commander, swift to see an

---

[1] Thucydides, VI, 89-93.

The Life of Alcibiades

opportunity and to act on it, and, as Alcibiades knew, the conduct of the Athenian campaign was now in the hands of Nicias, who, honest and sound soldier as he was, was old and ill and dilatory. Here at Sparta his own abilities were fully recognized, and this "lover of Athens" enjoyed the highest reputation in the public life of her deadliest foe. King of Hate and High-Priest of Revenge though he was now in all that concerned Athens, he was still, we cannot help believing, her lover, who, through the storm of calamity which he raised against her, yet discerned, dim and distant through these ruinous tempests, the calm that should follow, when Athens would ask him to come home, and the crowded quays of Peiræus hail him with love and tears, even as indeed it happened. Just now he reciprocated to the full the hate with which she regarded him; she had flung vitriol on him, and he was flinging back deadlier stuff with far deadlier aim, but though he was devoting the utmost energy of that brilliant brain to compass her downfall, and though she had cursed and condemned him, yet through the savage glare of their mutual gaze there gleamed love. No man has ever lived who was consistent with himself; he is a polity of conflicting and contradictory motives which somehow he grafts on to the stock of his individual entity, and as such we must figure Alcibiades, inconsistency incarnate, hating Athens and loving her, and enjoying in the house of her enemy much honour for his superb strategy for her ruin.

Nor was this amazing man less honoured for the conduct of his private life; never was there anyone less Spartan either in the gaiety or quickness of his mind or in his luxury-loving tastes, but now he adapted himself instantaneously and exactly to the manners of life practised in this barbarous new home of his. He laid aside, like a doffed cloak, the extravagances and effeminacies of his habits, he let his hair grow long in the untidy Spartan fashion, he crunched their disgusting coarse bread with relish and smacked his lips over the abominable black broth; it was as if, so says Plutarch, he had never in his life eaten a meal prepared by a decent cook.

The tales of his mode in Athens, his lawlessness, his wit, his drunken revels and debaucheries, were known here, and Sparta could hardly believe that this was the man whose short sleek hair used to be drenched with perfumes, who used to wear Milesian wool "softer than sleep" next his delicate skin, whose sandals used to gleam with golden thongs, and on whose shield was the device of the invincible Eros. It was hardly possible that one so foppish should walk, as he did now, barefoot, like Socrates at Potidæa, as if he had never worn shoes, and his tunic was of rough goats' hair, and, winter and summer, he bathed in the repugnant Eurotas. All this was infinitely disarming; it was a huge (and apparently genuine) compliment he paid to Spartan manners, and his general demeanour was in keeping with this stern simplicity. He wore a grave face, who had always been laughing, and he spoke but little, and that without jest or unbecoming frivolity. For it "paid" to behave like a Spartan, it inspired confidence; he was like some supreme actor, who, when he treads the stage, so soaks himself in the character he impersonates that the audience say, "It is the man himself!"[1]

And then, apart from this convincing simplicity of manner and the high compliment it implied, and far more potent than that, was the charm which bewitched all on whom it shone. It ripened strange fruits for him, and though he had laid aside the shield of invincible Eros, as being too notably un-Spartan, he did not need that pretentious blazon. King Agis had become his most intimate friend and admirer, but now, with the building of the fort at Decelea, according to Alcibiades's most wise advice, the King was away from home with his armies, and so, without scruple, Alcibiades proceeded to make love to Queen Timæa. His intrigue prospered, she went crazy with adoration for him, and before the

---

[1] Plutarch, "Alcibiades," XXIII, 6.

The Life of Alcibiades

last year of his life at Sparta was over she had a son by him. At first it seems there was no scandal attaching to the birth of the Spartan prince, and he was given the name of Leotychides. But the Queen, distraught with her passion for the boy's real father, used to whisper to her friends and her maids that his true name was Alcibiades, as was eventually proved. Later, when Alcibiades had left Sparta, he used to shrug his shoulders over that base episode. "No, I never cared an atom for her," he said, "and indeed I did not—well—do it, for the pleasure of wronging that ass Agis. I only thought I should like to have a son who was King of Sparta."

Frankly, it must have been a hellish life for the man who had hitherto indulged every whim and fancy without restraint, knowing that in the eyes of Athens his charm would give him pardon for any outrageousness, to find himself now compelled to lead an idle existence in the city of Athens's deadliest enemy, and from morning till night, and till morning again, to be acting a part in which he had convincingly to repress every inclination that was natural to him. For his soft living and his luxurious table and his dandified clothes there were the bathe in the chilly Eurotas, the vile black broth and the coarse tunic; for his love of laughter and witty talk the assumed grave face and the long silences (for Spartans never said anything unless they had something to say), and for his flute-girls and courtesans the need of playing up to the passion of that boring royal mistress, who had no attraction whatever for him. He must have longed for an hour of those drunken and brilliant feasts of wine and wit, or a catechism from the man whom, in spite of his own lawlessness and consuming greed for popularity, he had respected and loved. "Socrates would approve of me now," he thought, "living this barbarous ascetic life, and showing myself superior to all the graces and pleasures of existence. I am becoming quite a little Socrates: I am like Socrates at Potidæa. I don't wear shoes, I am a ragged scarecrow, I eat stuff at which my tail-less dog would have turned up his nose, and I wash it down with a mouthful of sour wine. Athene! What a life!" ... And then perhaps, if he were alone, and could laugh without being thought light-minded, he must have laughed at the mere idea that this sad practitioner was Alcibiades.

But when he had laughed he thought it all over and decided that it was well worth it. Week by week now there flowed in news from Syracuse which made his eye kindle, for he, rubbing himself warm after his chilly immersion in the river, was the author of all these calamities which were driving, thick as the winter snow on Taygetus, upon his beloved Athens. That appointment of Gylippus was a master-stroke; till he had taken the defence of Syracuse in hand, the Athenians were progressing famously. They had seized the heights that commanded the town, and were building a wall across them which would soon cut off the city from any succour by land, while the fleet blockaded her by sea. But that arch-procrastinator Nicias had not pushed on the work as quickly as he might, and before it was finished Gylippus had brought the authority of Sparta and the spur of his own energy to bear on the situation. He instantly set to work on a cross-wall which would prevent Nicias from finishing his job, and raised fresh troops and ships from Sicilian towns. More reinforcements arrived too from Corinth and Sparta, and though Athens, by a splendid effort, sent out another fleet of seventy-three ships and five thousand more troops,[1] under the very capable General Demosthenes, the tide had turned and the fortunes of Athens ebbed swiftly. By the middle of the summer of B.C. 413 Demosthenes realized that the expedition had failed, that Syracuse and Sicily would never come under Athenian sway, and that the only wise course, before any overwhelming calamity occurred, was to give the whole thing up.

But then (and Alcibiades must have appreciated this) it was Nicias who opposed the notion of retreat: he had been sent out,

---

[1] Plutarch, "Nicias," XXI, 1.

The Life of Alcibiades

though most unwillingly, to take Syracuse, and he meant to persevere with it. In the course of his long service to the State he had never lost a battle, nor failed to return home victoriously, and his duty as a soldier was to carry out his orders. Besides, to retreat, apart from the disgrace of returning to Athens with his mission unaccomplished, would be doing something which required imagination and initiative, and he had neither. Alcibiades felt quite warmly towards the tired and ailing old man, for much as he himself had done to ruin Athens, it would be sheer jealousy to deny that Nicias was not doing more. But at last, when fresh reinforcements arrived for Gylippus, Nicias saw it was hopeless and consented to abandon the siege. The fleet would have started homewards next day, and Athens, except for a loss of prestige, would have sustained no real disaster, but an eclipse of the moon occurred, and the piety of Nicias dealt Athens the most staggering of all the blows which his belatedness had caused her. He sent for his astrologers and diviners, like Belshazzar at his feast, and in accordance with their interpretation of this celestial warning refused even to consider the question of retreat till a lunar month had passed. The fleet must stay where it was till once more the full moon shone out unshadowed.

Such news as this made sojourn at witless Sparta more bearable and gave savour to the unspeakable black broth. Alcibiades knew, too, by now, that his whim for a son who should be King of Sparta was likely to be fulfilled, for the Queen was pregnant. Moreover, the occupation of Decelea had been a grand success; thousands of slaves were deserting, and there was difficulty about provisioning Athens. And as this month waned, during which Nicias had decreed that the fleet must wait before retreating, the storm of calamity moved up and burst. It became known in Syracuse what his intention was, and the enemy determined to make impossible the escape of the fleet which Nicias's superstitions had kept here. The Syracusan and Corinthian navy formed a barricade of ships at the entrance of the harbour where the whole Athenian fleet lay, and now it must force its way through that before it could regain the open sea. All day the battle raged; sometimes it seemed as if it would win its way out, but while in one quarter the attempt bade fair to prosper, in another it was beaten back, and by evening failure was complete and the Athenians were helplessly cooped up without room to manoeuvre. Many of their ships were driven ashore, and a panic set in both in the fleet and in the land-forces which still manned the unfinished wall. Demosthenes proposed that at daybreak they should make another attempt to force the naval barricade, but now there was mutiny among the crews ashore and they refused to embark again. The only possible retreat was by land, in the hope of regaining some friendly city, or of taking one and establishing themselves there till some further fleet of rescue conveyed them back to Athens.

On the third day after the sea-fight the retreat began in circumstances the most depressing and desperate. The whole fleet was lost, their dead lay unburied, the wounded must be left behind, and provisions were short. There was hopeless failure in the past, and for the future but the faintest ray of hope, which, as the army pursued for eight days the *via dolorosa* of its flight, was engulfed in the blackest night. The cavalry and light-armed troops of the enemy harassed them on flank and rear, there was shortage of water as well as of food on the arid Sicilian hills, and as if in ironical supply of their needs a thunderstorm with volleying rain added discomfort to despair. But in these hours of long-drawn doom, Nicias, to whom the army's plight was mainly due, rose to the heroic. Prostrated as he was by his disease, he was never weary of exhorting and encouraging the troops; he passed along the depleted ranks and cheered men who were dropping out into a further endurance. He professed himself as being still of good hope for the future; bravery and pluck would enable them to raise again the fallen greatness of their city. Demosthenes, whose division followed Nicias, was not behind him in this courage of despair; he planned a ruse for escape from these incessant attacks,

The Life of Alcibiades

by lighting watch-fires as if they were encamped for the night, and under cover of the darkness setting forth again on a changed route. But soon the enemy were on their track, and though by daybreak they had reached the coast, they found the road blocked by troops which had headed them off.

Disaster followed on disaster; Demosthenes and the six thousand men with him were surrounded and surrendered; news of that was brought to Nicias next day, and after a futile attempt to negotiate, he surrendered also, and thus the whole Athenian force fell into the hands of the enemy. Gangs of prisoners were taken to work in the quarries, where exposure and overcrowding made an end of many of them. But the Athenian spirit, its grace and gentleness, caused the rescue of others; Sicilians and Syracusans were charmed by their breeding and fine manners, and they were set free again and given positions of service. Some won favour by being able to recite fragments of the poetry and choral hymns of Euripides, for whom the Sicilians had an immense admiration, and a few eventually reached Athens again, where, so the romantic little sequel runs, they paid their affectionate respects to the poet who had been their saviour.[1]

But the debacle was complete: "Fleet and army perished from the face of the earth."[2] The news was not credited when first it reached Athens; a stranger lately landed spoke of it in a barber's shop at the Peiræus, and the barber ran up to Athens and spread the story of the disaster in the marketplace. He was held to be a teller of idle and mischievous tales, and was tortured for this insult to the sovereign city. The news reached Sparta also, but good news is easier to believe than ill, and grim Sparta rejoiced. King Agis was with his troops at Decelea and perhaps it was Alcibiades who bore

---

[1] Plutarch, "Nicias," XXIX, 3.
[2] Thucydides, VIII, 87.

it to the Queen. The time of her child-bearing was near now; in a few months Alcibiades would, if the gods of adultery were favourable, look upon the son whom one day he thought to see King of Sparta.

They talked of him and of Agis, the blind and unknowing, who was doing Alcibiades's work for him in ravaging the plains of Attica, while he filled the King's conjugal role at home.

CHAPTER VIII

AT THE COURT OF THE TISSAPHERNES

CHAPTER VIII

AT THE COURT OF THE TISSAPHERNES

THE Sicilian disaster would have been enough to crush any city in Greece except one, and this was not the only calamity Athens had to face. The fort at Decelea had been completed early in the summer, and throughout the autumn King Agis and his troops had been encamped there, thus opening another theatre of war close to Athens. The invasion of Attica was no longer a short annual occupation, for the enemy were permanently installed, and the whole country was in their hands. Twenty thousand of the slaves on country farms had deserted, the entire stock of sheep and cattle had been wiped out, and provisions, hitherto brought overland from Eubœa, had now to be carried round to Peiræus by sea. Moreover, the silver mines at Laurium could no longer be worked, and fresh taxes must be raised to supply the deficit. The strictest economy had to be practised in civic expenditure; all that Athens domestically lived for—her festivals, her choric celebrations, her shows, and her processions—were curtailed. Not till the winter of B.C. 413 did Agis leave Attica, and even then troops remained at Decelea, while he collected money from cities to the north and from Thessaly for the building of a fleet to attack Athens on the waters of her Empire and raise the standards of revolt in the islands of her allies. At present her Empire was intact.

It looked, indeed, as if the hopes at Sparta of completing her overthrow during the next summer would be fulfilled, and that King Agis and his son after him would be Kings of Hellas. And there at Sparta, on Agis's hearth, sat the man who, like some magician of the air, had raised this cosmic tempest of calamity that was beating on his city. He ate the black bread, he yawned at the caresses of this stupid woman who adored him and he began to

The Life of Alcibiades

wonder what his next move would be, and whether Sparta was not getting a little unhealthy. There might be trouble for himself when Agis returned, and also he was beginning to feel, by that quick, unerring intuition of his, that, in spite of (or was it because of?) the huge success that had attended the advice he had given the Spartan Assembly on his first arrival, the ungrateful fellows were beginning to eye him jealously. For indeed it was he, not King Agis, who was King in Sparta, as everybody knew, from Queen Timæa downwards. Socrates had mocked him once for saying that he was as good as any king, but Socrates would not be so sarcastic now. ... Yet Athens was not sufficiently humbled yet for sending the "Salaminia" to fetch him home to die, and Sparta was clearly the best place from which to punish her. But something would turn up which he could shape to his own ends.

The Syracusan disaster, as was only natural, began to have its reaction on the cities of the Athenian Empire. For many years the title of "allies" had been a mere derision, and now that Athens seemed to be tottering, it is no wonder that they were ready to hasten her fall, as a means of recovering their own freedom. Envoys from Euboea and Lesbos approached King Agis, who was busy in the north of Greece with levying subscriptions from friendly cities to build a fleet, and asked for Spartan aid to throw off the yoke. He received them favourably and, without consulting his Government at home, sent one of his officers to Lesbos, with the promise of ships to follow.

Simultaneously there arrived at Sparta envoys from Chios on the same errand, and with them came representatives from Tissaphernes, the Persian military governor and satrap of Sardis. King Darius had ordered him to collect from the Hellenic cities in his province the revenues which hitherto the Athenian navy had prevented his obtaining, and Tissaphernes proposed a Spartan alliance against these cities of the coast and the adjacent islands, of which the most important was Chios. A similar deputation came from Pharnabazus, satrap of Phrygia, with the object of inducing the Greek towns in the Hellespont to revolt from Athens. All the world seemed courting a Spartan alliance, and Persia and the States of Hellas were hovering over stricken Athens, like eagles over the carcase on which they hoped to prey.

Instantly Alcibiades embraced this new opportunity for dealing Athens another blow. The sending of Gylippus to Syracuse, the fortification of Decelea, had been his devices, and she was staggering under the impact; a thrust at her naval Empire might cause her complete collapse, and the "lover of Athens" with Spartan support might then return to rule her, even as he had foreshadowed in his speech to the Assembly. ... The Spartan Government at home was divided as to which of these two projects—that of an attack on the northern towns of the Hellespont or that of an expedition to Chios—was the sounder, and probably, without this spur of Alcibiades's energy, would have continued to argue the matter indefinitely. He strongly urged the Chios scheme; Chios was the most powerful of Athens's island possessions, and if she revolted, others would be sure to follow, and the crumbling of the Empire would be rapid. Also Chios had sixty ships, and these would be a most valuable addition to those of Sparta and her allies in this new war in the theatre of Athens's naval Empire. Alcibiades got hold of his friend Endius, who was one of the Ephors for that year, and with his support Sparta voted that forty ships be sent to Chios, of which she would furnish ten and her allies the rest. Nothing could be done till the winter was over, and in the meantime the scheme was to be kept dark, for fear that Athens should learn about it.

There ensued an imbroglio of politics, naval movements and domestic disclosures, through which, in hot pursuit of his own ambitions, Alcibiades had to thread his way, and in the whole of history there is no record of a man who, in so complicated a welter of affairs, displayed such mastery in opportunism and simplifycation. He was playing his hand quite alone, condemned to death by his country, and an exile in the land of her enemies, who were

The Life of Alcibiades

beginning to regard him with suspicion, and his object now was to get safely away from Sparta (lest his ambitions should be extinguished, with himself, for ever), to remain for a while yet the arch-enemy of Athens, directing the war policy of Sparta against her and at the same time to be paving his way for his own return to Athens. We cannot conceive a more impossible programme; looking at it as he must have looked at it then, it reads like the affirmation of some conjurer who says he will bray in a mortar the watch he has borrowed from that gentleman in the audience and turn it into a live canary. But Alcibiades, like the conjurer, had movements which were a little quicker than any eye watching him could follow, and the history of Greece for the next few years is, in fact, an account of his conjuring tricks.

Let us, then, rid our minds of all moral prejudices (we can hastily clutch them to our bosoms afterwards) and try to follow his antic swiftness. It would be impossible for him to stay in Sparta much longer, for Queen Timæa had given birth to a son, and was whispering to her friends that others might call him Leotychides, but in the sight of the gods he was Alcibiades. There was corroborative evidence, too, of that, for it was ten months before the birth of the child since Agis had visited his wife's bed-chamber, and the date was fixed in the King's mind, for there had been an earthquake that night.[1] It was clear then that Alcibiades had better be gone from Sparta as soon as might be, for Agis was now at Corinth on his way homeward, and he had heard of the birth of Queen Timæa's child.

King Agis, it may be remembered, had arranged to send ships to Lesbos for the encouragement of the revolt, but a message from Sparta met him at Corinth saying that the Government advised the Chian expedition first; Alcibiades's hand can be traced here, for he

---

[1] Plutarch, "Alcibiades," XXIII, 8.

wanted to get away. Agis concurred, and, to save time, ships of the Peloponnesian League lying at Corinth were dragged across the Isthmus into Ægean waters. But the Isthmian games were being celebrated, and Corinth desired to postpone the sailing of this contingent to Chios till they were finished. These national games were periods of truce, and Athenian representatives at Corinth seem to have picked up valuable information as to whither this little fleet, so hurriedly dragged across the Isthmus, was bound. So when the sporting truce was over, and it took the sea, the Athenians knew all about it, and with a fleet of thirty-seven ships drove the whole lot ashore in a lonely harbour. And that, for the present, was the end of them.

Meantime a small contingent from Sparta (ten ships originally but now reduced to five) had been manned to join them and take command of the whole squadron; a Spartan officer, Chalcideus, and Alcibiades were in charge of it. But now news came that the Corinthians were all ashore, and it looked for the moment as if there would be no Chian expedition at all. This was extremely inconvenient for Alcibiades, who wanted, for domestic reasons, to be quit of Sparta before Agis's return, and (as planned) to be still directing Spartan hostilities against Athens. It was a serious difficulty, for Chios was expecting forty ships, and where was the use of sailing with five? But he had an admirable trick to settle that, and he got hold of his friend Endius again.

"Let Chalcideus and me sail at once with our five ships," he said. "We shall get there before they can hear at Chios that the rest are ashore, and we will say they are following. I'll tell them that Sparta is backing up their revolt, and that Athens is bleeding to death; they will believe me more than anyone. Besides (this was for Endius's ear alone), what kudos for you, if through you this revolt is raised and a Spartan alliance made with King Darius through Tissaphernes! Don't let King Agis have the credit for that. It's your plan; I of course am just your lieutenant."

The Life of Alcibiades

Such a simple argument, and quite effective. Alcibiades set off, never again to look on the dreary city of cold baths and black bread and love-lorn women, nor, indeed, on King Agis, and yet he was still directing the Spartan conduct of the war. He and Chalcideus captured all ships they met, for fear of the news of this very small squadron going ahead of them and causing disappointment till he arrived with his lucid statement, and after a preliminary meeting with some of the Government who were in the plot, they made their appearance in the city and went straight to the hall where the Council was sitting. Alcibiades assured them that a fine squadron of ships had started from Corinth (which was quite true), but forgot to mention that they were all ashore, with an Athenian fleet mounting guard over them. That was sufficient; the island of Chios proclaimed its revolt from the tyranny of Athens, and its example was immediately followed by Erythræ, on the coast of Asia Minor, and Clazomenæ. The three got busy with fortifying their towns.

The staggering news soon arrived at Athens. Chios, the most powerful of her islands, had revolted, the flag of Sparta was flying over the city and the man who had hoisted it was Alcibiades. Two years ago they had condemned him to death, and indeed he was showing that he was still alive. What a devil! What a master! They had been unwise to treat their superman like that, and to have thought that he would come back, like a sheep to the slaughter, when they sent the polite "Salaminia" to fetch him. They had driven him to the bosom of their enemy, and with his amazing adaptability he had made himself at home in the barbarous place and infused Spartan stupidity and slowness with the ichor of his brilliance. He had sent Gylippus to Syracuse, he had built that hornets' nest at Decelea, he was the father of the next King of Sparta, and now he had caused the revolt of the chief island of their Empire. And all this Pentecost of disaster had come upon them because they had been induced to believe that he had made parody of the Holy Mysteries. The whole priesthood had cursed him, and yet he seemed to prosper. ... Could it be that the Spirit of

God which abode at Eleusis knew that he had never profaned the holy ceremonies? Had the priesthood only lent itself to a political plot against an innocent man, and him the ablest of all the sons of Athens? No further shred of reliable evidence had been produced, and as for the mutilation of the Herms with which his name had been coupled, the authors of that were now believed to be Corinthian agents, whose design was to create such consternation in the city that the Syracusan expedition would not sail. ... Were they wrong from the first about Alcibiades? That doubt began to look them in the face, and when they scrutinized it, they met his steadfast eyes, still cruelly gay. "I asked to be tried," he seemed to say, "because I was innocent, and you would not try me till sufficient false witnesses were ready. You condemned me to death, and you reckoned me among the dead. Were you right ?"

And yet behind the cold, devilish purpose of those eyes was there some glint of regret and even of love? Some of them had begun to long for his return;[1] should they make some sort of sign to him and see if there was any answering signal?

Pride forbade it; the most intellectual city of Greece was up against the brains of one young man. The Treasury was nearly empty, but there was still that solid sum of one thousand talents (equivalent in modern value to over a million pounds) which Pericles had put by at the beginning of the war, passing a decree that it should not be touched unless the enemy attacked Athens with a fleet,[2] and that anyone who even proposed its expenditure on any lesser emergency should be executed. But the emergency in which Athens stood now was extreme and the Assembly resolved on its use, for ships and men were wanting, and the revolt of Chios, if acquiesced in, would mean that dusk would quickly

---

[1] Aristophanes, "Frogs," I, 1425.
[2] Thucydides, II, 24.

The Life of Alcibiades

deepen into night for the Empire. They could detach twelve ships from the fleet blockading the stranded Corinthian vessels, which that magnificent liar Alcibiades had assured the Chians were on the way, and with these funds at once furnish thirty ships more to send against Chios.

We cannot too warmly admire the resilience and tenacity of the great city in this fiery tempest of misfortune. She had lost the greater part of her navy and the flower of her troops at Syracuse, Attica was a desert, ravaged by the troops at Decelea, the Treasury was empty, and now, with the revolt of Chios, the coherence of her island kingdom was crumbling. If once that landslip of which the first runnels of earth had begun to flow was fairly started, she would be buried for ever in the *débris* of her own greatness. But as if the dusk were the early glimmer of the hour before dawn that would brighten into noonday, she shook off all presage of disaster and set forth with gallant confidence on new adventures. Admiral Strombichides with a squadron of eight ships went instantly off to Samos, which was the most important of the islands remaining to her, to ensure its fidelity and make it the headquarters for a new naval campaign; Admiral Thrasycles followed. But equally energetic and far more brilliant, both in strategy and tactics, was her chief antagonist. With five ships only, aided by that admirable ruse that a powerful fleet was coming, Alcibiades had already secured the revolt of Chios with its sixty ships, and now, leaving forty of the Chian fleet to protect the island, he set off with the remaining twenty to Miletus to spread revolt there. Two objects might be gained by the delivery of this lightning-stroke: Athens, swift though she had been in sending her new fleet out for the suppression of the revolt in Chios, would find that the ring of flame was spreading fast, while his own prestige at Sparta would soar heaven-high, if he, with his fellow-commander, Chalcideus, and those five ships, detached from Athenian allegiance not Chios alone, but Miletus also.

He slipped past Samos, where the two Athenian admirals had mobilized; they put out in pursuit, and were close behind him when he entered the harbour of Miletus. The Milesians must already have been ripe for revolt, for they would not let the ships of Athens into the harbour. Alcibiades had many influential friends here, and easily persuaded the town to join Chios, and that done, he doffed his naval uniform and became diplomatist again. He went up to Sardis with Chalcideus to interview the satrap Tissaphernes, whose envoys had come to Sparta to propose the alliance against Athens, and a treaty was made. By the terms of this monstrous agreement not only was Persia leagued with Greek against Greek, but the Hellenic cities of Asia Minor were ceded to Persia and their tribute was assigned to King Darius. This treaty was amended six months later, much to the advantage of Sparta, for the King agreed to pay the expenses of all Greek troops and ships for the recovery of these cities from Athens as long as they were serving on the Asian coasts.[1] Sparta, ever thrifty, thus incurred no outlay in this section of the war, which had for its object the dismemberment of the Athenian Empire. That was pleasant, and it was to Alcibiades that she owed both this alliance with the King of Persia and this inexpensive warfare. To Alcibiades also she soon owed the fact that these agreeable arrangements did not long continue.

Into the detailed movements of the Athenian and Peloponnesian fleets during this autumn of B.C. 412 and throughout B.C. 411 it is not necessary to enter, for most of these were unimportant skirmishes, productive of no real advantage to either side and indeed the very enumeration of them tends to obscure the real issues. Even Thucydides loses the habitual clarity of his narrative, and doubts have been raised as to whether the chapters

---

[1] Thucydides, VIII, 37

The Life of Alcibiades

in which he treats of them are really of his writing. Certain points of internal evidence, however, seem to prove their authenticity, and the later chapters of the eighth and concluding book of his history are quite unmistakably his. We may perhaps, then, hazard the conjecture that these very confused and ill-arranged chapters were notes made by him for some future revision which they never received. But out of this crowd of insignificant incidents a few solid events emerge: Athens sent out fresh reinforcements and recovered Lesbos; she established herself on a promontory of Chios, from which she ravaged Chian territory. The headquarters of her fleet were at Samos, which had hitherto been under an oligarchical government. But now, with the assistance of the crews of three Athenian vessels there, the people rose against it. Two hundred of the nobles were killed, four hundred were banished, and Samos became a democracy. This, of course, was a guarantee of her fidelity to Athens (just as the oligarchical revolution in Chios had declared for Sparta), and Athens granted Samos the status of an independent ally. In the crumbling of Empire a faithful ally was worth having without payment of tribute, and for the first time since the establishment of the Confederacy of Delos one of her islands became free instead of being a subject State.

These events were of the highest importance, not only for their actual value, but because they showed the Greek world, and now the Persian world as well, that in spite of the crushing disaster in Sicily, of the occupation of Decelea by the Spartans and of the revolt of Chios, Athens was not yet in her death-agony. It had been expected that before the year was out she would have bled to death from the wounds which would have been mortal to any but her. They had all been inflicted by the man whom she had condemned to death, and now, when we follow the splendid recuperation of the stricken city, we have to follow, even as we did in her disasters, the personal history of Alcibiades.

He had left behind him in Sparta statesmen and officials jealous of the successes he had won for her, and that jealousy had been deepened by his skill in procuring the revolt of Chios and Miletus and the treaty with Tissaphernes. And then there was King Agis, who now had disowned Queen Timæa's son as being no offspring of his. Alcibiades had indeed as bitter a company of foes in Sparta as he had in Athens when the "Salaminia" came to Catana to fetch him home, and once again the death sentence was passed upon him in Sparta as it had been in Athens, and an order was sent out by the Government to Astyochus, the Admiral of the Peloponnesian fleet, that he was to see to its execution. There was Alcibiades, the only Athenian in the fleet, and it would seem a simple matter that henceforth there should be none. But passing sentence of death on Alcibiades was not quite the same thing as preparing his corpse for burial. Once in his boyhood, Pericles had said he was as good as dead, once the Assembly at Athens had pronounced his sentence, and now Sparta followed suit, with precisely the same result, in that he showed himself more than ever alive. For though wherever he went he made deadly enemies, that charm of his made for him devoted friends, and from some such he must have heard of this amiable design on his life. He forestalled its accomplishment, and, secretly leaving the fleet, escaped to the Court of Tissaphernes at Sardis, which he had already visited in company with Chalcideus, and arrived there safely. Astyochus, who might have gathered from the sad example of Athens that Alcibiades's enemies went through depressing experiences, must bitterly have repented that he had not knocked him on the head first and talked about it afterwards.

So at last, after more than two years among these boorish Spartans, who lived on garbage, who washed in snow-fed Eurotas and were as unsociable as oysters each in his own laconic shell, Alcibiades proposed to enjoy the graces and luxuries of life again, and teach the Spartans what their jealousies had lost for them. Indeed he had cause to think them ungrateful dogs, for in his enmity to Athens he had served them magnificently; ever since he had come among them his inventiveness had been the source of all

The Life of Alcibiades

their success. Now they chose to turn against him, and they should see, as Athens had seen, how grievously idiotic that was. But the task before him was no easy one (though, perhaps, no harder than what he had so gaily accomplished at Sparta), for Tissaphernes was bound to Sparta's interests by the Treaty of Miletus, which Alcibiades proposed wonderfully to modify. But before getting to business he had first to win the satrap's confidence and esteem, and now, just as at Sparta he had munched black bread with relish and schooled his witty tongue to gravity or silence, he became, with that chameleon-like genius of his for suiting himself to his environment, a Persian of the true Orient. This was easier for him than his Lenten observances at Sparta, for his whole proclivities were towards luxury and splendour and debauchery, and in Tissaphernes he found a man who had never been called prude or Puritan. He exerted all that charm which even those who most feared and hated him found irresistible, he delighted him with the inimitable grace of his presence and his conversation, and soon he set about the business on which he had come. His host was fascinated by him; he had lately made himself a wonderful pleasance, full of cool streams and shady lawns and extravagant pavilions, and now he named the place "Alcibiades Park," in honour of his enchanting guest, and there at leisure the two conferred.[1]

Alcibiades's scheme was ready now; the main object of it was to injure Sparta's interests with the Persians in every possible way. Sparta had turned against him, and she must smart for it. That was sufficient in itself, but there was this as well—that by the same policy he brought nearer the day when Athens would long for him to come home again. He knew that already many regretted the sentence they had passed on him which had cost them such bitter

---

[1] Plutarch, "Alcibiades," XXIV, 5.

mintings, and now he was to show himself turning towards his city again with comfort for its afflictions and trouble for Sparta.

His tactics with Tissaphernes, as usual, were masterly. The pay, for instance, which, by the Treaty of Miletus, the King had contracted to give the Peloponnesian troops and sailors was a monstrous item; Alcibiades suggested that instead of giving each man a drachma a day, it should be cut down to half a drachma. Half a drachma was all that Athens, with her long naval experience, thought wise to give her sailors; higher pay was merely demoralizing, for the men spent their money on dissipated pleasures, which impaired their efficiency. It would be wise, too, not to let this economical pay-day occur with very great regularity, for that would guard against desertions; men who were thinking of deserting would know they would forfeit arrears.

This judicious parsimony strongly recommended itself to Tissaphernes; he thought it a remarkably able idea and one to be put into practice. And Alcibiades had other little notions of the kind, for when the captains of the Chian ships came to the satrap for their sailors' pay, he cried shame on them. There were they, the richest folk in all Greece, who had been delivered from that oppressive Athenian yoke by Spartans and Persians who nobly laid down their lives in fighting for them, and now they come and demand money as well! Out they went from his indignant presence, and when petitioners from other cities which had revolted from Athens came to ask the pay that had been promised their troops, he told them that it would be a crying scandal if they, who all these years had paid heavy tribute to Athens, were not eager to expend as much and more on this priceless benefit of freedom. He told them, too, that Tissaphernes was paying all the expenses of their ships and troops out of his own pocket, a statement which may perhaps have been true to the extent that the satrap might be supplying these moneys out of levies squeezed from the satrapy. We must not therefore dismiss this statement as being one of Alcibiades's lies.

The Life of Alcibiades

That was a good day's work, for he had sown fruitful seeds of discontent in the Peloponnesian fleet, while Tissaphernes was more pleased than ever with this fascinating fellow, his grace and his wit and his ability, for these were indeed admirable plans for saving expenditure. They supped in the pleasance that night, and Alcibiades, with his lisp and his brilliant manner, suggested to the satrap another new line of policy with regard to the war. He said that the wise thing to do was not to help this side or that at all, but to let both wear themselves out against each other. Of course, if Tissaphernes brought up that great Phoenician fleet and battalions of Persian soldiers to help Sparta, Athens would be quite wiped out. But was that wise? Sparta would then be supreme and without a rival in Greece both by land and sea; all the other Hellenic States would flock to her banner, and she would be truly formidable. As Tissaphernes knew, the ultimate aim of Persia was to annex the whole of Greece, islands and main alike, but if Athens were demolished, who would help Persia against Greece once more confederated under Sparta? It would be a big job to overthrow Sparta then; Tissaphernes might have to take the field himself, and that would entail great personal risk, for battles were nasty, dangerous affairs. And to think of the cost of a prolonged campaign in Greece![1]

We may plausibly picture to ourselves the setting and scene of these arguments; the two would be supping in one of these sumptuous pavilions in the newly-named Alcibiades Park. They had drunk a good deal, but the effect of sufficient wine on Alcibiades was only to give him, as we know, peculiar lucidity, and he had stated his views with admirable clearness and without too much insistence. Casual suggestions, made between the cups, were far more potent than when given with emphasis and eagerness. He

---

[1] Thucydides, VIII, 46.

watched the effect, and saw that the hint that the satrap might have to take the field in person was very telling; Tissaphernes much disliked the idea. Admirably sound too was the proposed policy; it was far better to let Sparta exhaust herself and her resources in defeating Athens, than to give her such aid as would enable her to do so without a long and expensive effort. Then was the time to step in and crush Greece altogether and easily when drained of her strength.

"Let them exhaust themselves, my dear friend," said Alcibiades; "let them wear each other out without intervening at all. Don't help Sparta to crush Athens out of existence; if you do, she will federate all Greek States together under her supremacy, and Persia will have the devil of a job. Indeed I am not at all sure whether it would not be to your advantage to help Athens instead. Athens is a sea-Power; she will be content with a naval supremacy, and would gladly assist in subjecting the Hellenic towns in Asia to the King, whereas Sparta is employed in liberating them, and would never leave them—if you will excuse the expression—in the hands of the barbarians." He yawned with elaborate carelessness. "Really, if you back anybody," he said, "you had better back Athens."

In all history there was never a "lone hand," such as Alcibiades was playing, more consummately played. All these arguments by which he was gaining Tissaphernes's sympathy, and was hoping to gain his support, were, from the Persian point of view, well worth thinking over. It was no wonder, as the satrap knew, that his brilliant guest had this animosity against Greece, Sparta and Athens alike, for first his own city had denounced and condemned him, and then the city of his exile to which he had rendered such splendid service had given the order for his death. How fully too he appreciated Persian aims! Indeed in his appearance, even as in his counsel, he was more Persian than Greek. There he lounged in trews and mitre, with his page-boy fanning him, dipping in that dish of sweetmeats by his couch, with the Persian flute-girl ready to

The Life of Alcibiades

play to him, and the two dancing girls waiting for his nod to begin the slow, sensuous movements that were so unlike the vigour of Greek dancing. Tissaphernes could hardly believe he was a Greek at all, so Persian were his luxurious habits, and it was so natural that he should be a friend of Greece's foes after the way he had been treated.

Tissaphernes was much impressed; indeed he was convinced of the wisdom of the course Alcibiades had suggested, and at once proceeded to act on it. He cut down the pay of the Peloponnesian troops and sailors, and was remiss in its distribution; above all, he kept idle and out of action the Phoenician fleet, which, in conjunction with the Spartan ships, could have made an end of the sea-power of Athens in one engagement. The effect was that the Peloponnesian navy, lately very efficient, began rapidly to deteriorate; the men, with their pay cut down by half, and that often in arrears, grew sullen and discontented, while Athens, already heartened up by recent successes, began to wonder what this meant. It was known that Alcibiades had the ear of Tissaphernes and was in high favour with him, and now, instead of backing up the Spartan fleet, the satrap was withholding their pay and giving them no assistance whatever. What did it mean?

Alcibiades knew what it meant. Behind that sound and specious diplomacy which had already convinced Tissaphernes, there was his own design swiftly ripening. He let the demonstrated effect of his influence with the satrap take hold of the quick Athenian wits, and then played the card he had been holding up. He sent confidential messages to various officers of the fleet at Samos, saying that he wanted to return to Athens and that he could bring with him the friendship of Tissaphernes and through him of King Darius. But there was one condition attached: the democracy which had driven him into exile must be put down, for while it was in power he could never come back. He sent his greeting to all good men and true at Samos and asked them seriously to ponder what he said.

He was thus now at work on the final item of his conjuror's programme, namely, his recall to Athens. When first he had addressed the Spartan Assembly he had planned that it should be Sparta who, after crushing his country, should restore him, but since then Sparta had signed his death-warrant, for which piece of impertinence he was now brilliantly injuring her interests. But his programme remained precisely the same, though the technique of this final trick was changed. He could no longer accomplish it that way; it did not matter, and he would do it by some other sleight. ...

The officers of the fleet and of the troops at Samos discussed his proposal first among themselves and then with the leading civilians of the place, and the nucleus of a conspiracy to restore the lately-deposed oligarchy was formed. Then the feeling of the troops was carefully tested, and the prospect of receiving pay from Persia was found to be acceptable. But Phrynichus, one of the generals, disapproved of and distrusted the whole project. Why, he argued, should Persia suddenly wish to break with Sparta, whose fleet was now quite as powerful as that of Athens, and why should she make the condition that the oligarchy must be restored? Alcibiades, he believed, was working, not for Athens at all, but simply for himself. But Phrynichus convinced nobody, and an embassy, with General Peisander at its head, was sent to Athens to lay before the Assembly the glittering prospect of detaching Persia from her alliance with Sparta, and of securing the aid of her money and her ships. Only Alcibiades could do that for them, and thus staunch with triumph the war which was bleeding them to death, and Alcibiades, whose influence with the satrap was acknowledgedly paramount, would not stir a finger unless he was recalled to Athens and the democratic Government which had condemned him and which was responsible for all the mismanagement of the war was overthrown.

The scene in the Assembly when Peisander spoke in this wise must have been intensely dramatic. Alcibiades's name had been last mentioned there when the decree was passed which confiscated his

The Life of Alcibiades

property, ordered that he should be publicly cursed by all priests and priestesses of the High Gods and condemned him to death, amid yells of approving execration. Three years and more had passed since then, and now, on the mere suggestion that he should be allowed to return, the members of the sacred families of Eleusis, the Eumolpidæ and Ceryces protested in the name of heaven and earth against restoring a man who had been condemned for sacrilege, but who, as everyone knew, had never been tried for it. Again, at the suggestion of changing the democratic government, there was outcry and violent expressions of dissent; speaker after speaker opposed it. But Peisander replied to each of them in turn. Sparta had a fleet as large as that of Athens and a much larger backing of allied cities; Tissaphernes found for them the expenses of the war, but the Athenian Treasury was now nearly emptied of the last thousand talents reserved for dire emergency. Could any one tell him what hope of salvation there was for Athens except with the help of Persia?

The tumult raised by the suggestion of changing the whole form of government died down; not one of those who had yelled repudiation could find any answer to the demands of one exiled Athenian, and Peisander, in an aside, reminded them that they could revert to democracy when the peril of Athens was over. Then came again the central and cardinal point, "We must recall Alcibiades," he said, "for he is the only man who can save us," and now, when he repeated that, even those who had protested most loudly were dumb. They knew that it was so; only the man who had dealt Athens the wounds of which she was bleeding to death could staunch them. They had hated and reviled him, they had loaded his name with infamy, and now they yearned for him and longed to have him again.[1] Athens had drunk deep of the waters of

---

[1] Aristophanes, "Frogs," I, 1425.

affliction for her treatment of him, and it was he who, as they were beginning to see, was ready to forgive. It was not her favour and forgiveness he asked; he offered them his—on conditions. And the Assembly that had opened in violent protest against Peisander's proposal passed a vote that he and ten others should negotiate with Tissaphernes and Alcibiades to the best of their power, accepting these terms. There would be difficulties, Peisander knew, at Samos, where General Phrynichus was flatly opposed to having any dealings with Alcibiades, and before Peisander left on this mission the Assembly passed a vote depriving Phrynichus of his command, thus getting rid of official opposition. Athens would suffer no obstacle to interfere with the return of her beloved exile. Phrynichus must go, the democratic Constitution of Athens must go, the charges of impiety for which Alcibiades had been condemned must go in order to secure his return. They yearned for him. If ever in the course of history there was a necessary man, it was now.

But while this revolution was being accepted in principle at Athens a vat of cross-purposes and counter-plots was fermenting at Samos and in the garden of Tissaphernes. Phrynichus, not yet deposed from his office as general, fully expected that the Athenian Assembly would carry this proposal for Alcibiades's return, and as he had opposed it, he was not feeling very comfortable, for Alcibiades's enemies had a habit of coming to grief; it so often happened like that. ... So, with a tender regard for his own safety, he sent a despatch to Astyochus, Admiral of the Spartan fleet, with full details of how Alcibiades was trying to detach Tissaphernes from the Spartan alliance and contrive one between him and Athens. A ranker treachery than that an Athenian general should inform the head of the enemies' forces of this scheme by which Athens would so hugely benefit can scarcely be imagined, and in this despatch he excused himself for so doing on the plea that he was mortally afraid of Alcibiades. But this treachery amazingly miscarried, for Astyochus was perfectly

The Life of Alcibiades

powerless to undermine Alcibiades's position with the satrap, and it is also possible that he was in the plot himself.[1] So, with a high sense of comedy, he merely went to Alcibiades and showed him this letter. Alcibiades instantly denounced Phrynichus to the Athenian generals at Samos, as being in treasonable correspondence with the enemy, and demanded that he should be put to death. That was a nasty stroke, for if now Alcibiades (as seemed most probable) should be restored, he would doubtless enforce this demand. Phrynichus, more alarmed for himself than ever, capped one piece of treachery by another, and again wrote to Astyochus giving him the plans of the fortifications of Samos, and indicating where a successful attack could be made by the Spartan fleet. Luckily for Athens this Athenian traitor was dealing with a Spartan traitor, and Astyochus treated this second letter as he had treated the first, and forwarded it to Alcibiades. Phrynichus's plan had thus completely failed, and he made the best of a very bad job by telling his fellow generals that an attack would be made on the defences at Samos at that weak point in them which he had indicated to Astyochus, and urged them instantly to make it stronger. This rehabilitated his loyalty, and when Alcibiades sent a second despatch to Samos warning them of this danger-spot which Phrynichus had recommended to Astyochus, he was too late, for Phrynichus had already caused it to be repaired. ... This comedy of traitors, which reads like a page of Aristophanes, then terminated.

Before we pursue the unravelling of the main thread of our story it will assist its simplification to glance at the three focuses of energy, so to speak, which direct it. First comes Alcibiades himself, now definitely detached from Sparta and devoting himself to the interests of Athens, in the furtherance of which lay his chance of furthering his own interests and of being recalled there as the one,

---

[1] Thucydides, VIII, 50.

the only man who could help her. He had promised to obtain for Athens the help of Tissaphernes against Sparta, but the democracy, which had banished him, must be overthrown before his return. At present he was at the Court of the satrap at Sardis, who had listened favourably to his argument that Persia would be wise not to support Sparta against Athens, but not to his recommendation to break the existing alliance to support the other. Tissaphernes had taken his advice, in so far that he had already cut down the pay of the Spartan fleet and had withheld from it the assistance of the Phoenician fleet, which would, if employed, have terminated the war at once with the destruction of the Athenian navy. To have neutralized that fleet was in itself a notable accomplishment, and bade fair for the fulfilment of the satrap's promise actively to aid Athens. ... The second focus of energy was Samos, where a few weeks ago Alcibiades had sent his message that he was willing to return to his country, bringing the help of Tissaphernes, on condition that the democracy was strongly modified. Samos just now was the headquarters of the fleet and army of Athens, and was indeed more truly the seat of government than Athens itself, for at home there were not more troops than were necessary to man the long walls, nor more ships than the protection of the Peiræus demanded. The troops and the civilian population generally, with the exception of Phrynichus and such following as he may have had, were favourable to Alcibiades's proposal, and, as we have seen, had sent General Peisander to Athens to lay their scheme before the Assembly. ... The third focus of energy was Athens, where the Assembly had voted in favour of the exile's return and was now sending Peisander out to Sardis to confer with the satrap and Alcibiades.

Peisander and his deputation arrived at Alcibiades Park, expecting the ratification of the promise transmitted to them. That pleasant dream was rudely shattered. There were three conferences, at each of which Tissaphernes by the mouth of Alcibiades made increasingly monstrous conditions. As the price of the Persian-

The Life of Alcibiades

Athenian alliance, he demanded that the whole of Ionia, coast towns and islands alike, should be ceded to the King of Persia. Though this implied that Athens would lose the greater part of her naval empire, Peisander consented to this, for Sparta, with the help of the Persian fleet, would be crushed, and there would still remain to Athens her Thracian colonies and the cities of the Hellespont. Other conditions followed, which were also accepted, and then came a demand on the part of Persia which was intolerable, namely, that the King should build what ships he pleased and send them when he wished "along his coasts." This clearly meant nothing else than that when Sparta had been crushed the King would prepare an armada to wipe off from the seas the fleet of his new allies. Peisander refused to accept this condition and broke the conference up, believing that Alcibiades had duped him into organizing his return and a revolution at Athens, with a promise of help from Persia for which there was no foundation. He and his deputation went back to Samos furious against the man who had cheated them into believing it.

Now historians have taken the view that Tissaphernes had never made such a promise, but that Alcibiades had invented it in order to get the democratic government at Athens which had condemned him overthrown and himself recalled.[1] But if we try to reconstruct, not only the material, but also the psychological situation, it seems unlikely to the verge of the impossible that he had represented the satrap as promising to break with Sparta and ally himself with Athens unless he had really done so. For whatever we may think about Alcibiades's moral character, it is difficult to suppose that a man of his ability could have been guilty of so arrant a folly. For if his assertion that Tissaphernes was ready to side with Athens on the condition of his own restoration and the

---

[1] Grote, "History of Greece," VII, 27, etc.; Bury, "History of Greece," p. 491.

establishment of oligarchy was unfounded, what would his position have been when, returning to Athens, as he was eager to do on the city's invitation, this promise proved valueless or loaded with such conditions as made it impossible to accept it? Athens might have recalled him at once, without this preliminary conference, and without doubt he would have gone. Then, when it was seen that he could not perform his part of the bargain in producing Persian assistance, every party in the State, oligarchs, democrats and the keepers of the Eleusinian Mysteries, would have been leagued against him, and Athens would have been more determined on his death than she was when she sent the "Salaminia" to fetch him from Catana. He must have known, if Tissaphernes's promise was an invention of his own, that he was powerless to fulfil his contract and that there was no place in the wide world, not even the palace of Agis at Sparta, where his life was more certainly forfeit. Granting that his first ambition was always his own power and popularity, he could no more have dreamed of going back to Athens on the promise of Tissaphernes's support, had he not received it, than he could have returned to Sparta. It seems impossible to doubt that Tissaphernes had given this promise and that Alcibiades had believed it.

The account given by Thucydides amply confirms this view.[1] He tells us that the satrap had "full confidence in Alcibiades, and approved his views," and that on this knowledge Alcibiades opened the original negotiations with Samos. But subsequently (so runs the only reconstruction which seems to hold water), after Peisander had gone to Athens, securing the vote of the Assembly for Alcibiades's recall and setting the oligarchical plot afoot, Tissaphernes began to waver. The Peloponnesian alliance was still in existence, and he remembered a very sound argument which

---

[1] Thucydides, VIII, 46.

The Life of Alcibiades

Alcibiades had used as they talked together before he induced him to promise active support to Athens instead of the neutral support of general abstention, namely, that there was much to be said for letting both sides, Spartan and Athenian, wear each other down before intervening for the one or the other. That had appeared a very wise counsel, and though later Tissaphernes had agreed that the better course was to support Athens actively, that would be a serious step, and the previous proposition appeared a sounder policy.[1] But Alcibiades had already acted on his promise, and Athens had voted for his recall. Before Peisander and his colleagues arrived on this abortive embassy to Sardis he knew that Tissaphernes had drawn back and was not prepared to support an Athenian alliance actively. The conference therefore was bound to end in a fiasco, and the only way in which he could save his face at all was by prompting the satrap to ask impossible conditions, so that the rupture might seem to come from the Athenian side by the refusal of the envoys to entertain them. In this way only can we reconcile the process with the result.

But no one can have been more disappointed at the outcome than Alcibiades himself. His super-humanly clever scheme, founded on the pledge of Tissaphernes, had promised brilliantly, and its breakdown left him not where he was before, but at a serious disadvantage. The magic of his name coupled with the hopes he had held out had raised for him a party in Athens which, as Peisander had told him, had caused the Assembly to vote for his recall, for the abolition of the democratic government and for the deposition of General Phrynichus, his arch-enemy at Samos. Now the scheme had completely miscarried, and the embassy which should have taken him back in triumph to Athens had gone to Samos, furious at the deception which he seemed to have practised

---

[1] Thucydides, VIII, 56.

on them. Nothing could have been more humiliating; not since the days of his boyhood, when he had mistaken the character of Socrates's affection for him, had he experienced so staggering a rebuff. But not for a moment did he give up his determination to get back to Athens, though the contact he had established had been temporarily broken. He, the deadliest of her injurers, had said he was willing to come, she, the deadliest of his foes, had passed a vote of welcome. That particular avenue of approach was barred now, but some other opportunity would gleam before long from another quarter, as yet unconjectured, and like a hawk, far-seeing and poised invisible in a remote sky, he would drop on it and seize it. Till then, alert and watchful, he must play the complete Persian still, just as he had played the complete Spartan, and listen to the dreary bawdiness of the fat satrap.[1]

The focus of energy shifts to Athens. Peisander and his disgusted deputation put in at Samos on their way home and discussed the situation with the oligarchical clique there. They decided that, though they would have nothing more to do with Alcibiades, they would continue this conspiracy, both here and at Athens, to overthrow the democracy, for they were deeply compromised already, and their only safety lay in carrying it through to a successful conclusion; to abandon it was to put themselves in the power of the democrats. On arrival at Athens they found that the movement which they had begun had been zealously organized in their absence by the secret political clubs and had made great progress. To clear the way for Alcibiades's return, Androcles, who had originally indicted him for sacrilege, had been assassinated, and though the return of Alcibiades was no longer part of the programme, a firm and influential supporter of the democracy had been removed and his murder was followed by

---

[1] Plutarch, Alcibiades, XXIV.

The Life of Alcibiades

those of others who were known to be opposed to the establishment of oligarchy. All was skilfully and secretly contrived; none except the chief conspirators knew who was in the plot, and an intelligent minority, precisely like the Bolshevists of the Russian Revolution, acting cleverly and ruthlessly, had soon got the city in the grip of terror. The time was ripe, when Peisander returned, for the open declaration of the oligarchy, and there was set up an oligarchical Council of Four Hundred, controlled by five leaders, of whom Phrynichus was one. He had lately been deposed from his generalship owing to his opposition to Alcibiades, but now that Alcibiades had failed, he was reinstated as a leader. In the hands of these five was vested the whole direction of the revolution, and they upheld it by sentencing to death or banishment any who were likely to be dangerous. Instead of the Assembly in which every free citizen of Athens had a vote, a new Assembly was constituted consisting of five thousand members, but it had no real function, and only met when summoned to do so by the Four Hundred. The new Constitution was not yet framed, but here was the machinery for framing it. Athens, for a hundred years a democracy, had become for the moment a Bolshevist oligarchy.

Its reign was of the shortest; three months later it had ceased to exist. For at Samos the oligarchical conspiracy, initiated by Alcibiades's promise of help from Tissaphernes, and organized to some extent by Peisander, had not prospered. A club of three hundred had been formed whose design it was to overthrow the democracy, but it must be remembered that this had been a condition of Alcibiades's return, and there was now no reason why the condition on which it depended should be fulfilled. A reign of terror similar to that at Athens had no doubt been the intended means of establishing the oligarchy, but after the murder of the democrat Hyperbolus, who some years before had been ostracized from Athens and was living at Samos, the population, which included the bulk of the Athenian troops, discovered the plot which lay behind this senseless assassination, and at the instance of their generals rose against the three hundred. They killed thirty, they banished three and forgave the rest of these faint-hearted revolutionists.

News had to be sent to Athens of this attempt at establishing an oligarchy and of its failure, and the ship "Paralus," the whole crew of which were free-born Athenians, was despatched there. On their arrival they found that the oligarchy had prospered better there than at Samos and that the city was in the hands of the Four Hundred. Two or three of the crew, who were all democrats, were imprisoned, and also their captain Chæreas. He managed to escape and get back to Samos, where, being a gentleman of lurid imagination, he reported to the troops that Athens was in the hands of rank Bolshevists. They whipped free-born men, they outraged their wives and children, a word of criticism against the Government spelt death and the Four Hundred were intending to imprison the families of all the men serving at Samos, and, if the troops did not accept their rule, to kill them. All this was quite untrue, but it served its purpose, and not less the purpose of Alcibiades, whom we have left at the Court of Tissaphernes waiting for his opportunity.

The immediate effect at Samos was that the army saw red; it was with difficulty that they were restrained from stoning those of the oligarchical three hundred whom, out of mere contempt, they had forgiven. But their leaders, Generals Thrasybulus and Thrasyllus, were wise and moderate men and managed to keep them in hand. Among the troops and crews were many of oligarchical views, but the generals represented to all alike that if quarrels broke out among them here, ruin awaited both Samos and Athens, for the enemy's ships were lying near by the island, and they would take instant advantage of any disunion. The indignant democrats were in the large majority, and now the generals went from ship to ship binding the men individually by the most solemn oaths to maintain a democracy and to be of one mind, to prosecute vigorously the war with the Peloponnese, to be enemies to the

The Life of Alcibiades

Four Hundred and to hold no parley with them by heralds. For indeed quarrels in the fleet meant utter ruin, and since the majority were democrats, the Four Hundred at Athens were for the time as much their enemies as were the Spartan ships lying at Miletus. Amid all the mismanagement and imbecile leadership of the Athenian State from the day that Nicias had been sent to Syracuse and Athens had made an enemy of Alcibiades, this firm dealing with a most perilous situation shines conspicuous for its wisdom.

An Assembly was held, and a new board of democratic generals was elected. After all, so ran the debate, there was no cause for despair. The troops and ships now at Samos were far more powerful than the naval and military forces at Athens; it would be truer to say that Athens had revolted from Samos than that Samos had revolted from Athens. The Peiræus would have been taken long ago by the Peloponnesian fleet if Samos had not acted as guard to it, and it was Athens which had overthrown the Constitution which Samos upheld. Their position here was strong, and there was no need to fear the enemy's navy while their own held together. But one step must be taken at once: Alcibiades must be recalled and pardoned, for he alone could procure the help they needed. Athens, where was the seat of government, and Samos, where was the bulk of her army and navy, were on the brink of civil war, but they were both agreed that no one could save the Empire but he.

Nothing could more vividly demonstrate Alcibiades's prestige; history furnishes no parallel to this incident of his recall. Quite lately he had failed to produce the help from Tissaphernes which he had promised, and yet the people's belief in himself was unshaken. More than that, he had only lately sent to Samos to say that the establishment of an oligarchy was the irreducible condition of his return, and here was the Assembly of democrats who had just overthrown the oligarchy demanding his recall. They voted his full pardon for the crime for which he had been sentenced to death four years ago at Athens, thus assuming the authority of the renegade city, and General Thrasybulus was sent to the Court of Tissaphernes to beg the exile to come back.

Now a man who was only clever might easily have suspected that this was a trap, baited with the promise of his pardon, to get him into the hands of the democracy, from whom he would surely receive short shrift, since he had insisted on the establishment of an oligarchy. There was a formidable indictment against him; who but he had profaned the Mysteries, had been the cause of the ruin of the Sicilian expedition, had induced Sparta to build the fort at Decelea whereby Attica was now desolate, had caused the revolt of Chios and this crumbling of Empire, and who but he had declared himself an irreconcilable foe to the democracy? Surely a very clever man would have laughed at so patent and undisguised a trap, but it took a man of genius to see that there was no trap at all. Did he perhaps trust to that charm of his which even those who feared and hated him could not resist, or did he not rather see, with the intuition that never once failed him, that the Athenian troops and sailors at Samos, democrats though they were, yearned for him? He too, yearned for them, and he went.

CHAPTER IX

THE SAMIAN COMMAND

CHAPTER IX

THE SAMIAN COMMAND

AN Assembly was convened as soon as Alcibiades arrived at Samos; not since he begged in vain to be allowed to stand his trial on the charge of blasphemy before he set forth in joint command of the Sicilian expedition had he addressed his fellow-citizens. After a personal statement, in which he said that the fate which had driven him from Athens was cruel and unjust, he went straight to the present situation. Tissaphernes was the main topic; again he assured them of his influence with the satrap, and, if Thucydides's brief and rather contemptuous resume of his speech is to be trusted, indulged in some remarkable statements about Tissaphernes's devoted friendship for Athens. If he could only trust the Athenians, the satrap declared he would pawn his own bed rather than that they should lack food, and he would bring up the Phoenician ships to their support. But he could not trust them unless Alcibiades guaranteed their sincerity.

In spite of its bombast and rodomontade, this speech clearly shows one thing, namely, that Alcibiades still believed he could bring Tissaphernes to intervene actively on behalf of Athens, for it would have been incredibly foolish of him in this first hour of his restoration if, having just failed once, he should reiterate the same promise unless he thought that he could fulfil it. His speech roused the wildest enthusiasm both as regards the prospects of Athens in the war and as regards the cause of democracy against the newly-declared oligarchy at home. Under the spell of his words, his audience (largely troops and sailors) thought scorn of the fleet of Sparta, now that Tissaphernes was ready to befriend them, and wanted to sail at once for the Peiræus, to visit with a swift retribution the atrocities of the Four Hundred. Alcibiades was

The Life of Alcibiades

instantly appointed general, and the whole direction of the fleet was put into his hands. In an hour, from being an exiled felon, he had become supreme commander over the navy of Athens and once more the idol of the people. But where a lesser man, intoxicated with the dizzy wine of popularity, would have yielded to the troops who clamoured for him to take them to the Peiræus, he was firm in his refusal. He loved wine, he loved popularity, but neither ever went to his head. As general he told them that his first duty was the prosecution of the war, and to sail to Athens now, with the enemy's fleet close at hand in the harbour of Miletus, would be a ruinous mistake. His immediate business was to see Tissaphernes, and straight from the Assembly he took ship for this errand. His acting thus appears a further proof that he sincerely believed that he could obtain for Athens the promised support. Now though Alcibiades never procured a practical alliance between Tissaphernes and Athens, and to that extent failed in making good his promise, most historians have minimized or altogether overlooked the immense service he had rendered Athens with regard to the satrap. For we must not forget that in those conferences with him in Alcibiades Park he had advised him to cut down the pay of the Peloponnesian forces and to be irregular in disbursing it. This counsel had greatly benefited Athens, for Tissaphernes had followed it to the letter, and the result had been to cause friction and want of unity between Spartans and Persians. Moreover, though Alcibiades had not secured the active co-operation of the Phoenician fleet with Athens, he had persuaded the satrap not to bring it into action against her, and he had thus saved Athens from an overwhelming defeat. His fellow-commanders and the forces generally at Samos must have recognized this, for their confidence in him remained unabated, and we do not find a single murmur against him that he had failed for the second time to fulfil his promise; they saw that negatively, at any rate, his achievement had been of the highest value. The Spartan commanders were aware that he was deep in intrigues with

Tissaphernes, who was doing nothing to help them, but in every way hindering the prosecution of the war with Athens, and officers and rank and file alike were thoroughly discontented. The Spartan Admiral Astyochus was also suspected of disaffection, and complaints were made at Sparta that he was in the pay of Tissaphernes. In consequence the Spartan Government superseded him, and sent out Mindarus to take his place.

These dissensions and squabbles certainly made good news for Alcibiades to take back to Samos on his return from his visit to Tissaphernes. But though he himself had been restored and was general of the Athenian army, it was clear that the satrap did not intend to intervene actively, and that no more than neutrality and a steady determination not to assist Sparta according to the terms of the Treaty of Miletus were to be expected. Still the outlook (thanks to this neutrality) was by no means bad, for though the Peloponnesian fleet was as strong as Alcibiades's, it was riddled with discontent and disunion, whereas at Samos all dissensions had been healed by the blind devotion of the troops to him personally. A proof of this was immediately forth-coming, for there arrived envoys of the Four Hundred from Athens who were anxious to reconcile the democratic army with the Government at home. They had, indeed, good cause for misgivings, for the fleet and troops at Samos constituted far the greater part of the strength of Athens both by land and sea, and, as far as the Government at Athens was concerned, they were in a state of insurrection. They were on oath to take no orders from home, and had placed themselves under the command of a man who was still, in the eyes of the Government at Athens, an exile under sentence of death. The Four Hundred, in fact, felt far from comfortable collectively, owing to their repudiation by the fleet at Samos, and far from comfortable individually, since among them were several personal enemies of Alcibiades, such as Phrynichus, who had so strenuously opposed his return. Phrynichus had spoken his mind on this point; he had said that Alcibiades was a selfish, unscrupulous scoundrel

The Life of Alcibiades

who cared not two straws for oligarchy or democracy, but only played for his own hand. Possibly that was quite true, but there was no denying that he had played that hand with singular skill in that he was now the adored commander of Athens's forces, and Phrynichus wondered whether he had been quite wise in being so very explicit.

The reception of these apprehensive envoys by the Samian Assembly was far from encouraging. They represented the supreme Government at home, but when they tried to speak, loud cries of "Death to the traitors" went up. At last they got a hearing and explained that they were animated by the best intentions, and that the stories which Chasreas had brought to Samos about Bolshevist floggings and outrages and imprisonments and executions were pure fabrications. But the more they explained the less were they believed, and again the Assembly clamoured that the fleet should sail to the Peiræus and make an end of oligarchy. Had not Alcibiades been there, and had not the whole army pinned their devoted confidence on him, there is no doubt that this popular cry would have carried the day. Athens would have blazed with the flames of civil war, and her Empire, no longer guarded by the fleet at Samos, would have fallen, like a soft fruit from a shaken bough, into the hands of the Peloponnesian navy. But as Thucydides, with one of his rare flashes of enthusiasm, tells us, no man ever did so signal a service to the State as did Alcibiades at that crucial meeting. Once again, at the risk of being deposed from the supreme leadership to which he had just been appointed, he withstood the will of the angry Assembly. No one else at that moment could have controlled them,[1] but he succeeded in doing so by the sheer force of his personality; the devotion he had inspired he used, not for the furtherance of his own popularity, but

---

[1] Thucydides, VIII, 86.

in the service of true patriotism. As before, he insisted that if the fleet left Samos now, the whole island Empire would surrender to the Peloponnesian fleet. He then saved the envoys from the furious crowd that threatened violence and gave them his own orders. The Assembly of the Five Thousand which they had set up in Athens was unobjectionable and might stand, but the Four Hundred must go. That was the only way of preserving Athens from civil war, and when that was done they would look for some mode of reconciliation between Athens and her democratic army at Samos. He concluded with a thoroughly Alcibiadean touch. "If anything happens to our army here, or to you at Athens," he said, "there will be no one to be reconciled with."

Back went the envoys to Athens; they were lucky to have escaped with their lives, and these they owed to Alcibiades. Athens, no less than they, owed her existence to him.

The three focuses of energy which we have been following are now condensed to two: Alcibiades and Samos are merged into one; Athens is the other. These two, with their strongly-flowing stream of rapid movement, must still be followed separately, till they finally join in the recall of Alcibiades, by the will of the people, to Athens itself. At Samos we have the democratic fleet and army with him as dictator, at Athens the oligarchy still under the rule of the Four Hundred; of the two, it is necessary first to trace the current of events at Athens.

There were already, during the few weeks in which the Four Hundred had been in office, signs of disunion between the extreme oligarchs, headed by Peisander, Phrynichus and Antiphon, and those who, like Theramenes, were of more moderate views. This fissure in policy was widened by the return of their envoys from Samos, with the news of their reception there. The extremists took two steps: they at once sent an embassy to Sparta as representing an oligarchical Athens (which would be more likely to meet a favourable reception), giving it power to make peace on any terms that could possibly be accepted, and they pushed on with all speed the building of a fort on the mole of the Peiræus, which commanded the narrow opening into the harbour and could close it against the entrance of any fleet. This fort was defended against attack by land and also served the purpose of a storehouse for corn coming into the city by sea. Its ostensible object was to bar the Peiræus to the entry of the fleet from Samos if it should arrive with hostile intention against the oligarchy.

The embassy to Sparta returned without having been able to make peace on any terms, and now the breach between the two parties rapidly widened. Theramenes and the moderates affirmed that the extremists meant treachery and that this new and formidable fort at the Peiræus was built with the object of admitting Peloponnesian ships into the harbour and then closing the entrance against the Athenian fleet from Samos. This suspicion was confirmed by the news that Eubœa, which now was the main granary of Athens, had asked that a Peloponnesian fleet should be sent there. At the best this was an ominous request, for it certainly portended trouble in Eubœa, but a far more sinister interpretation could be put on it. A fleet of forty-two ships, now known to be on the point of sailing from a Spartan port, was not, so Theramenes caused it to be whispered, destined for Eubœa at all, but had been invited by the extremists to enter the Peiræus. Suddenly these whispers flared up into open and public talk and into more than talk; Phrynichus, one of the leaders of the extremists, was murdered in the full market-place and fresh news came of the suspicious fleet. It had not sailed to Eubœa, but, having made a raid on Ægina, was waiting off Epidaurus, ready to pounce on the Peiræus. What need was there, so the excited rumour ran, of further witness as to the intention of the extremists? Threatened at home by the insurrection against their supposed treachery, threatened from Samos by the democratic forces under Alcibiades, they had given up all thought of saving Athens if by her betrayal they could purchase immunity for themselves.

This Spartan fleet had now left Epidaurus and was come into sight from the Peiræus; news of its approach flew up to the city, and came back again winged with this sinister construction. There were soldiers employed on the building of the fort, and they struck work and made a hostile cordon round the house of one of the oligarchical generals. The extremists of the Four Hundred, who were in session, ordered the forcible suppression of this strike, amid the protests of the moderates, who were convinced that treachery was brewing, and the whole city buzzed with alarms. Was it true that the Spartan ships had entered the harbour? Was it true that they were now occupying the fort? And were the Four Hundred in collusion with them? Civil war was imminent, and Theramenes rushed down to the Peiræus. The strikers met him, and demanded to know for what purpose this fort had been built. The reaction against the extremists which he had engineered was already beyond his power to quell, and the crowds began demolishing the walls of the fort to the slogan, "Whoever is for the Assembly of the Five Thousand and against the Four Hundred, let him come and help. The Four Hundred must go, and the democratic Five Thousand be established." The mob, with the soldiers in support, were echoing precisely the orders that Alcibiades had given to the envoys at Samos.

The Four Hundred held a moribund meeting next morning and their sitting was interrupted by news of a kind highly disquieting for the extremists. The demonstration in the Peiræus against their rule had taken organized shape, and the troops there, having demolished the fort, had now marched into Athens and encamped there with their arms. Civil war had moved a step nearer, and the Four Hundred made their practical surrender by sending a deputation to the troops with the promise of appointing the democratic Assembly at once, and, as a guarantee of its reality, of publishing the names of its members. A meeting between the two parties was arranged, but before it could assemble came further news which postponed it. The fleet from Sparta, sighted

The Life of Alcibiades

yesterday, was advancing on the Peiræus from Salamis. No one doubted that its intention was to sail, on the invitation of the extremists, into the harbour and establish itself there, under the protection of the fort. The fort, happily, had been demolished, but the Peiræus was undefended. The only chance for the extremists now was to join in the defence of the city, and all able-bodied men in Athens were rushed down to the port to prevent the entrance of the fleet. Ships were hastily manned and a body of troops was drawn up on the quays. The Spartan fleet was now close outside the harbour, ready to row in.

Now, judging as we best can from these data, it seems certain that the extremists had been in treason-able correspondence with the enemy, and had told them, on that embassy to Sparta, that everything would be ready ; they had but to enter the Peiræus and take possession of the fort. But the Spartan Admiral, Agesandridas, could now see that the fort had been demolished, that the quays were humming with troops and that ships were being launched. All this looked as if some hitch had occurred, and so, instead of sailing into the Peiræus, he reverted to the original design and proceeded in the direction of Eubœa, according to invitation, there to raise the standard of revolt against Athens. Serious danger, therefore, still threatened the State, for the Spartan garrison at Decelea held Attica, and if Eubœa was taken, food supplies would be largely cut off. The ships that were being launched in the harbour were hastily equipped, and thirty-six vessels, ill-provisioned and with untrained crews, set off on the trail of the Spartan fleet. Two days afterwards an action took place; the Athenians were utterly routed and twenty-two of their thirty-six ships were lost.

No blacker hour nor one so near to total eclipse had ever come on the city. When Themistocles had evacuated it before the Persian advance, there was a fleet to carry off the fugitive population; when disaster had overtaken the Sicilian expedition, the island Empire still remained; when Decelea was occupied by the enemy, Athens was still impregnable by land and her ships could protect her harbour. But now the navy was at Samos, Eubœa, on which she chiefly depended for supplies, had revolted, and the Peiræus was unguarded. Had the victorious Peloponnesian fleet sailed for Athens, the city must have fallen, and it was only the slowness of Spartan wits which saved it. Admiral Agesandridas did not seize the greatest opportunity that had ever presented itself to the Spartan command, and, just as the Germans in 1918 did not realize that there was nothing to prevent their taking at least two of the French channel ports, so he failed to see that Athens, after the defeat of her last scratch squadron of ships, was defenceless. He contented himself with occupying Eubœa, and did not sail straight back to Peiræus. In this respite Athens by a final effort armed twenty ships to guard the Peiræus, and formally deposed the Four Hundred, entrusting the government to the Assembly of the Five Thousand. The Assembly passed a vote recalling Alcibiades, and a ship was sent to Samos bearing this message with the entreaty that he would prosecute the war with all vigour. He was already doing so, and in consequence was not at Samos when his recall to Athens arrived.

Meantime the flow of the second stream of events at Samos towards this point up to which (with the recall of Alcibiades) we have been following events at Athens was roaring down the channel he had made for it. He no longer believed that Tissaphernes intended actively to break the Treaty with Sparta, or to employ the Phoenician fleet on the side of Athens, and the best that could be done (and that was supremely good) was to ensure that it should not be used against her. This fleet, originally a hundred ships, had been increased to a hundred and forty-seven, and was now stationed at Aspendus; if it joined up with the Peloponnesian navy Athens must certainly be beaten by so overwhelming an addition to a fleet already equal to her own. Hardly had the envoys from Athens escaped, thanks to Alcibiades, from the hornets' nest at Samos and gone home with his autocratic message that he approved of the Assembly of the Five Thousand, but that the Bolshevist committee of Four Hundred must commit hari-kari as a political institution, when a most disconcerting piece of news arrived at Samos. The whole object of his policy at sea was to sow and foster dissension between the satrap and the Peloponnesian fleet, and now the tidings came that Tissaphernes was on his way to Aspendus, where this powerful armada lay, and was taking with him the Spartan commander Lichas, who had succeeded in amending the original treaty between Persia and Sparta, vastly to the advantage of Sparta. This looked as bad as it could be; the only, inference that a sensible man could draw was that the quarrel between Tissaphernes and the Spartan fleet over the pay of the sailors had been made up and that the satrap was about to order the Phoenician fleet to join up with the other and, at its will, either to sail to the Peiræus, or, as a preliminary measure, to engage the Athenian fleet at Samos. No other interpretation could reasonably be put on these sinister tidings: Athens in the one case must fall, and, in the other, the fleet at Samos had not a chance against the combined navies.

Of all Alcibiades's intuitions that which came to him now was perhaps the most brilliant, and this flash of perception which so illuminated for him the whole situation, and showed him how to deal with it, has never been justly appreciated. The only chance, so a sensible commander would have argued, was to keep the entire Athenian fleet together and hope by some miracle of skill or luck to defeat the hugely superior force of the enemy. But in this meaning of the word Alcibiades was not a sensible commander; he was a genius, and genius sees things which are invisible to sensible folk. Instead of sailing for Athens and trying to prevent the effective blockade of the city; instead of remaining at Samos and trying to save the island Empire; instead of keeping the whole fleet together, he took thirteen of the ships at Samos and went off with them to meet Tissaphernes on his way to join the Phœnician fleet. He was full of gaiety, assuring the troops that he was about to do Athens a great service. Perhaps he might bring the Phœnician fleet back with him as allies, and at the least it would not be as enemies. Such exactly was the lamentable situation at the time of his blithe departure, and study it as we may without consulting the sequel, it is impossible to guess what his plan was.

At first sight his detaching these ships from the navy seems quite futile except on the supposition that he was brewing a further treachery and that he meant to join the Spartan cause once more and persuade Tissaphernes that the time was come to wipe Athens out. Personal ambition, always a leading motive with him, would make such a conjecture reasonable, for he had done Sparta untold service already, and now if he brought the Phœnician fleet into the Peiræus, he might well expect some signal reward for this crowning ministry. The way to supreme power lay open to him, and should Sparta annex Athens he might at least be President of the oligarchical Government there; should Persia take possession of it, he would surely be satrap of Attica. For years, if we consider his past record, he had showered this rain of calamity on his city, and it would be logical to predict this final blow which his high favour with Tissaphernes made it well within his power to deliver.

But his purpose was precisely the opposite, entirely patriotic, and the means whereby he effected it were so simple that only the most far-seeing genius could have thought of them. The Spartan fleet, already at loggerheads with the satrap over the question of the pay of their crews, was at Miletus, checking and in check to the Athenian fleet at Samos. News came to it that Alcibiades with thirteen ships had joined up with Tissaphernes and the Phœnician fleet at Aspendus. The effect of that was exactly what Alcibiades had foreseen. The Peloponnesian commanders, swindled by Tissaphernes and deeply disgusted with him, were already more than half convinced that he meant to do nothing for them, and the new Admiral, Mindarus, eager to get to work, saw that, with Alcibiades at the satrap's ear again, it was no use wasting time in the hope either of getting the long-overdue pay for the crews or of securing the help of the satrap's Phœnician fleet. But there was a

The Life of Alcibiades

field for profitable activity further north, for Pharnabazus, whose satrapy included the Hellespont, on the shores of which were numerous cities subject to Athens, was inviting the co-operation of the Peloponnesian fleet against them. Good solid work might be done there in conjunction with Pharnabazus's forces on land, and Mindarus, despairing of assistance here, sailed from Miletus for the Hellespont with seventy-three ships. He was afraid of his movement being known at Samos, and went speedily and secretly. Alcibiades's stroke of genius had succeeded; the Peloponnesian Admiral had given up all idea of getting Tissaphernes to join him, because Alcibiades had joined Tissaphernes. Examine it as we will in the light of the results of it, this most simple of manœuvres was a flawless piece of strategy. The menace was over, and, after some adroit flatteries for the satrap,[1] Alcibiades went back with his thirteen ships to Samos. There he found the despatch from Athens recalling him from exile, and entreating him to prosecute the war vigorously. He was a citizen of Athens again, instead of being a pariah sentenced to death, and the Assembly had endorsed his Samian appointment as supreme commander over the Athenian forces. He had realized all he had planned, and had, without a flaw, accomplished his amazing programme of conjuring tricks.

Now we may, if we wish, take Plutarch's view of the reason why he did not instantly return to Athens, and attribute it to pride. Athens perhaps was just sorry for him, and out of pity allowed him to return. He was one whose nature it was to grant favours or to deal deadly blows, rather than accept favours or suffer under blows; it was incompatible with his pride to go back like a naughty child who has been forgiven, and he had no taste for so humble an epiphany.[2] But there was surely another consideration which

---

[1] Plutarch, "Alcibiades," XXIV, 5.
[2] Plutarch, "Alcibiades," XXVII, 1.

weighed with him: Athens was at war, and now that he was again a citizen of hers he must serve her. Besides, this message that recalled him had begged him to conduct the war. He was a brilliant commander, unrivalled in the field,[1] and his service was needed at the front more than in the argle-bargle of debate on the Pnyx. Off he went with five or possibly nine ships (the accounts differ) in addition to those he had taken to Aspendus, and having fortified the important island of Cos, raised funds for the fleet (and funds were sorely needed) in Halicarnassus. What arguments he used, we do not know; if persuasion was useless, no doubt his squadron of twenty ships or thereabouts was seen to be a strong argument against adopting a false economy. While there, he learned for certain where the Peloponnesian fleet had gone, and, abandoning this financial mission, he set sail northwards for the Hellespont. Samos, in the interval, had also received news of its movements, and seventy-six ships of the Athenian fleet had started in pursuit. Before Alcibiades, from further south, could join up with them, an action was fought at Cynossema, and though the Peloponnesians lost twenty-one ships against a loss of fifteen on the Athenian side, this battle was an indecisive affair. But a trireme was dispatched to Athens with tidings of a great victory, and after the storm of calamity which for three years now, since the hopeless defeat of the Sicilian expedition in B.C. 413, had beaten down on her, this caused just the stimulus she needed. At last the tide had turned. Besides, Alcibiades was hers again now, and Athens waited eagerly for more splendid news. It came.

Neither fleet had been driven off the field at Cynossema, and small skirmishes, gradually intensifying and becoming more general, succeeded the battle, until, once more, both fleets were fully engaged again in the narrows opposite Abydos on the Asiatic

---

[1] Thucydides, VI, 15.

The Life of Alcibiades

side of the straits. To-day they had been in fierce action, but the engagement was a dog-fight, with scurryings and snarlings, with a snap here and a momentary hold there, followed by a successful wriggle to disengage. Towards the decline of day there came ruffling up the straits a new squadron of eighteen ships, and as they approached it was seen that they were Athenian and that they were indeed none other than those which Alcibiades had taken to Aspendus on his visit to Tissaphernes, with a few more in addition. For the moment (and no wonder) the Athenian commanders were in doubt as to what his sudden arrival here meant. For what was his record after all? What deadly wounds he had inflicted on the city; was this another thrust at her, perhaps the deadliest of all? Was the treacherous devil leading the van of the Phoenician ships which would spell annihilation to Athens? And high for that moment rose the hopes of the Peloponnesians;[1] they knew his bitter feud with Athens, and his brilliant strokes against her, and it was like him to arrive at this climax when the whole fleet of Athens was engaged and the fortune of battle wavered. Surely there would be an end of Athens now. ... And then from the fore-mast of his flagship streamed out the ensign of Athens, and his ships drove from windward on the Peloponnesian line. They turned from their pursuit and ran before him, and he chased them landwards; some he rammed and sank and some he engaged at close quarters. Others grounded in shoal water and the crews swam ashore, and Pharnabazus with his troops came up to defend such ships as were beached. By the time that night fell the Athenians had recovered all their ships which had been taken and captured thirty of the

---

[1] Plutarch, "Alcibiades," XXVII, 3.

Peloponnesian vessels. Alcibiades had turned the indecisive action at Cynossema into a brilliant victory.[1]

This success was not only important in itself, but was of the highest moral significance. For the last three years, since, at Alcibiades's urgent representations, Gylippus had been sent by Sparta to Syracuse, disaster after disaster had overtaken the arms of Athens. Now, the moment that she revoked her savage sentence against him for a crime which had never yet been proved against him and of which he was probably innocent, the glittering tide of victory began to flow over these sands of tribulations. But she was not to welcome him home for more than three years yet; he was to work for her now as brilliantly and successfully as in that black night of their mutual hate he had worked against her, and of that devilish industry there was much to be undone. He had brought Athens very low, he had whelmed her in deep waters, and in his refusal to go back yet we may discern, not only the pride which Plutarch attributes to him, but, as Admiral of her fleet, the will to repair the vast injuries he had done her. Even as he had said to the Spartan Assembly in the first days of his exile, he loved her, and throughout these next three years, until, in one of her childish petulances, Athens once more turned her back on him, he served her with untiring devotion. Neither Themistocles nor Pericles did nobler work for her in the building up of her Empire than did Alcibiades in restoring her to the position which, chiefly owing to him, she had lost, and her final rejection of him was far more disastrous for her than her rejection of her other two great statesmen. Both of them were elderly and had done their best work, but Alcibiades was still in full vigour of life and ability, and he might have raised her to such supremacy as she had never

---

[1] The different accounts of the battle by Diodorus, Thucydides and Plutarch are hard to reconcile: the above only gives a probable reconstruction.

attained yet. At the least, if he had continued directing and executing her naval policy, as in these three years which now followed the reconciliation, the disaster that lost her the Empire could never possibly have happened.

CHAPTER X

THE CAMPAIGN IN THE HELLESPONT

CHAPTER X

THE CAMPAIGN IN THE HELLESPONT

TISSAPHERNES meantime was not altogether pleased at this alliance between Pharnabazus and the Peloponnesians. He had meant to keep them dangling indefinitely round Chios and Miletus, wearing out themselves and the Athenians, according to that ingenious idea suggested to him by Alcibiades. An admirable scheme; when they were exhausted, Tissaphernes proposed to step in and crush them both, for that would earn him high favour with King Darius.

But now, disgusted with his parsimonies and procrastinations, the Spartan Admiral had given up all idea of getting help from him, and was co-operating with the energetic Pharnabazus. In spite of the set-back (a serious one) which had followed on the battle of Cynossema, Pharnabazus had met with considerable success in operations against the Athenian cities of the Hellespont, and Tissaphernes thought that he might as well have a hand in it, and, distasteful as it was to one of so notable an indolence, be doing something. Jealousy of Pharnabazus was an incentive; also the King had ordered him to co-operate with Sparta, and his co-operation at present had been limited to withholding the pay of Sparta's crews. Complaints of his conduct had been made at Susa, and the King, not grasping the value of his attrition policy, might think he was disobeying orders in not using the Phœnician fleet against Athens. So he left Magnesia and pleasant Alcibiades Park to go up to the Hellespont and confer with his more energetic colleague.

Alcibiades, in command of the Athenian navy at Sestos, heard of his coming, and determined to make one more effort to get hold

The Life of Alcibiades

of that Phœnician fleet. This naval victory had altered the aspect of affairs, and since it was clearly to the advantage of Persia to throw her weight on to the winning side, he might be able to persuade Tissaphernes that an alliance with Athens was in his best interests. So with his love of pomp and splendour, Alcibiades set out to meet the satrap, attended by an imperial retinue and loaded with gifts. But for the first time in all his wide webs of intrigue, his judgment was at fault, for Tissaphernes was at last really uneasy about his own dilatoriness in aiding Sparta and about the complaints made of him,[1] and in this sumptuous visit of Alcibiades he saw a convenient opportunity of putting himself right and showing his tardy zeal for the Peloponnesian cause. So instead of welcoming him, he instantly arrested him and sent him to Sardis as a prisoner. That would show the King how false were these reports that he was friendly with the Athenian General. For the fourth time in his life of forty years Alcibiades was "as good as dead," and as alive as ever.

It was now the winter of B.C. 410; the Spartan fleet at Abydos, protected by the land forces of Pharnabazus, had received reinforcements and the Athenian position at Sestos was none too secure. The whole theatre of the war had shifted toward the north, so, instead of going back to Samos, the bulk of their fleet sailed west round the Chersonese, where it would be less liable to attack, and wintered there, while small squadrons cruised about collecting money from allied cities. But long before the end of the winter Alcibiades was very much alive again; he had escaped from Sardis within a month of his incarceration there, had got hold of a horse and ridden to Clazomenæ, an Athenian city on the coast. But he felt vexed with his dear friend the satrap for doing this treacherous thing, and, hitting upon a truly Alcibiadean reprisal, let it be widely

---

[1] Plutarch, "Alcibiades," XXVII, 4, 5.

known that it was Tissaphernes who had arranged his escape. That would be very unpleasant for his dear friend, for it was indeed most awkward evidence as showing his pro-Athenian sympathies.[1] "It was a mistake to treat me like that," thought Alcibiades very cheerfully.

From Clazomenæ he crossed to Lesbos, which was now again an Athenian island, and, with a squadron of five triremes, rejoined the Athenian fleet and resumed command. On the approach of spring he recalled the roving units, and went through the fleet raising everybody's spirits by his own high confidence. He told his soldiers that they had got to smash the Peloponnesians, and that without delay, for money was short, whereas the enemy was in the pay of the King.[2] They had all to be soldiers as well as sailors, sailors as well as soldiers, and conduct siege operations, too, if that were necessary. "And now come and look for the Peloponnesian fleet," said he.

There was news of the enemy at once. Mindarus with all his fleet had left Abydos and was blockading the town of Cyzicus on the Asiatic side of the Propontis: Pharnabazus was supporting him on land. The united Athenian fleet navigated the Hellespont at night, so that no enemy ship might see their approach,[3] and on their way they captured all trading vessels that they overtook so that none should carry the news of their stealthy advent.

They made the passage of the straits undetected, and crept along by the shore, favoured by thick fog and rain, till they were near Cyzicus. Here, still out of sight of the town, Alcibiades landed his heavy-armed troops to support the fleet on shore and hold Pharnabazus's army in check. When this had been done, the ships went out to sea again, but now in a new formation, for Alcibiades

---

[1] Plutarch, "Alcibiades," XXVIII, 1.
[2] Xenophon, "Hellenica," I, i. 14.
[3] Diodorus Siculus, XIII, 5.

The Life of Alcibiades

split the fleet up into three divisions. He himself was in command of the first of these, numbering forty ships, while the other two, numbering fifty between them, he ordered to keep well in the rear. Presently the fog lifted, and the Peloponnesians, lying off the harbour of Cyzicus, which had now fallen, saw the first division approaching. They took it, as Alcibiades had intended, to be the entire fleet, and put out to engage it. Alcibiades, feigning retreat, drew them out from the coast in pursuit of him, and the two other divisions sailed up and disclosed themselves.

The complete and annihilating defeat of the Peloponnesians followed. Alcibiades went about, and while engaging the line of the enemy with half his division, broke through it with the other half and threw it into utter confusion. Some of the ships put to shore, and their crews landed, but now the body of heavy-armed troops which had marched along the coast came into action and routed the infantry which Pharnabazus sent to their aid. The satrap fled, the Spartan Admiral Mindarus was killed, and his entire fleet, with the exception of some ships from Syracuse which were scuttled by their own crews, was captured. In the whole of the Hellespont and Propontis not a single ship remained out of this great naval concentration of the enemy, and all the coast towns, with Cyzicus, which at once surrendered, were at the mercy of Athens. A despatch from Mindarus's staff-captain to the Government at Sparta presented the disaster with laconic simplicity. "Our ships are lost; Mindarus is killed; our men are starving; we know not what to do."[1] This despatch was captured and read out in the Assembly at Athens.

The news, however, soon reached Sparta, and Diodorus[2] tells us that an embassy was sent to Athens to offer terms of peace; he

---

[1] Plutarch, "Alcibiades," XXVII, 6.
[2] Diodorus Siculus, III, 6.

gives the oration made by Endius, the ephor, who was concerned with Alcibiades in the revolt of Chios. But as neither Xenophon nor Plutarch mentions this incident at all, it must be considered doubtful whether it actually took place. In any case, Sparta's treaty with Persia forbade her to make peace without the consent of the King, and clearly therefore this embassy cannot have gone further than to discuss unofficially possible terms. These were based upon the status quo ante helium, which Athens, intoxicated by her huge victory, was not at all in the mood to accept. Historians have argued ever since as to whether she would have been wise to do so, and grow passionately oratorical over the question. Certainly it would have been a great thing to have got rid of the Spartan occupation at Decelea, but, on the other hand, Sparta, even if she had violated the treaty of Miletus and gone out of the war, could only have signed for herself; both Persia and the other Peloponnesian allies would have been at liberty to repudiate the peace.

But what all historians alike seem to have over-looked is that at this moment of huge triumph the Assembly at Athens was absolutely powerless to make any effective decision at all. The will of Athens did not reside in the city, but in the victorious fleet and army, and if the Government had sent a deputation to Cyzicus to inform Alcibiades that peace had been made, he would without doubt have treated it exactly as he treated the embassy that came to Samos on behalf of the Four Hundred. It would have been sent back to Athens again (without violence) and he would have continued righting to restore her Empire to her, precisely as he did. Indeed it may be doubted whether even he, for all his magical hold over his men, could have induced them to go tamely home just now, and it is quite certain that he would not have tried. As it was, the rejection of the Spartan proposals (if they were ever made) by the democratic party in the Assembly under the leadership of Cleophon put the democrats into complete power again. The Constitution of Theramenes, with its mixture of oligarchical and

The Life of Alcibiades

democratic principles, was upset and universal franchise restored. The last trace of oligarchy at Athens vanished, and the home Government came into line with the principles of its naval and military forces as established at Samos.

For three years, dating from this great victory at Cyzicus, Alcibiades conducted a campaign of unvarying success in the north of the Ægean, the Hellespont, the Propontis and the Bosphorus, and no one but he who had so sorely injured his country could, as all Athens was agreed, have made so magnificent an atonement. It is important in estimating his character, no less than his abilities, to realize what his position was in these three years, during which, in spite of the Aristotelian gibe,[1] Athenian history was what Alcibiades did. He was what we should call First Lord of the Admiralty, as well as Lord High Admiral of the Fleet: he was Secretary of State for War and Commander-in-Chief of the Army. The whole policy of the war, in fact, was in his hands, as well as the strategy and tactics by which it was carried out. As far as we can tell, no orders whatever reached him from home, and his colleagues were merely his staff officers, ready, no doubt, with advice if he asked for it, but without the power (even had they the will) to reverse any of his decisions. The entire strategy and execution of the campaign during these wonderful three years, which raised Athens from the lowest ebb of her fortunes (for which also Alcibiades had been responsible) to the full tide again, were his. In the actual operations of the war his success was unclouded by a single failure, however trivial, but what most we must admire was the far-sightedness of the statesmanship which directed them. Never yet had his authority been supreme, for previous to his exile in Sparta, Nicias had been an antagonistic colleague; now the complete control of Athenian fortunes was

---

[1] Aristotle, "Poetics," IX, 1451.

vested in him, and he wielded it with a consummate wisdom. An immense scope had come within the horizon of his ambitions, and for the moment they were occupied: an autocracy without rival was his, and his a huge work of reconstruction and consolidation to accomplish. He exercised this autocracy with prudence and daring and moderation; daring had always been his habit, but it is surprising to find the soberer qualities there, especially when, as now, he was at last in supreme authority. It may fairly be said that henceforth his own reputation was his only rival; he had to live up to the prestige that attends a man who is believed to be able to accomplish anything. He was unlike the lion to which both he and his countrymen had compared him in this, that he never dozed or licked his chops after such full meal of victory as he had gulped down at Cyzicus. He only paused to set up the formal trophy of triumph and was off again on an imperial chase. No partisan of his would deny that he sought his own glory, but no detractor could point to any patriot of whatever age who served his country with such unique and brilliant success. The objects which underlay the movements of his army and navy—his they indeed were—were to regain all the revolted cities in the northern part of the Athenian Empire, chiefly round Thrace and the Propontis, and to secure the command of the two straits, the Bosphorus and the Hellespont. This latter was of the highest importance, for with Decelea still in the hands of the Spartans, no harvests could be garnered from Attica, and with Eubœa still in revolt, Athens depended for her supplies on the corn-ships from the Black Sea. But the annihilation of the Peloponnesian fleet at Cyzicus made it unnecessary to keep his navy together, since there was no fear of any attack, and Alcibiades constantly split it up into three divisions under himself, Theramenes and Thrasybulus. Thus several widely-sundered operations were often going on simultaneously, and the bewildering and apparently contradictory accounts of these, as given by Xenophon, Diodorus and Plutarch, are considerably smoothed out if we remember this.

The Life of Alcibiades

With a view to securing the free passage of the Bosphorus, Alcibiades at once sent a portion of the fleet to Chalcedon, a town a few miles inland at the southern entrance of the straits on the Asiatic side, which had revolted from Athens in the previous year, B.C. 411. There was a Spartan governor there and a Spartan garrison, and, on the approach of the Athenian ships which landed soldiers in front of the town, friendly Pharnabazus brought troops up to defend it. Simultaneously Alcibiades with his division of the fleet blockaded Perinthus on the European side of the Propontis, which at once surrendered. He then attacked Selymbria, another revolted town, but abandoned the blockade for the present on payment of a sum of money.[1] We have no details of this odd transaction; probably Selymbria paid the tribute due to Athens for the current year, and hoped that by the next the fleet would have vanished from these waters. Alcibiades, for his part, had more important work on hand, for it was now early autumn and the season for the grain-ships to come through the Bosphorus. Selymbria, isolated and insignificant, could wait, and he went to see how the siege of Chalcedon, which was close to the southern end of the straits, was progressing.

It was evident that it would not be taken without difficulty, and the immediate business was to secure the passage of the corn-ships to Athens. So he fortified a small seaport town, Chrysopolis, to guard the southern end of the straits, and stationed Theramenes there with thirty ships, who kept the straits open and exacted a toll equivalent to one-tenth of their cargo from the corn-ships; this came in useful for the pay of his men. Another detachment of ships guarded the Hellespont, and supplies, of which there would be sore need at Athens, could come safely through to Peiræus. Thus the occupation of Decelea by the Spartans (suggested to

---

[1] Xenophon, "Hellenica," I, i, 21.

them by Alcibiades) failed in one of its main purposes, namely, in depriving Athens of its food supplies, and King Agis, from the heights where his fortress stood, might impotently observe the unimpeded procession of corn-ships into the port. He therefore sent a squadron of ships from Megara under a Spartan commander to attempt to loosen the hold of the Athenian fleet on the straits, which reached the Bosphorus with the loss of three ships out of fifteen, and established themselves at Byzantium. This idea of Agis's was a sound one, though the Megarian ships were not numerous enough to be effective. It is, however, only fair to mention the solitary instance of King Agis having hit upon any notion which could possibly be useful.

Alcibiades passed the winter on and about the Hellespont, collecting tribute from cities which had revolted from Athens during the last disastrous years, but which, after the annihilation of the Peloponnesian fleet, were only too glad to be allowed to rejoin the Empire again without reprisals. Another business also occupied him during this winter and the next, and though there is no mention by any historian of its execution, we shall find later on that he had accomplished it. As yet on the European side of the Propontis there was no Athenian post south of the colony at Perinthus; this was a long stretch of country, and it was highly desirable to build fortresses on the coast to bring the colonies on the Bosphorus into closer touch with those on the Hellespont. Alcibiades built one at Bisanthe, some thirty miles from Perinthus, to extend the Bosphorus-sphere southwards, and another at Pactye, at the north end of the Hellespont, to extend the Hellespontine sphere northwards. There were also intermediate fortresses, either built or contemplated, of which we know nothing beyond their names, Borni and Neontichus,[1] but we can certainly

---

[1] Cornelius Nepos, "Alcibiades," VII.

The Life of Alcibiades

infer the construction of Bisanthe and Pactye (though the building of them is not mentioned) from the fact that when Alcibiades left Athens finally in B.C. 407 they were in existence as "his" castles, and that he occupied both successively.[1] That he established them during these winters is fairly certain, since there is no other time when he could have done so, and we may look on their construction as items in a most statesman-like scheme for the consolidation of the power of Athens in the northern part of her Empire.

In the spring of B.C. 409 he went off to capture Selymbria, which by the payment of a tribute had purchased a temporary immunity the year before. Like Sir Francis Drake, Alcibiades led in person the most hazardous of his operations, and in this no doubt lay part of the secret of the devotion which both of these supreme commanders inspired in their men. His exploit here was truly Drakian: they were blood-cousins in their genius for madcap adventure. He had got into communication with a pro-Athenian party in the revolted town, and it had been arranged that they should display a lighted torch at midnight above the wall, to show that they were ready to open the gate to him and his troops. But the plot leaked out, and the party opposed to surrender displayed the lighted torch, with high ingenuity, an hour before the time agreed on. Their hope was that Alcibiades's troops would not be ready yet, and that a small contingent only would arrive, whom they would keep as hostages. This was an admirable device, and it truly deserved to succeed. Indeed, up to a point it succeeded perfectly, for the moment the lighted torch was shown Alcibiades collected thirty men who happened to be ready and rushed off in a prodigious hurry, for fear that the friendly conspirators (who by some mistake, so he supposed, had shown their signal an hour too

---

[1] Xenophon, "Hellenica," I, v, 17; Plutarch, "Alcibiades," XXXVI, 2, 5.

soon) should think he was not coming and so shut the gate again. He told the rest of his men to follow as quickly as they could, and stole in with these thirty, to find himself confronted by a regiment under arms and ready to attack. It was indeed an awkward position, for to advance seemed certain death and to retreat would never do. ... Instead he thought of just such a plan as Drake might have conceived. He whispered to his trumpeter to blow the call for silence, and then, with colossal bluff, proclaimed that Selymbria must not take up arms against Athens. Now no one, it was obvious, could have made such a proclamation unless he had a body of troops ready to enforce it, and the Selymbrians supposed that they were waiting in the darkness just behind this little vanguard. His proclamation, too, had a pacific sound, and so there was a parley (Alcibiades extremely friendly, with great charm of manner and a pleasant smile), and while they parleyed up came the rest of his troops. There were some Thracians among them, who for private reasons had a grudge against Selymbria, but he would not allow these to enter the gate, for fear that they should plunder the city. The savage plan of Athens towards her revolted allies was to execute ringleaders freely, or, as in the case of Melos, to order wholesale massacre, and Alcibiades before now had taken the lead in such folly of vengeance. But that was no way to build up the lost Empire, and instead of a wild scene of butchery there followed just a business talk next morning. Selymbria had to pay, and she had to entertain an Athenian garrison, but she much preferred that to undergoing the fate of Melos. It was better for her to be a subject State of Athens than to cease to exist, and it was better, thought Alcibiades, for Athens to retain a tributary city than to gloat over a shambles.

The naval successes in the Hellespont and the knowledge that the most brilliant brain in Greece was now busy in her interests had made "glorious summer" for Athens, and early in B.C. 409, sanguine and resilient as ever, she sent out a fresh and noble armament under Thrasyllus to operate from Samos in Ionia and

The Life of Alcibiades

the satrapy of Tissaphernes. Tissaphernes had hoped that he would have been allowed a little quiet now that that most fatiguing young man Alcibiades had gone north and was worrying his colleague Pharnabazus: an amusing and licentious dog and convivial, but he always had some feverishly energetic scheme in his head, and if one clapped him into prison he escaped and spread false and damaging scandals. ... And here was another of these Athenians, with fifty ships and a thousand troops and five thousand sailors,[1] landing from Samos in the most impertinent manner and capturing Colophon, and he was now marching on Ephesus itself. Hitherto Tissaphernes had not taken the affairs of Athens and Sparta very seriously; they mattered very little to Persia, but this attack on an important city like Ephesus could not be tolerated, and for once Tissaphernes roused himself. He inflicted a smart defeat on Thrasyllus which sent him limping back to his ships, and he was pleased to hear that he had sailed quite away to join Alcibiades. Whether this raid on Ephesus was part of Thrasyllus's orders from Athens or whether he had been told to join Alcibiades at once, it was the most ill-advised adventure, and when he reported himself at Sestos he had a strange reception. For Alcibiades's troops were intoxicated with victory; they thought that they and their General were not as other men, and now these invincibles refused to make comradeship with defeated soldiers, and would neither drill nor share camp with Thrasyllus's men. Privately that pleased Alcibiades immensely, for from boyhood he had believed just that about himself, but as Commander-in-Chief he could not permit "swank," however justly founded, to interfere with military discipline. So he sent out Thrasyllus's troops to raid the country round Abydos, and when Pharnabazus brought up a strong force against them, he called out his invincibles, and they and the others together made

---

[1] Xenophon, "Hellenica," I, i, 34.

him run and joyously hunted him till dusk. This pleasant episode brought all the men back to camp together in the high spirits and comradeship of a joint success.[1]

Through this summer of B.C. 409 the siege of Chalcedon was going on, but ineffectively, and it was clear also that the command of the Bosphorus must be strengthened, for the Spartan Admiral Clearchus had slipped by the Athenian fort at Chrysopolis with his ships from Megara, and had established his troops in Byzantium and his ships in the harbour. This occupation, no less than the fact that there was again a squadron of the enemy in these waters, caused Alcibiades to reunite the scattered division of his fleet, now reinforced by the fifty ships Thrasyllus had brought from Athens, and set seriously to work to reduce Chalcedon and Byzantium. Not till that was done, nor till the straits were firmly held by loyal Athenian colony-cities, would his work here be finished.

Chalcedon was determined to save what she could, and on the appearance of this formidable fleet her citizens collected all that was of value in the place and smuggled it out of the town, entrusting it to the keeping of the friendly tribe of the Bithynians, whose territory lay adjacent. It would be pleasant to get hold of that booty, for money, as usual, was needed for the fleet, and so Alcibiades detailed a body of troops to enter the territory of the Bithynians and make them give it up. A herald, fulminating threats of what might otherwise happen to them, was a sufficient persuasion, and the citizens of Chalcedon observed with chagrin all their plate and valuables being carried on to Alcibiades's flagship. But this, though pleasant, did not bring the capture of the town any nearer, and he built a wooden stockade from the Bosphorus to the Propontis, cutting off the corner of land on which Chalcedon

---

[1] Plutarch, "Alcibiades," XXIX. Plutarch gets muddled over his chronology, making this adventure follow directly on the battle of Cyzicus. But Thrasyllus was not sent out from Athens for a year after that.

The Life of Alcibiades

stood. This was guarded by Athenian troops, so that neither supplies nor reinforcements could reach the town, just as Nicias had built a wall behind Syracuse, which, had it only been more expeditiously completed, would have caused the city to fall before the arrival of Gylippus. But there was no dawdling of that sort here, and when Pharnabazus brought up his army to relieve Chalcedon he could not pass the Athenian lines. The Spartan commander in the town made a simultaneous sally up the riverbed, where there was a gap in the stockade, but Alcibiades disposed his troops on a double front, one facing this outlet from the town, the other facing Pharnabazus. The satrap was driven off helter-skelter into Bithynia, and the party from the town had to retire inside it again. It was now only a question of time before it must surrender, and Alcibiades left the siege in the hands of his colleagues, while he went off for the capture of Selymbria, as already recounted, raised a large sum of money and made alliance with certain Thracian tribes, in connection, doubtless, with these fortresses of his along the coast.

After the capture of Selymbria he sailed back to Chalcedon, taking with him Thracian infantry and mounted troops. On arrival he found that Theramenes and Thrasybulus, whom he had left in charge of the operation, had come to terms with Pharnabazus regarding the surrender of the town. No punishment was to be inflicted on it for its revolt, and it was to become a subject city of Athens again, paying tribute as before, while Pharnabazus agreed to advance twenty talents on its behalf,[1] on condition that Alcibiades pledged himself not to overrun the territory of the satrap, and also promised to give safe escort up to Susa to an Athenian deputation. Pharnabazus, however, refused to recognize

---

[1] Xenophon, "Hellenica," I, iii., 8.

the authority of Theramenes and Thrasybulus, and the ratification of the treaty had been delayed until the return of Alcibiades.

This signing of the Covenant of Chalcedon, supplemented, as it was, with a private document of friendship between the satrap and Alcibiades, is a most illuminating incident. There is, first, the significant detail that Pharnabazus refused to regard as satisfactory any treaty not signed by Alcibiades, which gives us clear proof that in the eyes of Persia he was Athens; secondly, it defines the relative strength of Athens and Persia on the coast of the Propontis, for the satrap was willing to pay twenty talents as the price of the immunity of his district from attack. But, most of all, it illustrates for any who are not determined to see neither merit nor ability in Alcibiades[1] the statesmanlike wisdom of the man. The Propontis was far away from Athens, and the unhindered passage of corn-ships from the Black Sea of the highest importance to her, and by this friendly agreement with the satrap he ensured his good-will towards the Athenian colonies on the straits. Though he had never succeeded in getting the help of Tissaphernes against the Spartan fleet, that was needed no more, since the Spartan fleet had been wiped out at Cyzicus, and this friendship with the far more able and energetic Pharnabazus was a master-stroke. He might have earned for himself fresh enthusiasm in the camp by raids into the interior, but the satrap's good-will was far more worth having in the interests of Athens. Again and again we notice that when Alcibiades was in power that craze for popularity which was among his most besetting weaknesses troubled him no more; he invariably chose the wise course in preference, and we may reasonably wonder whether he lusted after popularity more as a means to get power than as an end in itself. He also established friendly relations with the Bithynians, and thus ensured security for

---

[1] Grote, "History of Greece," VIII, 180.

The Life of Alcibiades

Chalcedon. The Athenian deputation for Susa started at once, and met Pharnabazus at Cyzicus. Its precise object is nowhere stated; we may pre-sume that it was to arrive at some treaty with Persia.

As soon as the settlements at Chalcedon were finished Alcibiades took in hand the siege of Byzantium, which commanded the southern end of the Bosphorus on the European side. It had revolted in B.C. 411, and was now held by a garrison of Spartans, Megarians and Bœotians under the command of Clearchus, who had got past the Athenian guardships the year before with twelve ships from Megara, and it was essential for the security of the straits that Athens should regain it. As at Chalcedon, Alcibiades built a stockade round it, to starve it into submission, and when provisions began to run low, the Spartan commander commandeered the whole stock of food for the troops and let the unfortunate Byzantians starve.[1] His orders, of course, were to hold the town at any cost, but this Spartan callousness as to the fate of the population whom they had come to succour led to a revolt which might have been foreseen had Spartan wits ever been able, unaided, to foresee anything. The Byzantians had heard of the wise leniency with which Chalcedon had been treated, and got into communication with Alcibiades, who promised neither to plunder nor to punish if they would admit his troops. But the garrison was formidable, and Alcibiades invented a most pleasing Drakian device for getting a strong force into the city without heavy fighting. It had been arranged that one of the gates away from the harbour should be opened to him, and the morning before the appointed night when this was to be done he sailed off with the entire Athenian fleet, apparently raising the blockade, and letting it be known that a crisis had arisen in Ionia. Off they sailed out of sight of the town, and the moment it was dark they all hurried back

---

[1] Plutarch, "Alcibiades," XXXI, 2.

again. Alcibiades, who, as usual, led his men himself, was landed some little way down the coast, and with his troops made his way to the gate which was to be opened. Meantime the fleet went on into the harbour and entered it with all possible clamour. The Spartan commander naturally thought that this ruse of departure meant that an attack in force was coming from the harbour and hurried down all his troops to resist it. When they had all gone Alcibiades quietly entered the town. There was considerable fighting both at the harbour and in the city, but the feint was completely successful, and Byzantium was his. No punitive measures of any kind were taken against the inhabitants for their revolt: Byzantium simply resumed her place as a city of the Athenian Empire, and with Chalcedon and Chrysopolis controlled the straits. ... It is interesting to notice that Sir Francis Drake took Carthagena on the Spanish Main by a ruse identical in every particular, even down to the signal given to the troops that they were to advance. In his case the signal was given by a gun fired from the fleet; in the capture of Byzantium the shouting from the ships as they entered the harbour took its place.

By the autumn of B.C. 408, Alcibiades's mission in the north was over; there was nothing left to accomplish, for he had conquered and consolidated all the revolted cities there. Three years ago there had come to him from Athens the annulment of her sentence passed on him in his absence, and the invitation of the Assembly of the citizens that he should return. But coupled with that had been the entreaty that he should serve her, and, as we have seen, he had then determined not to go back empty-handed, like some chidden prodigal son, to a forbearing feather, but to come again with joy, bringing his sheaves with him. He had now reaped for her a golden harvest; he had annihilated the Peloponnesian fleet, he had restored to Athens her lost empire in the Propontis; Perinthus, Selym-bria, Cyzicus, Chalcedon and Byzantium, all of which towns had revolted in the days of his exile, had surrendered to him and were now tributary cities again. He had

The Life of Alcibiades

secured to Athens the straits through which the corn-ships must pass from the Black Sea, and had set Athenian forts there, he had made a treaty of friendship with the satrap Pharnabazus, an Athenian deputation was on the way to Susa and he had made fortresses to link up the outposts of her Empire in the north. Certainly no Athenian citizen had ever been so savage and brilliant an enemy of his country, but none had ever given her such succour and salvation. When, three years ago, Athens had revoked the sentence which had been no less savage than his reply to it, the last drops of her life-blood were already draining from her. Since then, first at Samos, in forbidding the exasperated democratic forces to avenge themselves on the oligarchy at home, and afterwards in these three years of brilliant military achievements, he had staunched the deadly wounds he had inflicted, and restored, as no one else could have done, the pulses of her vitality. It was time now to take his sheaves and lay them at the foot of the Goddess of the Acropolis.

There were a few preliminaries: he sent Thrasybulus to the Thracian coast, where Thasos was still in revolt, Thrasyllus took a squadron of the fleet with troops to Athens and he himself brought back the rest of the fleet, which for three years had been in the Propontis, to Samos. From it he detached twenty ships, and with them put across to the coast of Caria, where he collected tribute of a hundred talents (over £100,000 sterling in modern values) from allied cities, and then, for no apparent reason, put back into Samos again; we cannot help wondering if he was nervous about his return to Athens and of his reception there. Of course he would find enemies at home; no man who has achieved like him has ever lacked them. He loitered, and it was unlike him to loiter; he sailed to the island of Paros and from there sent to Athens the news of his coming, but once more he turned off and went down to Gythium on the Laconian coast, where Sparta was building a fresh fleet of thirty ships in replacement of that which he had so gaily annihilated. Then he sailed northwards again towards Athens and picked up news from home. The Assembly had officially confirmed him in his post as General, which he had held for the last three years on the mandate of Samos, and had elected him for the ensuing year. So now he could enter Athens, not as the forgiven prodigal, but as the Commander of her forces victoriously returning. He gave the order to sail for the Peiræus.

CHAPTER XI

THE RETURN TO ATHENS

CHAPTER XI

THE RETURN TO ATHENS

HE must enter (he would not otherwise have been Alcibiades) "terrible as an army with banners," and splendid as on the day when he broke all records at Olympia. But now he came with a nobler crown, for his ships were flashing with the captured shields of enemies and the trophies of victorious actions, and he had on board two hundred of the figureheads he had lopped from the triremes he had vanquished.[1] All these must be displayed, and he ranged them along the bulwarks of his ship and round his masts, and each was a symbol and sign of a captured vessel of the enemy. He took down his worn and sea-stained sail, and in place of it he put up one that was dyed purple for this pomp of festival. Chrysogenus, lately a victor in the Pythian games, had come out to meet him, and stood, decked in a Persian robe, on the prow of his flagship, blowing his flute to make music for the rowers, and with him was the great tragic actor Callipides, who by gesture and shout controlled their rhythm.[2] Alone and apart from the rest Alcibiades stood on deck, and his ship, leading the fleet, swept round the end of the mole where of late the treacherous fort had been, and the purple sail was furled, and the oars held water, and she slid up to the quayside.

From end to end the quay was a blur of massed faces and eager eyes, and all were turned to him, like a bed of flowers to the sun.

---

[1] Justin, V, 4.
[2] Athenæus, XII, 49. Athenæus is probably quoting from the history of Duris, which is not extant. See also Plutarch, "Alcibiades," XXXII, 2. Plutarch notes that Xenophon makes no mention of this magnificence, but the internal evidence is in its favour.

The Life of Alcibiades

His ship had been seen while yet far off, and the whole of Athens had trooped down to the harbour on the news of it. Ever since it was known that he was on his way home the city had buzzed with his name; there had been no topic except Alcibiades. Some said he was the noblest citizen that Athens had ever reared and had been treated with hideous injustice. He had been condemned without trial, he had been driven into the exile from which he was now returning loaded with imperial gifts for the city which had rejected him. They had sentenced him to a felon's death who had proved himself her saviour, and who had restored to her, when beaten to the dust, her dominion over the seas. None could gainsay that, but some shook their heads and pointed to where the strong walls of Decelea sparkled on the hills beyond the ravaged plain of Attica, for that was his doing too. Others again remembered that this was a strangely inauspicious day for his return, and this feeling was widely spread, for to-day was the celebration of the Plyntria, when the robes were taken from the most holy and venerable statue of Athene to be washed. To-day her image was veiled, and she seemed to hide her face and refuse to look on the return of Alcibiades.[1] But one and all trooped down to the waterside to witness the arrival of Athens's saviour and her most deadly foe. Eight years ago they had crowded the quay to speed his departure in command of the most gallant force that had ever left the Peiræus, and since then Athens had stumbled far into the valley of the shadow of death, but now he shined on them, a great light in their darkness.

The ship that bore him had come to her moorings; Chrysogenus's flute was silent and the great actor called no more on the rowers, and still that lonely and splendid figure remained

---

[1] Plutarch, "Alcibiades," XXXII; Diodorus, XIII, 9, 11; Xenophon, "Hellenica," I, iv, 12; Plutarch, "Alcibiades," XXXIV, i.

motionless on deck, while the buzz of talk ceased, and the huge crowd grew mute and tense. The years of hatred and exile were over; he was home again with his gift of Empire restored to Athens, but at this supreme hour the memory of the ruinous strokes he had dealt her surged round him and he was afraid. And then he raised his eyes and saw the familiar faces of friends and relations, and the smile leaped to his mouth, and he stretched out his hands to them. At that the roar of welcome broke out and all the quays were laughing and sobbing together because Alcibiades had come home. He sprang ashore, and once more his foot touched Attic soil.

His colleagues, generals and captains who had served with him in this rebuilding of the Empire, followed him, but they passed unnoticed. One will possessed the crowd, to get near Alcibiades, to crown him with the wreaths of gold and bronze[1] they had brought for his welcoming, to burn their eyes with the sight of him. A lane was cleared for his passage, a guard kept the throngs back and he went up to the city. The Assembly was summoned, and once more he faced the citizens of Athens on the hill below the Acropolis.

Both in boyhood and youth and maturity he was the most beautiful of men,[2] and he spoke to those with whom the love of beauty was a passion. There was that lisp in his enunciation still and the hesitation before he found the perfect phrase, and he held them in the enchantment of his personality. He told them at once that he had not committed the sacrilege for which he had been condemned and that he had been unjustly treated. But he did not blame anybody; all these sore troubles had come upon him—and he paused for the word, as was his wont—from some "envious genius of his own." And then the hesitating utterance of that

---

[1] Cornelius Nepos, "Alcibiades," VI.
[2] Plutarch, "Alcibiades," I, 3.

The Life of Alcibiades

golden voice quickened as he spoke of the broken hopes of their enemies at Sparta who had tried to crush Athens. Their power was shattered, their fleet destroyed, and Athens could lift her bowed head and gaze into the future with courage. He spoke long on this theme, kindling his hearers into the wildest enthusiasm. There were those who still hated and distrusted him and who remembered the bitter woes he had brought on Athens, but none dared raise a voice against him. Already he had been elected General, but now the Assembly voted him General-in-Chief, with sole and absolute command by land and sea; never yet had Athens given such authority to any of her sons. His property which had been confiscated was restored to him; he had been publicly cursed for sacrilege, and now the Heralds of the Mysteries were bidden to revoke their anathemas, and the lead tablets and the pillars on which the curses were engraved were ceremonially flung into the sea.[1] Alcibiades had made his peace with God and man, and the bitter feud was healed. To the citizens of Athens he seemed to be Victory incarnate, and it was with the honours due to a god rather than a man that they acclaimed him.[2]

But it would be a mistake in the very alphabet of psychology to suppose that he was satisfied. He had done all that he had dreamed of, and that in the most magnificent fashion, but true ambition proves its authenticity by the fact that it is never content. Content would be evidence that it was not the real stuff, for woven into the heart of ambition is the eternal striving for that which is not yet attained, and its successive achievements are but the stepping-stones to a goal that is never reached. Of actual power, military, naval or political, there was for the moment no more to be had, for when next he set out from the Peiræus, he would have behind him

---

[1] Cornelius Nepos, "Alcibiades," VI.
[2] Justin, V, 4.

the whole strength of Athens to execute any campaigns by sea or land that he chose to frame. He did not mean to stop here long in incense and idleness, for while the one fed his soul, the other starved it. His country had cast him out, and now he had come back to her with imperial gifts as balm for her sore folly. That seemed the summit of magnificence in this regard. The ministers of the Holy Mysteries had forgiven him for the sacrilege of which he solemnly declared himself innocent, and he must forgive them for their mistake by some splendid piety. ...

Now ever since the fort of Decelea (erected by his own insistent counsel while exile at Sparta) had dominated the Attic plain, the great annual celebration of the Holy Mysteries had been shorn of its sumptuous ritual. On the eve of the feast the mystics still went down to the sea for purification, but the great procession from Athens to Eleusis along the sacred way over the hills of Daphne, with its ceremonies and sacrifices and choral hymns and dances, had been abandoned. The unarmed troop of initiates would have been at the mercy of any attack from the Spartan garrison at Decelea, and for seven years now they had crept round by sea to the shrine where the sacred dramas were enacted and the holy symbols revealed. It was Ichabod: the glory had departed from the great spiritual festival, and Alcibiades (himself an initiate) bethought him to restore its splendour. It was not that he desired to make his peace with the Eumolpidæ,[1] for that had already been done, and they had solemnly revoked the curse pronounced on him and destroyed the record of it, but he desired to make this gesture of his acceptance of their forgiveness. He communicated his design to them, and they approved it.

The idea was one of his great pieces of magnificence; just as he had once entered more chariots in the games at Olympia than any

---

[1] Contra, Grote, "History of Greece," VIII, 204.

The Life of Alcibiades

king had ever done for the glory of Athens and of Alcibiades, so now (largely if not wholly for the sake of his own splendour) he must restore the glory of the Holy Mysteries. He posted sentries the evening before the processional day of the feast on the heights of Daphne to look out for any sign of activity in the direction of Decelea, and issued orders for troops to turn out next morning sufficient to guard the sacred way from Athens to Eleusis and protect the procession of the initiates. At daybreak the advance-guard would leave the city, followed by the main body. Perhaps King Agis would order an attack, and in that case Alcibiades meant to take command of his men and be seen by all Athens fighting on behalf of the great religious corporation in token of his forgiveness, and that would be pleasing in the eyes alike of gods and men. Or Agis might see that there was a formidable body of troops ready to engage him and would prudently keep quiet, and that would be a sore humiliation for him; Alcibiades liked humiliating Agis. For seven years the menace of his presence had caused the mystics to steal quietly round to Eleusis by sea, but now the exile was home again, and once more, under his protection, the white-robed procession would come forth with song and dance.

The morning of the festival dawned. The sentries had reported that all was quiet, and forth from the Dipylon gate came Alcibiades on horse-back, leading his troops, and the great procession streamed out behind him. There were many young boys in it, who had been under instruction and were now to be initiated, for the rite, like that of Christian Confirmation admitting to the Sacrament, was administered to the young; and there were many women and girls in it, for this was one of the few religious festivals in which they were permitted to take part, and there were those who, with aged hearts uplifted, saw again the resumption of the splendour of the feast. In front went the bearers of the image of Iacchus; his high priest followed and those who carried the emblems of the god, and then came the lines of white-robed mystics, wearing wreaths and holding torches as yet unlit. When they were clear of the gate they struck up the chants and hymns; there was the hymn to Iacchus and the hymn to the Holy Maiden, and to the Blessed Mother Demeter, and between the choruses the flutes and the cymbals beat the rhythm of the consecrated dances. Along the sacred way were many shrines where the procession halted to do sacrifice, and by the time they had reached the top of the hills, still in sight of Athens but now ten miles distant, night was falling. All day Alcibiades's troops had moved along with them, he, mounted, at their head, and now, looking back, the mystics could see the twinkling city illuminated in honour of the feast, and looking forward, the lights from the precinct of their pilgrimage. They kindled their torches, thick as the stars of the September night above their heads, and again the procession moved on its choric way. Eleusis, though in Attica, had its own independent territory, much like the Vatican at Rome, and when they came to the frontier the mystics were met by a company of priests, who gave to each an armlet and ankle-band to ensure admission, for none but they might enter the Holy Place.

And now Alcibiades gave his horse to his groom and his arms to his page and put on him the white robe of the initiate and his wreath of myrtle, and kindled his torch. All day as Commander-in-Chief of the army of Athens he had been at the head of his troops, but now they must remain outside the sanctuary and bivouac there while he, with his yellow riband bound about arm and ankle, entered with the worshippers to behold again the ineffable Mysteries. Next day he fasted and did sacrifice with them, purifying himself for the revelation, and when night fell he ate with the others of the sacred bread and drank of the hallowing wine. Then came the supreme hour, and once more, as in his boyhood, lord of Athens no more, but one of the crowd of men and boys and women and girls all equal in the sight of the immortal gods, he entered the Hall of the Mysteries which his guardian Pericles had built. When all were assembled, the lights were quenched and from the darkness came the chanted versicles from the priests and the

The Life of Alcibiades

responses from the congregation which none but they might hear and which none could understand but those who had been instructed in the hidden truths of life and death. "I have fed from the timbrel," chanted the priests; "I have drunk from the cymbal," muttered the worshippers. ... Silence again and darkness, and once more, as the hall leaped into a blaze of light, he looked on the tableaux of the final revelation which, to those who knew, made the passage from the familiar world of material things an entry into everlasting day.

Perhaps of all the triumphant achievements of his life, splendid and damnable alike, this was the supremest, that he who had been cursed and excommunicated by the ministers of the Mysteries, who had been condemned to death for the blackest impiety in their regard, should have brought the pilgrims to the shrine and have partaken again in the sacramental rites. If we consider this neutrally, we can hardly doubt that his admission here was equivalent to a full and final acquittal on the charge for which he had been refused trial, and that the Eumolpidæ themselves acknowledged his innocence. It may be argued that they had thought it wiser, in view of the wild enthusiasm of Athens at his return, to revoke the curse they had pronounced on him, but it was a very different matter to have allowed him to become a very steward of the Mysteries, and to have accepted his offer to guarantee the safety of the pilgrimage with all its old splendour of ritual. Had they not now been convinced of his innocence they could not have permitted such co-operation. We must remember, too, that he had never been tried, that the evidence against him was that of slaves who belonged to his bitterest enemies, and who could be tortured until they promised to give the desired information. He had entreated to be allowed to stand his trial, he had never ceased to protest his innocence, and the charge of the mutilation of the Herms, which had been coupled with that of the blasphemous parody of the Mysteries, had long ago been shown to have had nothing to do with him. Devilish indeed had been his reprisals for the wrong that had been done him, whether innocent or guilty, in his not being allowed to answer the charge at once; in his absence, his political opponents were able to weave such a net round him as none could escape from, but such reprisals do not touch the question of his guilt or innocence at all. So heinous was the crime of which he had been accused that the Eumolpidæ had once pronounced that no man ever accused of it ought to be allowed back in Athens again;[1] to-day they were indebted to him for the restoration of the rites themselves. Whether he was innocent can, of course, never be absolutely determined, but it is impossible to imagine stronger circumstantial evidence in his favour than the fact that the guardians of the Mysteries welcomed his co-operation in the conduct of the festival and his presence at Eleusis.

Alcibiades had doubtless calculated on the effect of this exploit (he always calculated), and the result justified him. Instead of being the condemned blasphemer, now forgiven by the Eumolpidæ, he appeared as the innocent and great-hearted man who in the plenitude of his forgiveness towards them had restored the long-dwindled honour of the festival and by the same stroke had restored the prestige of Athenian arms. Ever since the establishment of the fort at Decelea the troops of Athens had hardly set foot outside the town, and the circuit of the long walls on sentry-guard had been the limit of their marchings. The effect both on his men and on the common folk was prodigious; the army believed that with him at their head there was nothing they could not do (and Alcibiades fully shared their view), while the people saw in him the superman and saviour of the city. Years of twaddle-talk in the Assembly, of plot and counter-plot of oligarch and democrat, of frittering mismanagement of Athens's resources and opport-

---

[1] Thucydides, VIII, 53.

The Life of Alcibiades

unities had disgusted them with these shifting phantasms of government, mirages without substance, and they longed for the brain that could think on large lines and frame terrible and splendid dooms to be absolute master of the State.[1] Alcibiades's splendour and efficiency made a unique appeal to their imagination; he alone could bring final victory, and having restored peace to the war-weary city, rule it with authority. He had hammered the Spartan fleet into fragments, he had restored their Empire in the North, and as for the tragedies he had wrought for them, provoked by the false charges made against him and now magnificently refuted, they were all forgotten. The people conceived a passion for the idea of that wonderful personality being tyrant in Athens; it was openly spoken of, and he was sounded on the subject himself. Probably in this autumn of B.C. 407 it was within his power to establish himself as such, and it may plausibly be argued that he had considered if he wanted it. Undoubtedly it was his goal.

But the time was not come for that: Sparta was not yet done with, and by now there must have reached Athens disquieting rumours of her fresh activities in the islands and on the coasts of Asia Minor, and of the high favour in which the new Spartan Admiral Lysander stood with young Prince Cyrus, the second son of King Darius. The office of Admiral at Sparta was an annual one, and no one might hold it twice, but Lysander was certainly making the most of his year. Alcibiades lingered in Athens no more, but after these four months of triumph mobilized fleet and army, and during October returned to the seat of war.

As he must well have known, he left behind him, not only passionate devotion, but jealousies and distrust and, even more dangerous than they, his own colossal prestige. That was his chiefest rival.

---

[1] Plutarch, "Alcibiades," XXXIV, 6.

CHAPTER XII

THE FINAL DISASTER

CHAPTER XII

THE FINAL DISASTER

BEFORE leaving the Propontis, Alcibiades, it will be remembered, had every reason to hope that he had laid the foundation for a friendly understanding between Athens and Persia. He had come to an agreement of amity, backed by professions of personal friendship, with Pharnabazus, who was to take an Athenian deputation up to Susa to wait on King Darius, and without doubt the satrap was prepared to urge this policy. But on the way there a very serious set-back had occurred. He met, coming away from Susa, Prince Cyrus, who carried with him his own appointment, under the royal seal of his father, to the satrapy of Lydia, and, what was more ominous, his own determination to support the Spartans to the utmost of his power. He refused to allow the Athenian embassy either to proceed to Susa or to go back to Athens, and they were interned for three years.[1] Cyrus then went on to Sardis and sent for Lysander, who was at Ephesus with a new fleet of ninety vessels, thirty of which had lately been launched at Gythium. Their meeting was the death-blow to the hopes of friendly relations between Athens and Persia which Alcibiades had so long been trying to establish.

Lysander was received by the pro-Spartan Cyrus in the most friendly manner, and his complaints about the way in which Tissaphernes had withheld the pay of the Peloponnesian sailors, contracted for in the Treaty of Miletus, was a happy topic, since Prince Cyrus detested and distrusted the satrap. Unlike most Spartans, Lysander could wear, when convenient, courtly and

---

[1] Xenophon, "Hellenica," I, iv, 7.

The Life of Alcibiades

deferential manners, and he flattered Cyrus to the top of his bent. He knew that money to be expended in liberal pay to the sailors was the first necessity, for Athens was very short of funds, and a higher scale of wages on Spartan ships would induce the hired oarsmen of the Athenian fleet to desert. He begged the Prince therefore to raise his sailors' pay to a drachma a day, which would really save money in the end, for the ships of Athens would soon be empty.[1] This was too expensive for Cyrus's enthusiasm, but in spite of his refusal relations remained extremely cordial, and when, at the end of Lysander's visit, the Prince gave him a banquet, and asked him, when he drank his health, what he could do for him, Lysander made no personal request, but in a truly Oriental manner returned to his bargaining with a diminished demand. An extra obol a day (four instead of three) for his seamen would please him, he said, more than any personal gift. Cyrus thought this very public-spirited, and agreed.

Such was the news, wholly disagreeable, which met Alcibiades when he arrived from Athens at Samos, which, as heretofore, was again the head-quarters of the fleet. He had made a raid en route on the island of Andros, and though he had defeated the islanders and their garrison of Spartan troops, he had not succeeded in taking the town, and ill-success was a most unwelcome stranger to him, and one whom he knew his countrymen would resent. But this rapprochement between Persia and Sparta disquieted him more, and clinging to the hope that something might still be done through Tissaphernes, who was all for the policy, suggested originally by himself, of letting the Greek States wear themselves out against each other without Persian interference, he sent an embassy up to Sardis to try to arrange through the satrap an

---

[1] Xenophon, "Hellenica," I, v, 5. This was not merely "rather a high wage" (Glover, "From Pericles to Philip," p. 46), but double the usual rate.

interview with Prince Cyrus. But Lysander had seen to it that Tissaphernes should be ill-looked on; moreover, such policy of inaction was altogether distasteful to young Cyrus's energy, and he refused to receive the deputation. News of the higher pay provided by Persian gold seems to have caused a certain amount of desertion and discontent among the Athenian sailors, and, very wisely, Alcibiades did his best to provoke an engagement with Lysander while he was still superior in the matter of efficient ships, and while his name was still magic. But Lysander refused to be enticed from his protected harbourage at Ephesus. Time was on his side now, for he had the eager support of Cyrus, his men were well-paid and content, and he was reorganizing his fleet. Time, on the other hand, was dead against Alcibiades, for discontent was spreading in his ships; since he left Athens he had done nothing to justify the enormous enthusiasm which had made him lord of all her forces by sea and land; his hopes of securing even a continuance of neutrality on the part of Persia had faded, and, above all, funds were so low that he could barely pay the smaller wage of his sailors. The first necessity, since Lysander could not be induced to give battle, was to get money, and he sailed off with a few ships, first to confer with Thrasybulus, the commander whom he had left with a squadron on the coasts of Thrace when he went to Athens. Thrasybulus had finished his work of consolidation there, and was now blockading Phocæa,[1] a revolted Athenian town on the coast of Lydia. There Alcibiades sailed, with the object of inspecting Thrasybulus's fleet and receiving the commander's report. He then proceeded to the coasts of Caria, which had provided a hundred talents earlier in the year, to attempt to raise a further levy.[2] Money

---

[1] Xenophon, "Hellenica," I, v. 4.
[2] Pultarch, "Alcibiades," XXXV, 3.

The Life of Alcibiades

was absolutely essential, and it was his duty, if the fleet was to be maintained, to raise it.

Now the historian Diodorus[1] tells us that Alcibiades, when at Phocæa, made a raid on the city of Cyme, which was close by, and was, he tells us, a faithful ally of Athens. He attacked the town and sacked it, taking a number of prisoners. But the citizens made a counter-attack and defeated his troops and recaptured the loot and the prisoners. Alcibiades then besieged the town, but being unable to take it, ravaged the territory. When he had gone, Cyme sent despatches to Athens protesting against such an attack made by the Athenian Commander-in-Chief on a faithful ally.

This incident, we must notice, is only given by Diodorus, and neither Xenophon nor Plutarch record it. We should therefore, in such circumstances, be cautious in accepting it, and when we come to consider the nature of it, there can hardly be a doubt that it must be rejected. To begin with, though we may grant that Alcibiades was perfectly unscrupulous, he was not imbecile, and wantonly to attack a friendly city when it was all important to retain good relations with the faithful dependencies of the Empire would have been an incredible folly. Moreover, as his campaign in the Hellespont shows, such an act would have been utterly inconsistent with his policy; he had treated even revolted cities, like Chalcedon and Byzantium, with extreme leniency in order to cement their friendly relations with Athens, and that he pillaged a small and faithful ally and was with all his troops beaten and driven back to his ships passes the bounds of any reasonable demand on our credulity. We cannot envisage the Commander-in-Chief returning to his fleet with the news that he had suffered defeat from an Athenian ally. Mr. Grote,[2] it is true, prefers to accept Diodorus as against the

---

[1] Diodorus Siculus, XIII, 10.
[2] Grote, "History of Greece," VIII, 208, etc.

complete silence of Xenophon and Plutarch, whose witness he eagerly adopts when he can construe into it fresh condemnation for all that Alcibiades did or was; and he tells us that this raid on Cyme was among the causes which led to Alcibiades being presently deprived of his command. But both Xenophon and Plutarch give in detail what those causes were, and the sack of Cyme does not appear among them. Mr. Grote's further suggestion that Diodorus copied this story from the Cymæan historian Ephorus cannot be considered to carry much weight, for no extant fragment of Ephorus alludes to it. His comment that Alcibiades's visit to Phocæa could have had no purpose unless he meant to plunder Cyme disregards the fact that Thrasybulus was there with his squadron from Thrace, and that it was not wholly unreasonable of the Commander-in-Chief to visit so substantial a portion of his fleet.[1]

The whole episode is obscure, and it may be that Nepos gives us the clue to it when he says that the Athenians were displeased with Alcibiades because "he did not manage affairs at Cyme as they wished," and that they thought he did not take Cyme because he had been bribed not to by the King of Persia.[2] It is possible therefore that Cyme had revolted, and he had been ordered to punish it. Support is given to this view by a passage in Thucydides which is consistent with it.[3]

But before leaving Samos Alcibiades had made a very serious error of judgment which led to disastrous consequences. He appointed to command the fleet in his absence, not one of his staff, or a captain of some other ship, but his pilot Antiochus.[4] This was the man who, years ago, had captured for him the quail

---

[1] Grote, 208, etc.
[2] Cornelius Nepos, "Alcibiades," VII.
[3] Thucydides, VIII, 31.
[4] Plutarch, "Lysander," V, 1.

The Life of Alcibiades

which had escaped from his cloak in the Assembly at Athens, and who, since then, had been a great favourite of his. Such an appointment was very ill-advised and was likely, as proved to be the case, to provoke keen and justifiable resentment among his officers; it was in the most insolent style of his boyhood. It is true that he gave Antiochus strict orders not to engage the enemy in his absence, whatever opportunity presented itself, but to appoint such a man at all, who, though a good sailor, had no commissioned rank, and by all accounts was no more than a roystering braggart, was a piece of ultra-Alcibiadean impertinence, inviting the Nemesis which speedily followed.

As soon as he had gone, Antiochus put out from Samos with two triremes and sailed over to the harbour at Ephesus, where Lysander's entire fleet was lying. He cruised across the mouth of the harbour, crossing close to the bows of the enemy's ships with insulting cries and gesticulations. Lysander sent out two or three ships in pursuit, upon which more Athenian triremes put out to go to the rescue, and Lysander, seeing the chance of an important capture, and knowing that Alcibiades was not in command of such haphazard work,[1] came out of the harbour of Ephesus, from which Alcibiades had in vain tried to tempt him, with his fleet of ninety triremes and formed line of battle. On this the rest of the Athenian navy joined in, and the action became general. But while Lysander's fleet was in good order and controlled by him, there was no command on the Athenian side; their ships were scattered units without any sort of formation or tactical plan. In consequence, they suffered a severe defeat and lost fifteen ships; many prisoners were taken and Antiochus was killed. It was the most disastrous affair, and though Alcibiades had ordered Antiochus on no account to provoke or accept an engagement, the brunt of the

---

[1] Diodorus, XIII, 9.

blame must certainly attach to him for putting such a man in command. High-handed insolence alone can have made him do it.

Such was the news that awaited Alcibiades when he came back from Caria, and well he knew that when tidings of this gratuitous defeat reached Athens his prestige would suffer a staggering shock. The only possible way of restoring it and of repairing the error he had made was by overscoring this disaster with some signal success. He set sail at once with his whole fleet and cruised off the harbour at Ephesus in the hope of again enticing Lysander to come out. But this was a very different affair, and Lysander had no mind to attack a well-handled line, still equal to him in numbers, instead of scattered ships under no command. He did not stir from the harbour.

There had been, as was only natural, strong resentment in the fleet against Alcibiades for this appointment of Antiochus, and its consequences gave one of those who were always jealous of his ascendancy a rare opportunity. Thrasybulus, son of Thrasus (not Alcibiades's colleague of the same name in the Hellespont), went back to Athens from Samos with a wealth of damning information. The idol of the people had set out from Athens three months ago supreme commander of all her forces by sea and land, and with the implicit confidence of the city to back him. Instead of exercising his functions with any sense of the noble responsibility that rested on him, he had turned the fleet over to the command of a man who was not even an officer, and whose sole merit was his capacity for drinking and amusing the Admiral with bawdy stories, while he himself, though the enemy's fleet was close at hand, went off to Caria and the more congenial society of dissolute women. Where, too, were those old reiterated promises of securing Persian neutrality if not Persian alliance? It was Lysander now, not he, who had the ear of Prince Cyrus and the control of Persian funds. Had the Athenians also heard of the castle he had built at Bisanthe in Thrace? What did

The Life of Alcibiades

Alcibiades want with a castle in Thrace, except as a refuge against the day when Athens would no longer tolerate him?[1]

Now there was a solid and awkward measure of truth in these denunciations. Alcibiades had appointed, during his absence in Caria, a man totally unfit to command, and the disaster at Notium which followed was the consequence of it. But what was utterly unjust was the reason assigned for this "spree" to Caria. From all we know of Alcibiades it is likely to the verge of certainty that his private life there was most unedifying, but it was in the interests of public edification that he had gone there. He had to pay his crews, and the money was not forthcoming from Athens. He had to get it elsewhere, and he went to the rich cities of Caria, where a year before he had raised a hundred talents. But what told against him most was his loss of prestige, for the worst enemy he had left behind at Athens was his own supreme reputation. Never before had he failed in any enterprise, whether it was to the benefit or to the dismal undoing of Athens, and she would not believe that he could now have failed if his will had been set to serve her. She could find no excuse for the man to whom she had pinned her unlimited faith. The Assembly gave its vote as to what should be done with him, and the message went out to Samos that he was deposed from his command. In place of him in whom had been vested the sole command, ten new generals were appointed, according to the usual custom. Alcibiades left the island at once in the trireme which, like his father Cleinias, he had furnished at his own expense, and sailed to his castle at Bisanthe on the coast of the Propontis, which in his felicitous campaign there he had built to be a link in the chain of fortresses which should bring the Athenian colonies on

---

[1] Plutarch, "Alcibiades," XXXVI, 3.

the Bosphorus into closer touch with those on the Hellespont. Perhaps at the back of that ever-calculating mind he had foreseen the possibility of a day when he would be sorely in need of some refuge, and the day had come. Athens, Sparta and Persia were all close to him; each of the three Powers which at one time or another had courted and caressed him would have rejoiced to see his head brought them on a charger. Tissaphernes, who had called his new pleasance Alcibiades Park, had already imprisoned him, and would like nothing better than to be able to make favour with Prince Cyrus by handing him over; Sparta, with excellent cause, regarded him as her deadliest and most capable enemy, and Athens, who not a year ago had made him sole lord of her navies and her armies, had deposed him. For two years he made his home in remote and barbarous Thrace.

It was not, of course, in the power of the man to be idle; he was capable of almost anything except inaction in the pursuit of some immeasurable ambition. Unfortunately, we know next to nothing of the details of his days, which must have been highly picturesque. He arrived at Bisanthe with his trireme,[1] and got together a body of mercenary troops, with the slave-oarsmen of his ship as nucleus. Thrace was inhabited by independent tribes and scattered settlements under no unified Government, and Alcibiades made raids on these, and reaped plunder of considerable value. With other local chieftains, too strong, perhaps, to spoil, he made alliances; Medocus and Seuthes, whom he calls "Kings" of Thrace, were among them,[2] and just as at Sparta he had lived as Spartans live, so now in Thrace he made himself a Thracian in his mode of life. Since

---

[1] Xenophon, "Hellenica," I, v, 17.
[2] Diodorus, XIII, 15; Cornelius Nepos, "Alcibiades," XI.

The Life of Alcibiades

drink and sensuality were characteristics of them, he found existence more congenial than it had been at Sparta, and it is not surprising to hear that he was more Thracian than any native-born.[1] He organized some of these districts under an effective control, and stopped barbarian inroads on Greek settlements,[2] such as Perinthus. Purpose, as Thucydides remarks, always lurked behind his deeds, and it seems only reasonable to conjecture that these were the first steps towards founding some sort of kingdom here; indeed, when we consider the astonishing ability and energy of the man, it is hardly possible to doubt that some such scheme, whether for the ultimate benefit of Athens or for his own, was maturing. What its scope was, whether he meant to draw into it the northern colonies of Athens, which he had re-established in her Empire in that brilliant campaign on the Propontis, we have no idea, but in this control and consolidation of these Thracian districts there was certainly some such design. He moved from fortress to fortress; we find him, for instance, later on at the castle of Pactye on the Hellespont, but before his schemes disclosed themselves the course of the war made him once more a wanderer.

In August B.C. 406 Athens scored a great naval victory off the Arginusæ islands. It did not approach in importance the victory at Cyzicus, but seventy Spartan ships were sunk, and it altered the balance of power in the east of the Ægean, where now again Athens was ascendant. The year of Lysander's command was over, and Callicratidas, who had succeeded him, was killed in this battle, but though, according to the law

---

[1] Athenæus, XII, 47 (quoting from Satyrus.)
[2] Plutarch, "Alcibiades," XXXVI, 3.

of Sparta, a man could not hold the office twice,[1] it was felt that Lysander, with his known influence over Prince Cyrus, must continue the conduct of the war. To get out of the legal difficulty, he was given the title of Vice-Admiral to an admiral of straw, and went out to Ephesus again in actual, though not nominal command. Soon after his arrival Cyrus was sent for to the death-bed of his father, King Darius, and for the period of his absence he appointed Lysander Deputy-Satrap of Lydia, with complete control of its revenues. He still refused battle with the Athenian fleet, which, in spite of further Spartan reinforcements, far out-numbered his, but took advantage of its dispersing from Samos to slip across to the coast of Attica, where he conferred with King Agis, who came down from Decelea to the coast. But he learned that the Athenian fleet was in pursuit, and still refusing to engage, sailed northwards instead of going straight back to Ephesus. With the whole of the resources of Lydia to draw on, he could afford to wait till an opportunity of giving battle on advantageous terms presented itself. On his way home he learned that the Hellespont was unguarded and he took Lampsacus, a town on the Asian side of the strait, and established himself there. The scene was set for the huge catastrophe which ended the war.

The Athenian fleet, magnificent with its hundred and eighty sail, followed him up. It put in at Sestos to revictual and then took up a singularly ill-chosen station at Ægospotami, on the European side of the strait, exactly opposite the enemy. There was no proper harbourage there—the nearest place for obtaining provisions was Sestos, a couple of miles distant; we can only suppose that the Athenian admirals felt sure that

---

[1] Plutarch, "Lysander," VII, 2.

The Life of Alcibiades

Lysander would still refuse to engage, and that they despised the smaller number of the enemy's fleet. A few miles away to the north there stood a castle, and from the walls of Pactye Alcibiades looked out, and saw his country's fleet, over which so lately he had been in supreme command, anchored at this most unstrategic spot. Once he had fought for Sparta, and grievous were the wounds he had inflicted on Athens; since then in these waters he had sunk the Spartan fleet and established Athenian supremacy again, and now, in the strange disposition of destiny, he was a mere spectator, without authority on either side.

For four days he watched the two fleets. In the Spartan navy there was perfect discipline; at sunrise the triremes were manned, and all day they remained ready to start on the word of command, and behind them along the shore the troops were drawn up. Every morning the Athenian fleet sailed out, challenging them to battle but failing to provoke an engagement, and in the evening went back to its anchorage. But Alcibiades saw also that as they returned two or three Spartan triremes hung about in the straits till the Athenian troops and sailors had disembarked, leaving only a few guards on their ships, while the rest strayed and scattered about on land, or went into Sestos for provisions and diversion. It was evident that they held the enemy in contempt, and though they were the more formidable in point of numbers, their generals were allowing slackness to take the place of discipline, and were presuming on Lysander's refusal to be engaged. At the least, the position of the Athenian fleet was most ill-advised, and such slack handling in the presence of the enemy was fraught with grave danger. He made up his mind, though he risked insult and rebuff, to interfere and warn the generals, and on the evening of the fourth day he rode out of Pactye across the few miles of country to Ægospotami.

Now we have no data as to his motive in doing that except from what knowledge we have acquired of his character, and the more we study that, the more difficult is it to decide which of two widely-sundered desires prompted him. It may have been pure patriotism, the love of the city of his birth, which he now believed to be in the greatest peril. But if we incline to that, we must not forget that it was he who of all men had most injured her, and though the quarrel had been made up, after he had rendered her such services as no other could have done, and had been received back with such apotheosis as she had never given to any of her sons, that she had turned him out again, and that he did not easily forget. ... If, then, we reject patriotism as prompting his action, we must suppose that ambition was his main motive, and that he expected that, on this sudden and amazing epiphany of the vanished Alcibiades with all his glamour and all his un-chequered success when he fought for Athens, he would repeat the triumph of his previous return and once more be put at the head of her navy. And yet that seems ultra-sanguine even for him, for since his disappearance two years ago Athens had got on very well without him; the battle of Arginusæ was no mean achievement. But, primarily, it was either for the sake of Athens or of Alcibiades that he rode now to Ægospotami.

It was evening; the most of the crews and of the troops had landed and were strolling and wandering about,[1] and we may picture groups of them staring open-mouthed at the gallant figure they knew so well, magically coming out of nowhere and riding into the lines. Yes; he was Alcibiades, and he wished to speak with the generals of the fleet. The message was taken

---

[1] Plutarch, "Alcibiades," XXXVI, 5.

The Life of Alcibiades

to them and they settled to receive him. Whatever his motive was, he was in earnest, and in the old autocratic style he found fault with all their dispositions. Their anchorage was bad, they had no harbour and no provisioning town close at hand; everything had to come from Sestos. And look at their discipline! At this moment there was scarcely a man on their ships; they were all skylarking on shore, or amusing themselves in Sestos. It was madness to behave like this in the presence of a powerful and alert enemy; they did not know what dangers they were running. "Shift your anchorage to Sestos at once," he said, "or it may be too late. With the protection of a harbour, you will be able to fight when you please; as it is, the enemy can force an engage-ment at any moment he chooses, and he will find you unprepared."

The news of his amazing arrival had spread, and the soldiers had gathered round the group.[1] The generals heard him, they laughed at him, and Tydeus scornfully told him that he had better take himself off, for he was General no longer, and the interview was over. Some friends of his escorted him out of the camp, and as they went, he swore to them that but for this insolent reception he would within a few days have forced the Spartan fleet to give battle. He had friendly Thracian chieftains, too, at his back, Medocus and Seuthes, who had offered him an army of troops and cavalry and had begged him to lead them against the Spartans.[2] Some thought that this was his boastful habit; others believed him,[3] and he mounted and rode back to Pactye. But if the generals had taken his advice, whether they co-opted him again or not, the disaster of Ægospotami would never have happened.

---

[1] Cornelius Nepos, "Alcibiades," VII.
[2] Diodorus, XIII, 15.
[3] Plutarch, "Alcibiades," XXXVII, 1.

He had done his best to save Athens, whatever his motive, and the very next day, from the walls of Pactye, he saw his disregarded warning terribly fulfilled. Once more, and for the last time, the Athenian fleet tried to entice Lysander out, and once more, on its return towards evening, two or three Spartan triremes followed it, and waited in mid-strait till they saw that the crews had disembarked for their evening diversion, some to market, some to stroll about on shore. But to-night those Spartan triremes did not return to their anchorage, and on the prow of one a brazen shield was hoisted and flashed its signal to Lysander, that the Athenian fleet was at his mercy. The trumpeter on the Admiral's flagship sounded the call to put out to sea, and every ship in the Spartan navy came foaming forth, rowed at top speed. Straight across the narrow water they raced, and they were more than halfway over when Conon, one of the Athenian generals, saw the huge disaster imminent, and it was in vain that he shouted for the men to return to the ships, for they were scattered and dispersed. Eight only out of that great armada could be fully manned and put to sea, and across the water came the sound of the racing oars and the Spartan battle-cry. The Athenian troops, all unarmed, for they had left their weapons on their ships, were streaming back now, but it was too late, for the enemy was on them. Some got aboard, and were killed before they could arm, others fled and were pursued and slaughtered. The whole fleet, with the exception of the eight ships under Conon and the State galley, the "Paralus," was captured with all the other generals, and three thousand men were made prisoners. Just twenty-four hours ago Alcibiades had uttered his warning to deaf ears, and was scoffed at for his interference with the fleet of the sovereign people, in which he no longer held command. Now the day of wrath had come for Athens, the fleet was wiped out, the long war was over, and Alcibiades saw the

The Life of Alcibiades

last scene of it from his fortress. The "Paralus" carried the news to Athens, and as the tidings spread from Peiræus to the city, there rose and swelled the sound of lamentation and great mourning, and that night no man slept.[1]

---

[1] Xenophon, "Hellenica," II, ii, 3.

CHAPTER XIII

"MAGNUS CIVIS OBIT"

CHAPTER XIII

"*MAGNUS CIVIS OBIT*"

IT must be admitted even by those who throughout Alcibiades's career see in his genius no more than an infinite capacity for securing his own advantage, that he had done what he could to avert from Athens this final and overwhelming disaster, and now he had to think for his own safety. There was not a single Athenian ship left in the whole region of Bosphorus, Propontis and Hellespont; the imperial gift which, after three years of fighting, he had brought to Athens was in the hands of the Spartans, whose fleet he had sunk off Cyzicus, and those castles in Thrace which he had designed to be links in the chain of Athenian dominion were already like little sundered rocks surrounded and soon to be submerged by the flood-tide of Spartan victory. He bethought him of the pact of friendship he had made with Pharnabazus, and made haste to be gone. The dream of establishing a new kingdom here, or at least a province of Athens, was shattered, and collecting such property as he could carry with him, but leaving behind the bulk of his acquisitions of these last two years, he set off. Apparently he still had the trireme in which he had sailed from Samos after his deposition, but the Spartan fleet was once more mistress of the sea, and to have crossed the Propontis to Phrygia would have meant certain capture. So he struck inland and travelled through Thrace up to the Hellespont, and then slipped across the straits.

His plan, maturing as he journeyed, was to go to Pharnabazus, and in the name of their treaty of friendship to seek sanctuary with him. And yet he could not imagine for himself a life of indolence without those schemings and

The Life of Alcibiades

intrigues which to him were the salt of existence. He had known the lazy languor of Persian days before, when Tissaphernes had made much of him, but then there had been an object in playing the perfect Persian, just as there had been in playing the perfect Spartan at that damned barrack of a town on the Eurotas. He had been busy then with his great plan of procuring for Athens the support of the satrap in her war with Sparta, but now there was nothing to occupy him. What was he to *do* (he never counted wine and women as more than relaxations) even if Pharnabazus received him with friendliness and welcome?

His brain began to seethe with projects. There was that embassy of Athenians which Pharnabazus had promised to conduct to the Court of King Darius at Susa. It had never got there, for there had been some hitch; Prince Cyrus, who was so zealous a pro-Spartan, had stopped it, and the Athenians had been interned. But why should not he manage to get to Susa? Themistocles had done so when Athens ostracized him, and surely Alcibiades could accomplish the same. Indeed the parallel was strangely close, for Themistocles had gone to Susa just when a former Artaxerxes had succeeded his father, and now another Artaxerxes had but lately come to the throne. But Themistocles had asked to be allowed to wait for a year, during which time he should learn to conform to Persian ways and speak their talk, but Alcibiades needed no such time for tuition, for he had all that at his fingers' ends. And Themistocles had made a success of it; he had been received with high honour, and had been appointed Governor of Magnesia. "And why should not I do the same and better?" thought Alcibiades.[1] "But I shall not, like Themis-

---

[1] Plutarch, "Alcibiades," XXXVII, 4.

tocles, be working against Athens, but for her."

Alcibiades was, in fact, contemplating again the old project for which he had vainly tried to get the help of Tissaphernes. But now it was the great King himself whose ear he hoped to gain and whose favour to win. And the scheme was one which, when advanced by the charms of that persuasive speech, might easily appeal to Artaxerxes. Alcibiades meant to represent to him that Sparta, now that Athens was crushed, was a dangerously powerful kingdom, and one that was only too likely to prove a menace to Persia. All Greece would be hers with the naval Empire of Athens added, and the great King might be reminded, very tactfully, of course, that united Greece had once proved herself more than a match for his ancestor. It would be far wiser of him not to permit so powerful a supremacy, but to break with Sparta and restore Athens, now helpless and defenceless, and thus constitute a check on what would otherwise be Sparta's unchallenged Hellenic dominion.

It was with this idea at work in his mind that Alcibiades left Thrace directly after the battle of Ægospotami at the end of September B.C. 405, for there was no time to be lost in getting out of a country now potentially in possession of Sparta. He suffered further loss, in his journey through Bithynia, of the valuables he had been able to carry away with him, but reached Phrygia in safety, and was warmly welcomed by Pharnabazus. But his request to be given protection and facilities for his journey to Susa on such an errand as this must have been exceedingly embarrassing to the satrap, for this immense Spartan victory at Ægospotami had restored to the King of Persia all the coast towns of Asia Minor which had once been subjects of the Athenian Empire, and it was thus highly unlikely that Artaxerxes would listen favourably to any anti-Spartan policy or approve of the conduct of a satrap who was abetting the author of it. Pharnabazus therefore refused to give sanction or protection to his guest on such an errand.

Such is the story as given by Plutarch of Alcibiades's attempt to get to Susa, which differs entirely from that recorded by Diodorus,[1] on the authority of the historian Ephorus, and it seems probable, since there is confirmatory evidence for both, that both are true, and that Alcibiades, having failed to get Pharnabazus's support for his first purpose, looked about for another, which the satrap might approve, and conceived the project recorded by Diodorus. According to the latter, Alcibiades found out that Prince Cyrus was conspiring to dethrone his brother with the aid of Spartan troops and seize the sovereignty for himself; and at once he saw in that a golden opportunity. It should be his to reveal this plot to Artaxerxes, and this should be the primary purpose of his journey to Susa. All his life he had lived in the limelight; he breathed limelight as others breathe air, and what more splendid illumination could he desire than that which would stream on the noble Athenian exile revealing to the King of Persia the treason of his brother? ... He went with his new idea to Pharnabazus, but again he met with a refusal. Perhaps the satrap thought that he would himself like to play so sumptuous a role; perhaps he feared some miscarriage of the message, for, should it be known that he was instrumental in sending Alcibiades to Susa on such an errand and anything went wrong, his own position would be highly hazardous. There was Prince Cyrus, satrap of Lydia and Cappadocia, and if Alcibiades's information was not credited, where would Pharnabazus be? So he would have nothing to do with this journey, though he remained in friendly relations with Alcibiades, giving him a house in some Phrygian village, probably

---

[1] Diodorus, XIV, 3. See also Cornelius Nepos, "Alcibiades," IX.

Melissa,[1] and the revenues derived from the fortified town of Grunium. These brought the exile an income of fifty talents a year.[2] He could live on that as befitted his magnificence, for in the modern equivalent it would amount to £50,000.

It soon became known that Alcibiades had a suitable establishment in Phrygia. Whether the satrap felt that with Sparta in such high favour at the Court of Prince Cyrus he was too dangerous a guest, and gave information of his whereabouts, we do not know. If he did, he was certainly breaking the laws of hospitality towards one who thought he was protected by them. On the other hand, he may have told Alcibiades that, frankly, he did not desire to be held responsible for his presence, and that if he chose to remain he must take his chance. Or again—it is quite likely—Alcibiades himself, with that monstrous arrogance which was so characteristic of him, may have made no secret of his sojournings and of his mission, and proclaimed right and left that here was Alcibiades himself, who was presently journeying to Susa, where he would give straight talk to the great King and advise him for his good. He could not live out of the limelight, and thought the limelight would fade into darkness if it was not illuminating him. ...

However it happened, his presence in this village of Phrygia became widely known. Word came of his whereabouts to Athens, now shorn of her long walls and fortifications, and dominated by the rule of the oligarchs whom Lysander had imposed upon her. There were many in the city who bitterly repented of her second rejection of Alcibiades, when, in a fit of rage, childish and unthinking, she had deposed him from his supreme command, because in his absence from the fleet

---

[1] Cornelius Nepos, "Alcibiades," IX.
[2] "Athenæus," XIII, 34.

The Life of Alcibiades

his pilot had disobeyed his orders. What an insensate petulance that had been, for there had never been anyone like him; success had been his handmaiden, never had he lost a single ship for Athens when he had been in command, nor an engagement on shore.[1] He had sunk the Spartan fleet at Cyzicus, he had regained Athens her Empire, and then they had slammed the door on him. Even after that he had done what he could; had not the generals at Ægospotami flouted and mocked him, that final disaster could never have occurred. And now they learned that after his long banishment he was the guest of Pharnabazus, and, at the thought of that, a ray of hope shone through the darkness. Everything was not lost while Alcibiades was alive. Again and again such talk as this was muttered in barber's shop and market-place. Was it possible that he could do something to save them yet, and bring down to the dust the insolent Spartans who had demolished the pride of their long walls to the sound of flutes?[2] With Alcibiades anything was possible.

It was not only among the common folk who had always worshipped him that such dreams were regarded as within the range of accomplishment. Athens was now in the hands of the oligarchical Thirty, who, though appointed only to frame the new Constitution of Athens in accordance with the ideas of Sparta, were determined to remain in power, and had already executed certain leading democrats. Yet even they felt uneasy when they heard that Alcibiades was still alive, for they feared that he might yet return to Athens, and, with the mob to whom his name was magic, set himself up as head of a democracy. Nothing shows more vividly the extraordinary

---

[1] Isocrates, "De Bigis," 23.
[2] Xenophon, "Hellenica," II, ii, 23.

hold that he had over men's imagination than that a man like Critias, the leader of the extreme section of the oligarchs, could think that this solitary exile, far away in Persia, surrounded by the foes of Athens, was still a power to be feared, and that from that remoteness he might again mould the destinies of Athens. But such was Critias's opinion of his fellow-pupil in the tuitions of Socrates,[1] and he sent to Lysander to say that the oligarchy at Athens, which he had established, could not be considered safe while Alcibiades was still alive.

It became known at Sparta that Alcibiades was somewhere in the satrapy of Pharnabazus. King Agis was at home now, and as often as he looked on the bastard son of his Queen he thought of the boy's father. And who but he had sunk the Peloponnesian fleet at Cyzicus and led the mystics to Eleusis? Agis felt that nothing was safe while that man lived. The matter was brought before the Government, and on their approval a despatch was sent to Lysander, now with his fleet on the Asiatic coast, that Alcibiades must be killed. Such an order had gone out once before from Sparta in just such a manner to Astyochus, then Admiral of the Spartan navy. It had remained up till the present unexecuted, but Lysander was more business-like. The order reached him in due course, and he communicated it to Pharnabazus. The satrap knew the high favour in which Lysander stood with Prince Cyrus, and that though this order only came from the Spartan Admiral, it would certainly receive the Prince's endorsement and approval. He told himself, too, that though Alcibiades was his guest, he was the enemy of Persia's ally, and he sent for his brother Magæus and his uncle Sousamithras, who were officers in his satrapy, and told them to see to it. They got together a

---

[1] Xenophon, "Memorabilia," I, ii, 12.

The Life of Alcibiades

party of soldiers, and set off to the village where Alcibiades was living. On their way they held a conference as to their tactics, for he was an ill man to attack.

Alcibiades had been here about a year, and the prospect of getting up to Susa seemed as remote as ever from realization. He was comfortable enough as far as material considerations went; Pharnabazus had sent him a handsome girl called Timandra, and she lived with him and adored him. There was with him also a young Arcadian, who had a dog-like devotion for him, and never left him;[1] this was probably Axiochus, who had been with him in the campaign on the Hellespont.[2] But what a life it was in this provincial and barbarous village, a mere husk of existence without the kernel; the beasts that perished lived thus with their food and their mate. Even the two years at Sparta among those ascetic and witless bumpkins were better, for at least then his brain was busy and he saw the fruits of its invention ripening. The fire of his vitality burned bright and ardent as ever, though for so long no fuel of fierce living had been given it. He was eager for any adventure, but none beckoned, eager to scheme and contrive if only he could find any goal in sight. He had always been able to see a little further than others, and now for a year his vision had been starved, for there was nothing on which to focus his eyes, and for the flesh and blood of living he had been fed with sweetmeats. He was getting soft and womanish, too, in this slack backwater of existence, unable to swim out into the live and turbulent stream again, and his very dreams had taken the colour of this unmanly life. Just such a one had visited his siesta a couple of days before. He had dreamed that he was

---

[1] Cornelius Nepos, "Alcibiades," X.
[2] Athenæus, XI, 49.

wearing Timandra's clothes, and that she was holding his head while she painted and powdered his face like a woman's.[1] An odd dream, a disturbing dream; he did not know what it meant. It haunted him, and he told Timandra about it.

It was darkening towards evening, and still he mused over this dream and wondered what the interpretation of it was. Pindar had spoken somewhere in his Odes of that mysterious perception which in sleep "reveals a guerdon of joy or sorrow drawing near," and a diviner would have been glib with some plausible rigmarole of an explanation. Nicias would have had a consultation the moment he awoke after such a dream; he was always consulting his diviners, indeed he did so once too often when, owing to an eclipse of the moon, he stayed on at Syracuse for a month. Alcibiades did not much believe in prophecy and oracle, for had not an oracle said that Athens would annex all Sicily and capture every single Syracusan? And yet perhaps, according to Pindar, dreams were sent as a warning, even as Socrates claimed to have an interior sense which directed and prevented him. Socrates and those long catechisms! There was something wonderful about that old Silenus who loved him with so noble a devotion, and who alone of all men and women on this earth had ever made him ashamed of himself. Would he have done better to have lived more worthily of that love? He shrugged his shoulders; he did not care to cross-examine himself as Socrates would have done.

He strolled out in the scented, swift-falling dusk, and thought he saw several men hanging about in the garden. He called to them, asking their business, but got no answer; he

---

[1] Plutarch, "Alcibiades," XXXIX, 2. Plutarch gives other versions as well of Alcibiades's death.

The Life of Alcibiades

even searched a little for them, but he could see nothing of them. Loafing Persians, in any case. It was night now, and the lamps were lit in his house. Supper was ready, and Timandra should sup with him, and tell him if she had any interpretation of that dream of his. So Timandra and Axiochus and he supped together, and bedtime came. Perhaps the strange dream had unsettled his mind a little, for he looked for his sword to have it handy and could not find it, so the Arcadian left his with him.[1]

He woke to find the room dim with smoke and the glare of fire showing through it. There were little red tongues of flame shooting in under the door: he threw it open and a sheet of fire poured in from the kindled brushwood piled against the walls. He roused the girl, and pulling from the bed the coverlets and the thick mattress, he dumped them on the blaze outside the door to stifle it and give him egress. He snatched up his cloak and wrapped it round his left arm for a shield, and in his hand he took the sword his friend had left with him. Someone had fired his house with the intention of burning him to death, and outside in the darkness behind the blaze the brutes were no doubt hanging about to watch the consummation of their attempt. So his first business was with them. There might be a regiment of them for all he knew, but among all the damnable qualities which had been linked to his name—treachery, sensuality, drunkenness and unscrupulous perfidy—not even his worst enemy had included cowardice. Physical fear had never come near that dark and brilliant soul, and never was it further off than now, when he prepared to leap through the flames into the darkness and kill.

---

[1] Cornelius Nepos, "Alcibiades," X.

He drew back to gain speed and then ran straight for the furnace that roared on the threshold. He must step once on the burning embers with bare foot, and then on the smouldering bed-clothes, and now he was outside, naked and blackened with smoke, but unscathed by the fire. Close in front of him he saw in the brightness of the blaze the figures of the men he had seen like shadows in the dusk, and there were many of them, all armed with bows and javelins. Alone he rushed upon them, and they scattered this way and that, fleeing from the fierceness and the fearlessness of him, as if he had been a host of men and they the solitary combatant.

And then from the darkness into which they had vanished there came a javelin, and from another quarter an arrow. He was vividly outlined against the blaze behind him, and now a shower of weapons sang through the air. He fell and moved no more, and they left him lying there, and reported to Pharnabazus that they had dealt with his guest as he had ordered.

The fire died down; Alcibiades had quenched the most of it with mattress and bed-clothes, and now, when he did not return to her, Timandra came out into the still night, and found him lying there, blackened and bleeding and naked but for the cloak he had wound round his left arm. She wrapped her own garments about him, even as he had dreamed, and carried him back into the smouldering house. She held the dear head in her arm and washed the smoke and the blood-stains from the face, and with paint and powder restored to it, as the custom was, the semblance of the living. Next day she emptied her purse to give him such meet and honourable burial as it could furnish.

INDEX

A

Abydos, 209, 216, 217, 226
Acamantis, 24
Acharnians, 36, 62
Acharnæ, 69
Achilles, 44
Achæa, 96
Acropolis, 5, 9, 17, 146, 232, 239
Admiral, 8, 172, 193, 175, 183, 199, 204, 205, 207, 208, 211, 215, 218, 220, 227, 246, 255, 259, 263, 273, 259
Admiralty, 220
admiration, 36, 46, 47, 59, 89, 155, 160
adolescence, 50, 51
Adolph, 36
Adonis, 125
adoration, 25, 28, 33, 39, 38, 41, 43, 47, 73, 81, 87, 105, 120, 145, 155, 165, 200, 274
adulation, 51
adultery, 5, 76, 161
Ægean, 9, 10, 15, 106, 107, 114, 169, 220, 258
Ægina, 13, 63, 66, 71, 131, 202
Ægospotami, 89, 259, 260, 261, 262, 269, 272
Æschines, 30
affairs, 61, 85, 101, 113, 167, 178, 216, 226, 253
affections, 35, 37, 43, 44, 83, 152, 160, 189
Agariste, 138
Agatharchus, 100
Agathon, 48
Agesandridas, 204, 205
Agis, 70, 102, 155, 156, 160, 161, 165, 166, 168, 169, 170, 175, 187, 223, 242, 259, 273
Alcmæonid, 24
Alcmæonidæ, 65
allegiance, 62, 134, 143, 172
alliances, 14, 15, 61, 74, 90, 91, 92, 93, 95, 96, 99, 101, 102, 103, 104, 105, 108, 120, 121, 136, 166, 167, 169, 173, 181, 183, 185, 186, 187, 188, 198, 215, 216, 228, 255, 257
Ambassador, 103
ambitions, 15, 25, 51, 87, 81, 82, 88, 92, 118, 128, 146, 167, 168, 187, 207, 221, 240, 257, 261

Ammon, Shrine of, 123
Amphipolis, 89
Amycla, 29, 30, 47
anathemas, 240
Anaxagoras, 27, 39, 40, 76, 77
ancestors, 269
Andocides, 100, 126, 137, 138
Androcles, 127, 128, 129, 130, 138, 143, 189
Andros, 250
Antiochus, 85, 253, 254, 255
anti-Periclean, 86
Antiphon, 201
anti-Spartan, 269
Antisthenes, 37
Anytus, 46, 47, 51
Aphrodite, 116, 125
Apollo, 98, 136
appointments, 119, 157, 208, 249, 254, 255
Arcadian, 103, 274, 276
Archestratus, 8
Archidamus, 64, 69, 70, 102
Arginusæ, 258, 261
Argives, 74, 90, 91, 92, 95, 97, 98, 99, 101, 102, 103, 104, 105, 121, 129, 146
Argolis, 97
Argos, 82, 90, 91, 92, 93, 94, 95, 96, 97, 98, 102, 103, 104, 120, 148, 153
Ariphron, 29, 45
Aristides, 10
Aristophanes, 29, 34, 36, 48, 61, 62, 81, 105, 171, 182, 184
Aristophon, 100
Aristotelian, 220
Aristotle, 4, 56, 220
Armada, comparison, 122, 123, 126, 186, 131, 144, 151, 206, 263
Artaxerxes, 12, 268, 269, 270
Artemisium, 24
Asia, 9, 74, 170, 173, 179, 246, 269
Asiatic, 209, 217, 222, 273
Aspasia, 35, 36, 37, 38, 39, 40, 43, 76, 78
Aspendus, 205, 206, 207, 209, 210
Assembly, Athenian, 11, 19, 33, 38, 56, 66, 77, 84, 85, 93, 94, 95, 98, 108, 109, 115, 117, 118, 119, 120, 121, 122, 123, 127, 128, 130, 132, 136, 139, 144, 149, 150, 153, 166, 167, 171, 175, 181, 183, 185, 187, 188, 190, 192, 197, 198, 200, 201,

203, 205, 208, 211, 218, 219, 231, 233, 239, 240, 245, 254, 256
astrologers, 124, 158
Astyochus, 175, 183, 184, 199, 273
Athene, 4, 5, 15, 16, 17, 31, 75, 76, 124, 156, 238
Athenian, *passim*.
Athenians, *passim*.
Athenæus, 36, 37, 39, 77, 82, 237, 258, 271, 274
Attic, 4, 12, 25, 29, 30, 51, 153, 239, 241
Attica, 3, 13, 14, 15, 16, 17, 55, 56, 58, 62, 65, 66, 69, 71, 72, 73, 74, 91, 132, 151, 153, 161, 165, 172, 193, 204, 207, 221, 238, 243, 259
auguries, 124
Aurelius, 26
Auréle, 26
autocracy, 15, 221
autocratic, 205, 262
Axiochus, 36, 83, 274, 276

B

banishment, 12, 89, 105, 108, 152, 174, 185, 190, 191, 272
barbarians, 10, 151, 179, 258
barbarous conduct, 30, 154, 156, 170, 257, 274
bastard, 273
beauty, 3, 4, 5, 20, 27, 41, 43, 46, 47, 48, 49, 50, 60, 61, 132, 239
Belgium, 97
beloved, 43, 44, 49, 60, 125, 144, 157, 183
Belshazzar, 158
Bevan, 6
Bible, 44
Bigis, De, 272
birth, 16, 23, 24, 35, 55, 56, 81, 156, 168, 261
Bisanthe, 223, 224, 255, 256, 257
bishop, 38
Bithynia, 228, 269
Bithynians, 227, 229
blasphemy, 76, 128, 129, 197, 244, 245
blockades, 13, 113, 151, 157, 206, 217, 222, 230, 251
blood, 24, 224, 232, 274, 277
body, 9, 29, 31, 43, 44, 47, 51, 113, 122, 204, 218, 225, 227, 242, 257
Bolshevists, 138, 190, 191, 200, 206
Borni, fortress, 223
Bosphorus, 220, 221, 222, 223, 227, 230, 257, 267

boyhood, 23, 25, 28, 32, 40, 47, 51, 82, 83, 120, 175, 189, 226, 239, 243, 254
boys, 7, 23, 30, 31, 32, 34, 42, 43, 46, 49, 51, 57, 58, 242, 243
bride, 83
budget, 5, 33
Byzantians, 230
Byzantium, 223, 227, 230, 231, 252
Bürgermeister, 71
Bœotia, 4, 14, 24, 62, 69, 86, 91, 92, 139
Bœotian, 86, 93, 95, 96, 102, 151
Bœotians, 230

C

Cabinet, 11, 39, 87, 96
calamities, 125, 131, 154, 157, 158, 165, 207, 209
Callias, 83
Callicrates, 16
Callicratidas, 258
Callipides, 237
Camarina, 114, 136, 143
campaigns, 23, 60, 103, 132, 133, 134, 135, 144, 145, 146, 154, 172, 178, 213, 215, 220, 252, 256, 258, 274
Cappadocia, 270
captive, 137
Caria, 232, 251, 255, 256
Carthage, 114, 115, 124, 151
Carthagena, 231
castles, 224, 267
Catana, 135, 136, 139, 143, 145, 146, 147, 175, 187
catechisms, 47, 48, 60, 156, 275
Catholic, 129
cavalry, 57, 59, 86, 102, 103, 131, 159, 262
Cecrops, 9
celebrations, 6, 18, 165, 238, 241
Centaurs, 16
Cephallonia, 72
ceremonies, 72, 171, 240, 241
Ceryces, 182
Chalcedon, 222, 227, 228, 229, 230, 231, 252
Chalcideus, 169, 170, 172, 173, 175
Chalcidice, 61, 106
chants, 125, 131, 243, 243, 244
character, 7, 28, 35, 40, 59, 61, 64, 73, 96, 98, 137, 155, 186, 189, 220, 261
chariots, 49, 82, 101, 120, 145, 241
charm, 28, 33, 41, 46, 47, 50, 51, 61, 73, 81, 83, 93, 120, 132, 155, 156, 160, 175, 176, 193, 225

280

Charmides, 138, 144
Chasreas, 200
Cheiron, 36
Chersonese, 15, 216
Chians, 168, 169, 172, 174, 177
child, 10, 25, 64, 78, 83, 109, 161, 168, 208
children, 9, 16, 24, 38, 42, 83, 107, 191
Chios, 82, 166, 167, 169, 170, 171, 172, 173, 174, 175, 193, 215, 219
Chrysogenus, 237, 238
Chrysopolis, 222, 227, 231
Chæreas, 191
Cicero, 41
Cimon, 12
Clazomenæ, 124, 170, 216, 217
Clearchus, 227, 230
Cleinias, 24, 29, 55, 256
Cleon, 75, 76, 105, 108
Cleophon, 219
colonies, 11, 14, 61, 62, 64, 65, 71, 106, 113, 126, 153, 186, 223, 227, 229, 256, 258
Colophon, 226
commander, 102, 153, 172, 198, 200, 220, 206, 208, 209, 223, 226, 228, 230, 231, 233, 243, 251, 252, 253, 255
commanders, 147, 198, 207, 210, 224
commissariat, 59
Commons, House of, 85
companions, 35, 39, 42, 43, 46, 49,
comradeship, 43, 56, 226, 227
condemned, 134, 148, 149, 150, 154, 167, 170, 171, 174, 179, 181, 182, 183, 186, 238, 239, 244, 245, 253
confederacy, 10, 11, 15, 64, 72, 90, 102, 107, 108, 174, 178
conferences, 38, 39, 74, 116, 120, 185, 186, 187, 188, 198, 274
confession, 45, 49, 61, 137
confiscations, 103, 148, 149, 181, 240
Congress, 63
Conjugal role, 161
Conon, 263
conquests, 14, 108, 114, 123, 124, 133, 151, 152
conscription, 55, 135
conspiracy, 12, 130, 138, 139, 181, 189, 190
conspirators, 139, 190, 224
Constitution, Athenian, 56, 129, 139, 183, 190, 192, 219, 272
Consul, 86
Corcyra, 61, 131

Corinth, 14, 61, 69, 90, 91, 92, 97, 113, 126, 139, 149, 157, 168, 169, 170
Corinthian, 14, 61, 62, 74, 96, 97, 102, 149, 158, 171, 172
Corinthians, 62, 63, 65, 90, 126, 169
corn, 202, 221, 222, 223, 232
Cornelius, 28, 32, 126, 148, 149, 223, 239, 240, 253, 257, 262, 270, 271, 274, 276
Coronea, 24, 55
correspondences, 12, 184, 204
corruption, 7, 29
Council, Athenian, 18, 19, 38, 55, 64, 65, 93, 94, 101, 127, 128, 138, 170, 190
Courts, 175, 185, 191, 193, 268, 271
courtesans, 36, 37, 156
Covenant, 229
Cratetian, 39
Cratinus, 36
crews, 116, 117, 159, 174, 191, 204, 207, 210, 215, 218, 256, 261, 263
Critias, 48, 273
curriculum, school, 31
curses, 149, 150, 154, 170, 182, 240, 244
Cyllene, 148
cymbals, 243, 244
Cyme, 252, 253
Cymæan, 253
Cynossema, 209, 211, 215
Cyprus, 14
Cyrus, 246, 249, 250, 251, 255, 257, 259, 268, 270, 271, 273
Cythera, 96
Cyzicus, 217, 218, 219, 220, 221, 227, 229, 230, 231, 258, 267, 272, 273

D

Damon, 28
dandified, 156
Daphne, 241, 242
Darius, 166, 169, 173, 180, 215, 246, 249, 259, 268
dearly, 130
death, Alcibiades, 275, 276
Decelea, 151, 153, 155, 158, 160, 165, 167, 170, 172, 174, 193, 204, 219, 221, 222, 238, 241, 242, 245, 259
Deinomache, 24
Delium, 61, 86
Delos, 11, 174
Delphi, 9, 124
Delphic, 64, 70, 89, 124, 136
Demes, 36

281

Demeter, 9, 243
democracy, 12, 81, 88, 104, 138, 150, 152, 174, 180, 182, 185, 189, 190, 191, 193, 197, 200, 272
Demosthenes, 87, 157, 159, 160
Demostratus, 122
deputations, 61, 116, 166, 185, 186, 189, 203, 219, 228, 230, 232, 249, 251
Deputy-Satrap, of Lydia, 259
Derby, 119
desertions, 177, 251
Dialogues, 23
Diodorus, 24, 221, 217, 218, 221, 238, 252, 253, 254, 257, 262, 270
Diogenes, 6
Dionysius, 107
diplomacy, 65, 91, 93, 105, 173, 180
Dipylon, 242
disfranchisements, 35, 78
disgrace, 12, 33, 44, 56, 60, 73, 106, 158
divine, 4, 5, 8, 9, 16, 31, 74, 106, 124, 125
diviners, 88, 92, 101, 105, 113, 118, 123, 124, 143, 158, 275
doctrines, 5, 6
doctrines, 5
dominions, 8, 10, 14, 15, 62, 66, 95, 115, 144, 238, 267, 269
Dorian, 113
Doric, 16, 118
dowry, 83
drachmas, 108, 137, 177, 250
Drake, Sir Francis, 8, 65, 123, 224, 225, 230, 231
Duris, 237

E

earthquakes, 94, 95, 168
Educandis, 44
education, 7, 30, 32, 42, 43, 47
Edwyn, 6
effeminacies, 34, 100, 154
Egesta, 113, 114, 116, 117, 122, 124, 131, 133, 135, 143
Egesteans, 116, 117, 118, 122
egoism, 50, 118, 150
Egypt, 14
Eleans, 103
election, 11, 101
Eleusinian, 5, 127, 137, 187
Eleusis, 6, 18, 69, 144, 149, 171, 182, 241, 242, 243, 245, 273
Elis, 90, 92, 95, 148

Elizabeth, 8, 65
embassies, 63, 65, 66, 74, 75, 92, 93, 95, 117, 181, 188, 201, 202, 204, 218, 219, 249, 250, 268
Endius, 167, 169, 219
England, 31, 38, 64, 65
enmity, 15, 175
enslavement, 11, 49, 90, 107
envoys, 61, 62, 63, 69, 74, 90, 92, 93, 94, 95, 96, 101, 107, 109, 113, 115, 116, 118, 122, 123, 135, 149, 166, 173, 188, 199, 200, 201, 203, 205
Ephebes, 56, 57, 58, 115
Ephesians, 82
Ephesus, 226, 249, 251, 254, 255, 259
Ephors, 167, 219
Ephorus, 253, 270
Epidaurian, 98
Epidaurus, 76, 97, 98, 99, 202, 203
epiphany, 208, 261
epitaph, 149
Erchise, 56
Eros, 100, 146, 155
Erythræ, 170
Eryx, 116
escapades, Alcibiades, 28, 32, 41, 45, 127, 128
escapes, Alcibiades, 32, 126, 138, 148, 175, 201, 205, 216, 226, 254
Escurial, Spain, 65
estates, 26, 56, 70
Eubœa, 4, 165, 166, 202, 204, 205, 221
Eumolpidæ, 5, 182, 241, 244, 245
Euphronius, 57
Eupolis, 36
Euripides, 82, 160
Eurotas, 155, 156, 175, 268
Euryptolemus, 26
Euthydemus, 83
Evangelus, 26
evidence, against Alcibiades, 34, 36, 37, 51, 84, 127, 128, 130, 133, 137, 138, 139, 147, 168, 171, 174, 217, 237, 240, 244, 245, 270
excommunication, 148, 149, 244
executions, 3, 17, 130, 175, 200, 220, 223
exile, esp. of Alcibiades, 11, 12, 89, 107, 167, 179, 180, 182, 183, 185, 193, 198, 199, 208, 211, 220, 231, 238, 239, 241, 242, 270, 271, 273

F

fatherless, 29
fearlessness, 3, 32, 277
feasts, 16, 42, 48, 116, 117, 156,
festivals, 7, 18, 57, 100, 125, 165, 237, 241, 242, 245
flagship, 143, 144, 146, 210, 227, 237, 263
fleets, 8, 9, 10, 11, 13, 15, 19, 55, 61, 72, 73, 89, 92, 96, 99, 116, 117, 118, 125, 131, 133, 134, 135, 136, 139, 143, 146, 147, 148, 149, 151, 153, 157, 158, 159, 165, 166, 169, 170, 171, 172, 174, 175, 178, 180, 181, 182, 183, 184, 185, 186, 192, 197, 198, 199, 200, 201, 202, 203, 204, 205, 206, 207, 208, 209, 210, 211, 215, 216, 217, 218, 219, 221, 222, 223, 227, 229, 230, 231, 232, 237, 240, 246, 249, 250, 251, 252, 253, 254, 255, 259, 260, 261, 262, 263, 267, 271, 272, 273
flogging, 33, 82, 200
flutes, 31, 243, 272
forfeits, 38, 44, 147
forts, 69, 97, 153, 155, 165, 193, 202, 203, 204, 223, 227, 228, 232, 237, 241, 245, 256, 258, 264
fortifications, 10, 11, 13, 66, 69, 70, 184, 209, 222, 271
Foucart, 6
Freedman, 30
freedom, 14, 66, 84, 152, 166, 177
Freud, 24, 101
friends, 32, 46, 59, 60, 70, 76, 77, 78, 81,82, 91, 113, 127, 149, 155, 156, 167, 168, 169, 173, 175, 179, 180, 216, 217, 239, 262, 276
friendship, 44, 51, 86, 180, 197, 229, 232, 249, 267
Frogs, 171, 182
fugitives, 131, 204

G

Galahad, 47
garrisons, 11, 55, 58, 69, 99, 134, 204, 222, 225, 230, 241, 250
gates, 136, 224, 225, 230, 231, 242, 243
Gela, 114
generals, 11, 60, 87, 118, 122, 123, 130, 131, 136, 143, 157, 181, 183, 184, 185, 191, 192, 193, 203, 216, 226, 233, 239, 240, 256, 260, 261, 262, 263, 272
generalship, 63, 102, 190
genius, esp. of Alcibiades, 3, 4, 25, 41, 176, 193, 206, 207, 208, 224, 239, 267
gentleman, 26, 30, 116, 168, 191
Germans, 205
Germany, 97
girls, 7, 39, 42, 43, 46, 145, 156, 179, 180, 242, 274, 243, 276
glamour, 25, 77, 261
glory, 4, 5, 7, 10, 115, 116, 123, 145, 221, 225, 241, 242
Glover, 250
goal, 57, 240, 246, 274
goats, 155
gobbling, 97
goddesses, 4, 5, 15, 16, 17, 19, 41, 65, 132, 232
gods, 4, 5, 16, 49, 73, 74, 77, 98, 101, 106, 123, 125, 129, 131, 161, 168, 182, 242, 243
gold, 5, 17, 18, 46, 75, 116, 117, 124, 131, 145, 239, 251
government, 13, 63, 94, 95, 103, 106, 108, 136, 148, 152, 166, 167, 168, 170, 174, 175, 181, 182, 185, 188, 191, 192, 199, 200, 205, 207, 218, 219, 220, 246, 257, 273
governors, 12, 166, 222, 268
greatness, 77, 78, 105, 159, 172
Greece, 3, 8, 10, 12, 14, 15, 27, 29, 36, 37, 63, 72, 74, 82, 90, 95, 102, 114, 117, 120, 146, 148, 151, 165, 166, 168, 171, 177, 178, 179, 180, 186, 225, 229, 241, 252, 269
Greeks, 5, 6, 37
Grote, George, historian, 117, 186, 229, 241, 252, 253
Grunium, 271
guardians, 24, 28, 29, 33, 35, 40, 45, 46, 47, 61, 77, 144, 243, 245
guardianship, 24, 29, 55, 99
Gylippus, 153, 157, 158, 167, 170, 211, 228
gymnasia, 31, 38, 42, 47, 51, 126,
Gythium, 232, 249

H

Halicarnassus, 107, 209
Halieis, 14
handsome, 41, 81, 274
Hannah, 37, 39
harbours, 9, 62, 66, 97, 115, 131, 134, 135, 136, 139, 143, 145, 146, 148, 158, 169, 173, 198, 202, 203, 204, 205, 218, 227,

283

230, 231, 238, 251, 254, 255, 259, 262
Hector, 44
Hellas, 29, 30, 57, 63, 73, 91, 98, 165, 167
Hellenes, 66
Hellenic, 3, 8, 15, 74, 90, 102, 123, 151, 166, 173, 178, 179, 269
Hellenica, 217, 222, 224, 226, 228, 238, 249, 250, 251, 257, 264, 272
Hellespont, 167, 186, 208, 209, 215, 217, 218, 220, 221, 222, 223, 225, 252, 255, 257, 258, 259, 267, 274
Hellespontine, 223
Helots, 99
Henley, Regatta, 42
Heraclea, 114
Hercules, 115
Hermes, 4, 125
Hermippus, 36
Herms, 126, 127, 128, 129, 137, 138, 171, 244
Herodicus, 39
Herr, 36
Hesiod, 31
Hiero, 101
Hipparete, 83, 84
Hippias, 17
Hippodamus, 36
Hipponicus, 32, 33, 35, 51, 82, 83
historians, 89, 134, 145, 186, 198, 223, 219, 252, 253, 270
Homer, 4, 6, 30, 44, 46
hoplite, 10, 86
hoplites, 10
Hyperbolus, 105, 106, 190
hypochondriac, 101

I

Iacchus, 242, 243
Iberia, 151
Ichabod, 241
Ictinus, 16
Ilyssus, 49
imperial, 8, 14, 27, 64, 115, 132, 144, 151, 216, 221, 238, 241, 267
imperialism, 10, 11, 13, 15, 63, 118, 124
imprisoned, 191, 200, 257
indictment, 34, 189, 193
infidelities, 84
innocence, esp. of Alcibiades, 129, 130, 147, 244, 245
Ionian, 131, 148
Ionic, 10, 16, 18, 41

islanders, 63, 250
islands, 8, 9, 10, 90, 106, 108, 165, 166, 170, 172, 174, 178, 186, 246, 258
Isocrates, 272
Isthmian, 169
Isthmus, 69, 139, 169
isthmus, 35, 61
Italian, 4, 126
Italy, 151

J

Jews, 5
Jowett, Benjamin, 23, 24, 73, 119
Justin, 70, 237, 240

K

kings, 25, 82, 116, 137, 166, 242
kingdoms, 150, 172, 258, 267, 269
kinsman, 25, 26

L

Laches, 86
Laconia, 66, 96, 99, 103
Laconian, 232
Lamachus, 117, 134, 143, 145, 147
Lampsacus, 259
Lapiths, 16
Laurium, 56, 74, 88, 100, 151, 165
laws, 33, 56, 130, 271
leadership, 12, 77, 88, 101, 105, 123, 192, 200, 219
League, 14, 15, 62, 63, 91, 169
Lenten, 176
Leontini, 113, 117, 135
Leontinians, 135
Leotychides, 156, 168
Lesbos, 82, 166, 168, 174, 217
Levites, 5
Libya, 114, 115
Libyan, 123
Lichas, 206
lisp, esp. of Alcibiades, 81, 82, 83, 84, 94, 178, 239
lovers, esp. of Alcibiades, 4, 41, 43, 44, 45, 49, 50, 51, 73, 125, 154, 167
loyal, 124, 137, 227
loyalty, 61, 62, 124, 134, 137, 184, 227
luxuries, 100, 154, 156, 175, 176, 180
Lydia, 249, 251, 259, 270
lyre, 30, 31
Lysander, 246, 249, 250, 251, 253, 254, 255, 258, 259, 260, 263, 271, 273

Lærtius, 6

M

Madonna, 126, 129
magic, 4, 60, 165, 188, 251, 272
magician, 165
magistrates, 61, 84, 124
Magnesia, 12, 215, 268
magnificence, esp. of Alcibiades, 4, 5, 19, 81, 82, 116, 120, 123, 172, 220, 237, 240, 241, 259, 271
Magæus, 273
Mahaffy, 37
maidens, 7, 16, 41, 85, 243
maiden goddess, 7
manhood, esp. of Alcibiades, 4, 7, 16, 43, 47, 51, 73, 75
manners, 34, 154, 155, 160, 250
Mantinea, 86, 90, 92, 95, 96, 103, 120
Mantinean, 103, 129, 146
marbles, 16, 17, 73
Marc, 26
Marcus, 26
marriage, esp. of Alcibiades, 26, 35, 42, 83
Mediterranean, 114
Medocus, 257, 262
Megara, 14, 58, 62, 63, 65, 66, 71, 90, 114, 138, 223, 227, 230
Megarian, 62, 66, 72, 75, 223, 230
Meidias, 87
Melian, 106, 107, 108, 109
Melissa, 271
Melos, 15, 106, 107, 108, 109, 113, 114, 145, 225
Menexenus, 39
Messana, 135, 143, 147
Meton, 124, 125
Milesian, 35, 155, 173
Miletus, 172, 173, 175, 176, 177, 192, 198, 199, 207, 208, 215, 219, 249
Mindarus, 199, 207, 208, 217, 218
Mitylene, 108
Mnesicles, 18
monument, 16
motherhood, 30, 243
Munychia, 55, 115
mutilations, 81, 127, 126, 128, 129, 137, 138, 171, 244
mutiny, 145, 146, 159
Mysteries, 5, 6, 18, 127, 128, 129, 137, 138, 170, 187, 193, 240, 241, 242, 243, 244, 245

mystics, 49, 241, 242, 243, 273
Mystères, 6

N

Naupactus, 14
navy, esp. Athenian, 8, 10, 14, 15, 19, 71, 97, 117, 136, 158, 166, 172, 180, 185, 192, 198, 200, 205, 207, 215, 221, 254, 260, 261, 263, 273
Naxos, 11, 143
Nemea, 100
Nemean, 100
Nemesis, 254
Neontichus, 223
Nepos, 28, 32, 126, 148, 149, 223, 239, 240, 253, 257, 262, 270, 271, 274, 276
Nicias, 56, 86, 87, 88, 89, 90, 91, 92, 93, 94, 95, 96, 99, 100, 101, 102, 103, 104, 105, 106, 108, 109, 113, 115, 117, 118, 119, 120, 121, 122, 123, 124, 132, 133, 134, 135, 143, 145, 146, 147, 153, 154, 157, 158, 159, 160, 192, 220, 228, 275
Nike, 18
Nisæa, 72
nobility, 3, 4, 16, 19, 24, 25, 27, 28, 35, 38, 39, 42, 43, 50, 55, 60, 78, 81, 116, 225, 255, 270, 275
Notium, 256
nymphs, 100

O

oaths, 56, 191, 199
Odes, 275
Odeum, 18
Œconomica, 42, 83
Œnoe, 69
offences, 88, 95, 145, 150
oligarchy, 104, 126, 138, 150, 153, 174, 181, 187, 189, 190, 191, 192, 193, 197, 200, 201, 202, 203, 207, 219, 220, 232, 245, 271, 272, 273
Olympia, 4, 237, 241
Olympian, 19, 27, 34, 35, 38, 39, 45, 47, 70, 77
Olympic, 82, 120, 145
Olympus, 4, 5, 6, 40
omens, 28, 98, 124, 125, 127
oracles, 9, 64, 70, 89, 123, 124, 135, 275
orations/orator, 7, 39, 72, 78, 126, 137, 219
Orchomenus, 103
orgy, 127, 128
Orient, 176, 250

285

outrages, 28, 33, 125, 126, 128, 129, 137, 128, 200

P

Pactye, 223, 224, 258, 260, 262, 263
paganism, 49
pageant, 16
paintings, 4, 29, 100
Palladium, 124
Pallene, 61
Panathenaic, 5, 16, 18, 57
Paralus, 29, 77, 191, 263, 264
parentage, 36, 56, 78
parleyings, 10, 69, 106, 192, 225
parliament, 48
Parnes, 151
Paros, 232
Parthenon, 17, 18, 19, 41, 57, 75
passions, 28, 37, 43, 48, 50, 146, 156, 239, 246
Patras, 97
Patresians, 97
patriotism, esp. of Alcibiades, 24, 84, 87, 119, 152, 221, 201, 207, 261
Patroclus, 44
Patræ, 96, 97
peace, 14, 15, 58, 62, 65, 66, 74, 75, 86, 87, 88, 89, 90, 91, 92, 93, 96, 99, 101, 103, 104, 118, 121, 124, 153, 201, 202, 218, 219, 240, 241, 246
Peiræus, 9, 10, 13, 36, 55, 57, 66, 70, 71, 97, 131, 144, 154, 160, 165, 185, 192, 197, 198, 200, 202, 203, 204, 205, 206, 207, 222, 233, 238, 240, 264
Peisander, 181, 182, 183, 185, 186, 187, 188, 189, 190, 201
Pelasgic, 71
Peloponnese, 8, 63, 64, 90, 102, 105, 151, 191
Peloponnesian, 5, 8, 14, 15, 18, 55, 58, 61, 62, 63, 69, 72, 73, 74, 89, 96, 97, 103, 147, 169, 173, 175, 177, 178, 180, 187, 192, 198, 199, 200, 201, 202, 205, 206, 207, 208, 209, 210, 211, 216, 217, 219, 221, 223, 231, 249, 273
Peloponnesians, 209, 210, 215, 217, 218
Pentecost, 131, 170
Pentelicus, 16, 151
Periclean, 55, 64, 96, 97, 106
Pericles, 5, 7, 12, 13, 14, 15, 18, 19, 23, 24, 25, 26, 27, 29, 30, 32, 33, 34, 35, 36, 37, 38, 39, 40, 45, 47, 55, 60, 61, 62, 63, 65, 66, 70, 71, 72, 73, 75, 76, 77, 78, 84, 87, 106, 114, 132, 144, 171, 175, 211, 243, 250
Perinthus, 222, 223, 231, 258
Persia, 12, 15, 74, 108, 167, 173, 178, 179, 181, 182, 185, 186, 206, 207, 216, 219, 226, 229, 230, 249, 250, 251, 253, 257, 269, 270, 273
Persians, 8, 9, 10, 19, 24, 63, 64, 70, 74, 98, 108, 124, 166, 174, 176, 177, 178, 179, 180, 185, 186, 187, 189, 198, 204, 237, 250, 251, 255, 268, 176
perverted, 60
Pharnabazus, 166, 208, 210, 215, 216, 217, 218, 222, 226, 228, 229, 230, 232, 249, 267, 268, 269, 270, 272, 273, 274, 277
Pheidias, 5, 16, 17, 39, 75, 76, 77
Philip, 250
philosophers, 6, 25, 27, 35, 45, 59
philosophy, 3, 38, 40, 45, 59
Phliasian, 102
Phlius, 102
Phocæa, 251, 252, 253
Phoenician, 178, 180, 185, 197, 198, 205, 206, 210
Phrygia, 166, 267, 269, 271
Phrygian, 270
Phrynichus, 181, 183, 184, 185, 188, 190, 199, 200, 201, 202
Phædrus, 28, 44, 49
Phœnician, 9, 10, 206, 207, 215, 216
Phœnix, 10
Pindar, 4, 275
Plato, 5, 17, 23, 24, 28, 29, 33, 34, 36, 39, 43, 44, 46, 47, 48, 49, 50, 56, 59, 83, 86, 87
Platæa, 9
Pleiades, 57
Plutarch, 8, 13, 18, 19, 24, 25, 26, 27, 29, 31, 33, 35, 36, 37, 38, 39, 40, 44, 45, 46, 47, 50, 56, 75, 77, 82, 85, 86, 94, 97, 100, 101, 109, 115, 122, 123, 126, 130, 132, 135, 145, 146, 148, 149, 154, 155, 157, 160, 168, 176, 189, 208, 210, 211, 216, 217, 218, 219, 221, 224, 227, 230, 237, 238, 239, 246, 252, 253, 256, 258, 259, 261, 262, 268, 270, 275
Plyntria, 238
Pnyx, 209
poet, 48, 82, 160
Poetics, 220
poetry, 3, 160

poets/poetry, 2, 36, 48, 38, 82, 160
  9, 12, 14, 15, 63, 66, 69, 70, 71, 73, 75, 77,
  87, 88, 92, 93, 96, 101, 102, 103, 106, 114,
  118, 125, 133, 136, 143, 149, 150, 168,
  176, 178, 179, 188, 201, 206, 212, 215,
  220, 249, 250, 251, 252, 269
politics, 25, 47, 56, 77, 84, 96, 104, 126, 167
popularity, esp. of Alcibiades, 26, 50, 81, 82,
  87, 88, 119, 125, 156, 187, 198, 200, 229
Poseidon, 17
Potidæa, 23, 58, 59, 60, 61, 62, 64, 65, 66, 74,
  77, 81, 82, 83, 155, 156
Potidæan, 62
prestige, 158, 172, 192, 221, 245, 246, 255,
  256
pride, esp. of Alcibiades, 50, 88, 92, 132,
  171, 208, 211, 272
priests, 5, 6, 38, 98, 124, 127, 144, 148, 154,
  242, 243, 244
priestesses, 124, 148, 182
principles, 7, 12, 30, 64, 88, 118, 152, 183
prison, 76, 77, 126, 137, 138, 226
prisoners, 42, 75, 86, 100, 160, 216, 252,
  254, 263
proclivities, 176
promiscuity, 44, 75
property, esp. of Alcibiades, 26, 55, 56, 69,
  71, 83, 103, 148, 149, 182, 240, 267
prophecy, 89, 275
Propontis, 217, 218, 220, 221, 222, 223, 227,
  229, 231, 232, 249, 256, 258, 267
Propylæa, 18, 19
prosecution, 76, 151, 191, 198, 199, 205, 208
Protagoras, 29, 40
Pultarch, 251
Pulytion, 127, 138, 144
Puritans, 145, 176
Pylos, 93, 94, 99
Pythian, 9, 237
Pythoclides, 28
Pythonicus, 127

policy, 8,

Q

qualities, esp. of Alcibiades, 81, 120, 221,
  276
quarrels, 13, 76, 90, 93, 97, 98, 103, 113, 191,
  192, 206, 261

R

reinforcements, 157, 158, 174, 216, 228, 259
religion, 3, 4, 5, 6, 40
Renaissance, 4

Renan, 26
reputation, 27, 87, 88, 120, 154, 221, 256
revenge, 123, 154
Rhegium, 134, 135, 136, 139, 143
Rhium, 97
rites, 125, 128, 242, 244, 245
ritual, 241, 244
robes, 5, 17, 75, 83, 237, 238, 242, 243
Rome, 243
roysterers, 6, 60, 254
Russian, 190

S

sacraments, 6, 242, 244
sacred, 5, 6, 18, 128, 144, 149, 182, 241, 242,
  243
sacrilege, 126, 127, 128, 129, 137, 138, 144,
  145, 182, 189, 239, 240, 241
safety, 8, 9, 91, 101, 102, 132, 138, 183, 189,
  244, 267, 269
sagacity, 94, 153
sailors, 5, 145, 146, 177, 180, 193, 197, 206,
  217, 226, 249, 250, 251, 254, 260
Salaminia, 139, 145, 146, 147, 148, 166, 170,
  175, 187
Salamis, 9, 16, 63, 204
Samian, 195, 197, 200, 208
Samos, 15, 172, 173, 174, 180, 181, 183, 184,
  185, 186, 187, 188, 189, 190, 191, 192,
  193, 197, 198, 199, 200, 201, 202, 203,
  205, 206, 207, 208, 209, 216, 219, 220,
  225, 226, 232, 233, 250, 253, 254, 255,
  256, 259, 267
sanctuary, 103, 129, 243, 267
Sappho, 37
Sardis, 166, 173, 175, 185, 188, 216, 249, 250
satrap, 166, 173, 176, 177, 178, 179, 180,
  181, 184, 185, 186, 187, 188, 189, 197,
  198, 199, 206, 207, 208, 216, 218, 228,
  229, 232, 249, 250, 268, 269, 270, 271,
  273
satrapy, 63, 177, 208, 226, 249, 273
Satyr, 44, 50
Satyrus, 258
savagery, 107, 108, 154, 211, 225, 232
saviour, 51, 160, 238, 245
scandals, 36, 75, 81, 127, 156, 177, 226
scandals, 75, 226
schemes, 10, 86, 96, 105, 124, 134, 139, 143,
  151, 152, 153, 167, 176, 183, 185, 188,
  215, 224, 226, 258, 267, 269, 274
Schmidt, 35, 36

287

school/schooldays, 5, 31, 17, 29, 30, 37, 40, 42, 46, 51, 73, 176
sculptors, 4, 5, 17, 39, 43, 75, 76
sculptures, 3, 16, 17, 75
Scyllsæum, 97
seapower, 71, 96
security, 13, 108, 229, 230
seductions, 5, 75
segregation, 43
selfish, 60, 90, 199
Selinus, 113, 133, 143
Selym, 231
Selymbria, 222, 224, 225, 228
Selymbrians, 225
Sestos, 215, 216, 226, 259, 260, 262
settlements, 9, 151, 230, 257, 258
Seuthes, 257, 262
Sheba, 116
shrines, 16, 17, 70, 123, 126, 241, 243, 244
Sicilian, 65, 89, 113, 119, 121, 134, 143, 150, 157, 159, 160, 165, 193, 197, 204, 209
Sicily, 14, 113, 114, 115, 117, 118, 121, 123, 124, 133, 135, 136, 137, 139, 143, 144, 151, 153, 157, 174, 275
Siculus, 24, 217, 218, 252
sieges, 58, 61, 66, 77, 158, 217, 222, 227, 228, 230
Silenus, 47, 275
sincerity, 90, 95, 121, 197
Socrates, 23, 26, 33, 37, 39, 40, 41, 43, 44, 47, 48, 49, 50, 51, 56, 59, 60, 61, 81, 86, 87, 125, 155, 156, 166, 189, 273, 275
Socratic, 40
soldiers, 57, 59, 71, 118, 131, 134, 136, 145, 146, 154, 158, 178, 203, 217, 222, 226, 262, 274
Solomon, 116
soothsayers, 123, 135
sophists, 39, 123
Sophocles, 44
Sousamithras, 273
Spain, 65
Sparta, 8, 10, 12, 14, 15, 29, 30, 61, 62, 63, 64, 65, 66, 69, 71, 74, 75, 87, 88, 90, 91, 92, 93, 95, 96, 97, 98, 99, 102, 103, 104, 105, 106, 113, 118, 120, 121, 148, 149, 151, 152, 153, 154, 155, 156, 157, 158, 160, 161, 165, 166, 167, 168, 169, 170, 172, 173, 174, 175, 176, 177, 178, 179, 181, 182, 184, 185, 186, 187, 193, 197, 199, 201, 202, 203, 204, 205, 206, 207, 211, 215, 216, 218, 219, 220, 226, 232, 240, 241, 246, 250, 257, 258, 259, 260, 268, 269, 271, 272, 273, 274
Spartan, 29, 56, 58, 63, 71, 74, 86, 91, 92, 93, 94, 96, 97, 98, 99, 101, 102, 103, 139, 150, 151, 153, 154, 155, 156, 166, 167, 169, 170, 180, 181, 183, 184, 185, 188, 189, 192, 198, 199, 202, 203, 204, 205, 206, 207, 211, 215, 216, 218, 219, 222, 223, 227, 228, 229, 230, 231, 241, 246, 249, 250, 258, 259, 260, 262, 263, 267, 268, 269, 270, 272, 273
Spartans, 64, 65, 74, 86, 99, 103, 104, 156, 174, 175, 177, 198, 221, 222, 230, 249, 257, 262, 267, 272
speeches, 5, 9, 25, 37, 39, 63, 64, 72, 85, 119, 127, 149, 150, 152, 153, 167, 197, 269
Sphacteria, 86
spiritual, 3, 6, 41, 44, 51, 129, 241
splendours, esp. of Alcibiades, 5, 8, 15, 16, 17, 25, 28, 37, 61, 82, 87, 114, 116, 144, 145, 150, 176, 216, 241, 242, 244, 246
squadrons, 131, 136, 169, 170, 172, 205, 209, 210, 216, 217, 223, 227, 232, 251, 253
statesmanship, esp. of Alcibiades, 13, 40, 62, 75, 92, 96, 97, 99, 220, 224, 229
statesmen, 10, 90, 100, 174, 211
Stesimbrotus, 77
straits, 210, 217, 221, 222, 223, 227, 229, 230, 231, 232, 260, 267
strategy, 70, 143, 153, 154, 172, 208, 220
Strombichides, 172
successes, esp. of Alcibiades, 35, 41, 58, 71, 98, 122, 123, 158, 166, 174, 176, 180, 211, 215, 220, 221, 225, 227, 250, 255, 261, 268, 272
symposium, 23, 43, 44, 45, 46, 47, 48, 49, 59, 60, 61, 86, 87
Syracusan, 135, 136, 147, 149, 151, 158, 166, 171, 275
Syracusans, 134, 135, 136, 149, 160
Syracuse, 113, 114, 123, 124, 125, 126, 133, 134, 135, 136, 139, 143, 149, 151, 153, 157, 158, 167, 170, 172, 192, 211, 218, 228, 275

T

talents, esp. of Alcibiades, 4, 18, 76, 83, 116, 117, 135, 171, 182, 228, 229, 232, 251, 256, 271
tantrum, 77
Taygetus, 157

Tegea, 90, 91, 103
temples, 5, 16, 18, 56, 77, 98, 116, 124, 125
territory, 3, 14, 72, 95, 99, 153, 174, 227, 228, 243, 252
Teucer, 138
Thasos, 11, 232
theatre, 71, 136, 165, 167, 216
Thebes, 30, 31, 148
Themis, 268
Themistocles, 8, 9, 10, 11, 12, 13, 14, 15, 44, 66, 70, 89, 114, 124, 132, 204, 211, 268
Theodoras, 127
Theramenes, 201, 202, 203, 219, 221, 222, 228, 229
Thermopylæ, 8
Thessaly, 165
Thrace, 74, 221, 251, 253, 255, 256, 257, 267, 269
Thracian, 15, 29, 186, 225, 228, 232, 257, 258, 262
Thrasus, 255
Thrasybulus, 191, 193, 221, 228, 229, 232, 251, 253, 255
Thrasycles, 172
Thrasyllus, 102, 103, 191, 225, 226, 227, 232
Thucydidean, 121
Thucydides, 10, 11, 13, 18, 19, 24, 25, 32, 33, 58, 63, 64, 65, 69, 70, 72, 73, 86, 88, 89, 91, 98, 99, 100, 102, 104, 106, 107, 108, 114, 116, 117, 118, 119, 121, 123, 126, 129, 130, 133, 135, 148, 150, 152, 153, 160, 171, 173, 178, 184, 187, 188, 197, 200, 209, 211, 245, 253, 258
Thurii, 14, 148
Timandra, 274, 275, 276, 277
Timarchus, 30
Timæa, 155, 166, 168, 175
Timæus, 137, 138
Tissaphernes, 166, 169, 173, 175, 176, 177, 178, 179, 180, 182, 183, 185, 186, 187, 188, 190, 191, 192, 193, 197, 198, 199, 205, 206, 207, 208, 210, 215, 216, 217, 226, 229, 249, 250, 251, 257, 268, 269
Tory, 34
treason, 12, 70, 184, 204, 270
treaty, 64, 66, 88, 90, 91, 93, 94, 95, 96, 98, 99, 103, 173, 175, 206, 219, 229, 230, 232, 267
tribes, 24, 41, 57, 65, 227, 228, 257
tribute, 15, 18, 19, 25, 27, 61, 97, 144, 151, 173, 174, 176, 177, 199, 205, 222, 223, 224, 228, 232, 249
triremes, 24, 55, 100, 114, 116, 117, 122, 131, 209, 217, 237, 254, 256, 257, 260, 263, 267
triumph, 25, 27, 84, 101, 121, 132, 144, 181, 188, 219, 221, 244, 246, 261
troops, 14, 58, 59, 65, 69, 70, 71, 72, 75, 95, 96, 98, 99, 102, 103, 106, 114, 122, 123, 129, 131, 132, 135, 136, 139, 146, 151, 153, 157, 159, 160, 165, 172, 173, 177, 180, 181, 185, 190, 191, 192, 193, 197, 198, 199, 203, 204, 206, 210, 217, 218, 222, 224, 225, 226, 227, 228, 230, 231, 232, 242, 243, 245, 250, 252, 257, 260, 261, 262, 263, 270
truth, 6, 18, 42, 49, 116, 129, 136, 149, 256
Tydeus, 262
tyranny, 25, 63, 95, 138, 150, 152, 170, 246
Tænarus, 65

U

ugliness, 4, 31
unjust, 97, 152, 197, 239, 256
unnatural, 42, 44
unscrupulous, 62, 93, 96, 101, 103, 118, 199, 252, 276
Utopia, 88

V

vanity, 32, 41, 60, 81
Vatican, 243
veil, 16, 41, 43, 129, 238
vengeance, 87, 127, 147, 225
vessels, 16, 46, 116, 131, 135, 145, 148, 172, 174, 204, 211, 217, 237, 249
vice, 42, 259
viciousness, 47
victim, 32, 77
victims, 109, 116
victorious, 132, 144, 205, 219, 237
victories, 9, 16, 17, 18, 63, 96, 100, 209, 211, 216, 219, 220, 221, 226, 240, 246, 258, 267, 269
virgin, 15, 132
virtues, 31, 44
vision, 10, 15, 70, 114, 274

W

wedlock, 35
West, 115, 117, 123
Western, 121
wife, 7, 29, 30, 33, 35, 36, 38, 39, 43, 47, 83, 168, 191

289

wits, 39, 43, 46, 50, 81, 147, 156, 176, 180, 205, 230
women, 7, 9, 10, 29, 30, 31, 32, 35, 36, 37, 39, 42, 43, 44, 37, 72, 75, 76, 107, 109, 125, 138, 165, 170, 242, 243, 255, 268, 275

X

Xanthippe, 47
Xanthippus, 26, 29, 76
Xenophon, 34, 42, 49, 83, 217, 219, 221, 222, 224, 226, 228, 237, 238, 249, 250, 251, 252, 253, 257, 264, 272, 273

Y

Yorkshire, 4
youth, 7, 16, 28, 34, 38, 39, 41, 43, 44, 46, 47, 48, 51, 81, 82, 119, 120, 121, 131, 239
youthful, 85, 125
youths, 41, 42

Z

zeal, 216, 189, 268
Zeitalter, 35
Zeno, 6, 27
Zeus, 5, 6, 9, 17, 94, 135
Zimmern, 18
Zion, 77
Zopyrus, 29, 30, 32, 40, 47, 51

Printed in Germany
by Amazon Distribution
GmbH, Leipzig